LINCOLN'S LABELS

America's Best-Known Brands and the Civil War

Figure 1. Winslow Homer's engraving of "Christmas Boxes in Camp."
Source: *Harper's Weekly*

LINCOLN'S LABELS

America's Best-Known Brands and the Civil War

James M. Schmidt

EDINBOROUGH PRESS

2009

Edinborough Press
P. O. Box 13790
Roseville, Minnesota 55113-2293
1-888-251-6336
www.edinborough.com

The book is set in Font Bureau Whitman.

Cover image credits:

"Rally Round the Flag" from the Jack Smith Lincoln Graphics Collection, Indiana Historical Society, P0406

Brooks Brothers uniform label from the collection of Don Troiani, Military and Historical Image Bank, Southbury, Conn.

du Pont vintage gunpowder labels from Hagley Museum and Library, Wilmington, Delaware

Facsimile of wartime Borden's Condensed Milk label, from Sullivan Press, Morgantown, Pa.

Wartime Tiffany & Co. advertisement in *Army and Navy Journal* (1864), from Collection of Guy Hasegawa, Hagerstown, Maryland

LIBRARY OF CONGRESS CATALOGING-IN-PUBLICATION DATA
Schmidt, James M., 1964–
Lincoln's labels : America's best known brands and the Civil War / James M. Schmidt.
   p. cm.
Includes bibliographical references and index.
ISBN 978-1-889020-21-1 (casebound : alk. paper)
ISBN 978-1-889020-28-0 (softbound : alk. paper)
1. Brand name products–United States–History–19th century. 2. Business enterprises–United States–History–19th century. 3. United States–History–Civil War, 1861-1865–Economic aspects. I. Title.
HD69.B7S349 2008
                              973.7'1–dc22
                                                              2008007691

DEDICATION

To my wife, Susan,
and to our children,
Katherine, Robert, and Michael

Contents

Illustrations

Foreword

WHEN I WAS A CHILD, in the "Fabulous '50s," men wore hats—*real* hats; fedoras and such. My grandfather's dress hat was a Knox. He kept it in the original box, a large octagonal pale yellow carton with red trim, decorated on four sides and the cover with a rendering of the Knox coat-of-arms. I inherited it from him, being a hat person myself. The box stayed with me for decades, through several moves. Eventually, it disintegrated and was soon forgotten.

Meanwhile, I had become a student of the Civil War. Naturally, the "great" things (issues of slavery and secession, battles from Bull Run to Appomattox) and people (Lincoln, Lee, Douglass, Grant, Davis, and others), tended to be the focus of my work. But I liked more the "little" things: anecdotes casting light on issues, battles, and people; tricks of the soldier's trade; little differences in life between then and now, from the daily "growler" to the absence of deodorant.

Because of this interest, a decade ago Keith Poulter, publisher of *North & South* magazine, asked me to do a column of anecdota, curiosa, excerpta, minutia, and trivia. I think the column, called "The Knapsack," helps make the war more understandable and interesting in human terms. Thus when Jim Schmidt submitted a piece on the Procter & Gamble Company and the Civil War, it was a natural fit for the column. The piece ran in *N&S* in March 2001. More of Jim's essays on other enterprises have followed from time to time. So when Jim asked if I would write a foreword for *Lincoln's Labels*, an entire book on extant Civil War companies, I naturally agreed.

Lincoln's Labels tells how some businesses still operating today contributed to, and were affected by, the Civil War. It does this quite well. In the process, we get a look at mid-nineteenth-century business practices, some innovative people, the origins of several iconic American institutions, and a little insight into life in those distant days. But *Lincoln's Labels* is also about one of the many ways that we—Americans of the early twenty-first century—are linked inextricably to the great national epic. As such, *Lincoln's Labels* is a good read for anyone: scholar, "buff," or ordinary citizen.

So, you ask, what has this to do with Knox Hats? Well, years after the hat box had gone, I chanced to read an account of President-elect Lincoln's February 1861 trip from Springfield to Washington. On the afternoon of

Tuesday the 19th, the Lincolns arrived in New York. They spent less than forty-eight hours in Gotham, leaving on the morning of the twenty-first. In the interim, Lincoln met with various dignitaries, attended a number of political functions, made several speeches, and went to the opera with Mrs. Lincoln, who also toured the sights and shopped up a storm.

Abe himself did some shopping too. After politicking at City Hall, he wandered over to 110 Fulton Street and bought a hat at Charles Knox's little shop, which is still around, a few miles further north.

Ever since, I've wondered if Lincoln got the same box.

Albert A. Nofi

Preface

THE CIVIL WAR MAINTAINS an inimitable hold on the interest and imagination of Americans. Each year millions of people attempt to make a personal connection with the Civil War by visiting battlefields and museums, researching ancestors who fought in the war, participating as re-enactors in "living history" events, watching Civil War-related films and television programs, reading a seemingly unending stream of books and magazines, and collecting artifacts, photographs, and ephemera.

All Americans, if they wish, may make that same connection without leaving their homes. In their wallets, pantries, closets, jewelry boxes, magazine racks, and medicine cabinets are the products of companies that also supplied Union soldiers and sailors. They range from the obvious, such as gunpowder from du Pont and uniforms from Brooks Brothers, to seemingly mundane but equally necessary items, including soap and candles from Procter & Gamble and condensed milk from Borden's.

I had several objectives in writing *Lincoln's Labels*. First, I wanted to relate the rarely-told stories of companies that directly impacted the fighting, though they were far behind the battle lines. Their actions ranged from supplying food, medicine, and clothing, to providing services as grim and terrible as shipping home the bodies of the fallen.

Secondly, I also wished to explore how the war, in turn, affected the companies. The unique intersection of the lives of soldiers and sailors with our own is much more than curious trivia. I believe that a company of employees can have every bit as interesting (and sometimes as dangerous) a war story as a company of soldiers. Each of the subject firms has a tale that mirrored the war itself: family and friendships torn asunder, political intrigue, pitched battles, and paths crossed with this book's namesake—President Abraham Lincoln—and all leavened with the yeast of myth and lore.

Third, I hope the book will serve as a catalyst for a relatively unexplored area of research and scholarship. Historians have given consideration to all facets of the Civil War, yet scholars have paid the least attention to the war's "business end." The Civil War caused dramatic changes in the civilian American marketplace and forced the emergence of a unique mass market: the million-plus soldiers and sailors in the Union army and navy. However, no popular or scholarly book focuses solely on how well-known companies contributed to the war effort, and how in turn, the war affected these businesses. Attention, new or renewed, should be given to questions such as:

- How did some companies, close to the battlefields, secure their businesses from saboteurs or concerted military movements?
- How did other firms, farther from the battlefield, still help determine the war's outcome?
- How did the companies use their participation in the war to build brand image and new product acceptance?
- How did the companies meet uncertain, but rising, demand during the war, and then grapple with looming overcapacity at war's end?
- How did some companies avoid, let alone survive, charges of profiteering?
- How did companies boost morale by providing the comforts and contacts of home, given that soldiers and sailors spent more time in camp or aboard ship fighting boredom rather than Rebels?

Fourth, I hope the book will provide a new model for a combination of business and military history research and writing. While critically acclaimed and readily available histories exist for some of the subject companies, most devote less than a chapter (if any) to the Civil War years. Furthermore, they often ignore relevant sources familiar to military historians, such as official records, contemporary letters and photographs, and post-war memoirs. Likewise, traditional military histories of the Civil War often fail to take advantage of crucial corporate sources, including board meeting minutes, advertisements, and sales records. I have endeavored to use a healthy mix of these resources—including heretofore unpublished material—and hope the "Essay on Sources" will lead others to significant research and conclusions of their own.

I had three criteria in choosing the companies to be covered: First, they best exemplified the points I wished to make and contemporary records existed to tell their stories well; second, they continue to have broad consumer appeal with products or services used by today's average American; and lastly—and most important—their stories are worth telling because their actions had a direct and tremendous effect on the lives of individual soldiers and sailors, their families, and their comrades-in-arms, whether in camp, on the march, or in battle.

Jim Schmidt

LINCOLN'S LABELS

America's Best-Known Brands and the Civil War

Introduction

ON SEPTEMBER 17, 1861, a notice on the front page of Cincinnati's premier newspaper, the *Gazette*, attracted the interest of the city's businessmen. The long announcement—beginning just above the fold and continuing for several inches below—declared that proposals were being sought to supply a million pounds of bread, hundreds of thousands of pounds of bacon, rice, and sugar, and tens of thousands of pounds of hams, coffee, and apples. Also needed were "25,000 pounds first quality candles," and "80,000 pounds of good hard soap."[1]

In another year, the solicitation for so much in the way of food and staples might have signaled preparations for a magnificent autumn social befitting the Ohio River's "Queen City." But 1861 was no ordinary year, and a closer perusal of the paper would have belied any illusion of normalcy. Martial poems, including one entitled "The Picket," flanked the sides of the long list, and above and below were even more requests: for mess pans, infantry pants, and "gunboats for the western rivers." All this served as evidence that the Civil War—the first shots of which had been fired that spring, was in full gear. What's more, battles already waged from Missouri to Virginia to South Carolina were testament that the war would *not* be a picnic.[2]

The long advertisement in the *Gazette* was printed at the behest of Major A. B. Eaton, chief of the Office of the Commissary of Subsistence, with an eye towards building up stores to feed the Union armies in the coming campaigns. Still, Eaton's seemingly long list represented only a fraction of the needs of the army's subsistence department. Indeed, several such rolls, from "A to Z," were needed to outfit all of the departments of the rapidly growing Union Army and Navy: ambulances, badges, caissons, drums, envelopes, fifes, grapeshot, hardtack, insignia, johns tents, knapsacks, lamps, minie balls, needles, overcoats, pens, quinine, rammers, sabots, telescopes, uniforms, valises, wagons, yams, zouave caps, and so on.

To acquire these items, government authorities—state and federal—advertised widely in newspapers and then granted supply contracts to hundreds of companies. Most of these firms are long out of business, but a few still remain, as witnessed in another notice printed in the same newspaper a few months later. There, on the front page of the March 20, 1862, edition, was a list of contracts awarded the previous day by Major C. L. Kilburn, a commissary agent headquartered in the city: "30,000 lbs. new bacon sides to Brooks, Johnson & Co," "50,000 pounds lbs. hard bread to Brubeck & Height," and "7,000 lbs. Rio coffee to R. M. Bishop & Co." At the end, given contracts for "1,200 lbs. star candles" and "400 lbs. soap," was a Cincinnati company whose products (including soap) are found in an estimated ninety percent of American households *today*: The Procter & Gamble Company.[3]

P & G serves as a worthy model for introducing the other companies covered in this book, as its own story makes for something of an "everyman" experience of the various successes, challenges, and events, that drive the experiences of companies—famous and obscure—that did business in the Civil War: a "secession crisis," loss of a Southern base of materials or customers, competition for lucrative army contracts, the costs of doing business with the government, charges of profiteering, and the challenges of being close to the battlefields; all informed by an interesting company history and founding philosophy.

William Procter and James Gamble, immigrants from England and Ireland, respectively, arrived in Cincinnati, Ohio, in the early 1800s. James established himself as a soapmaker and William as a candlemaker. The men merged their businesses at the suggestion of their mutual father-in-law, Alexander Norris. A respected local candlemaker himself, Norris recognized both men competed for the animal fats from Cincinnati's many slaughterhouses (the city had been dubbed "Porkopolis"), necessary ingredients in the manufacture of soap and candles. On this advice, the partners gave birth to the Procter and Gamble Company in October 1837. By 1859, on the eve of southern secession, P & G sales had reached $1 million and the company employed eighty people in its manufactory.

When increasing sectional tensions made war seem possible, potential suppliers had an important decision of whether to invest in key raw materials in advance. It was not a sure bet: without the investment, they might not have sufficient stockpiles to manufacture their goods; with the investment, they might find themselves holding abundant inventory—but no demand—if the war ended after a short affair. "Whilst others timidly hung back until the article was needed, I went boldly into the market and bought all that was for sale," William Cozens, a leading tent manufacturer in Philadelphia, commented on his gamble of buying up cotton and linen duck in the war's early days. He also realized the consequences of the risk: "Had this enormous stock fallen upon my hands, my disaster would have been great," he added.[4]

For P & G, a critical raw material was rosin. A key ingredient in soapmaking, rosin came almost exclusively from the harvest of trees from forests in the Deep South, arriving in Cincinnati on boats from New Orleans, the principal center of the trade. War would stall P & G's relationship with southern rosin merchants, and thus stall the company's ability to continue its primary product. It was this concern that prompted the principals to send their sons, William Alexander Procter and James Norris Gamble, to New Orleans in 1860. The two young men managed to quickly purchase a huge cache of rosin at the low price of $1.00 a barrel.

The purchase the two young men managed was no small deed: it proved the largest single acquisition of rosin made by any Cincinnati soap manufacturer up to that time. Wartime P & G employee John M. Donnelly, in his reminisces, regarded the New Orleans episode as "one of the many instances of keen foresight so characteristic of members of this firm in all its history." Lacking the same foresight, the other local soap manufacturers considered the purchase extravagant and unnecessary, and—like tentmaker Cozens's competition—predicted the doom of P & G.[5]

The gamble paid off for P & G as it had for Cozens. When war broke out only months later, other soap manufacturers scrambled to find rosin so they could submit bids and samples to the government. Donnelly later recalled that "Rosin went up to eight, ten, and fifteen dollars a barrel, and there was none to be had anywhere. Procter and Gamble were the only people who had any." After close inspection of the P & G samples, officials gave the company contracts to furnish the western armies with soap and candles during the entire war.[6]

Still, lucrative government contracts had their own risks for the winning bidders. Before goods were shipped to the depots, they were subject to inspection, and the rigor and probity—or lack thereof—of the inspectors could have important consequences for the contractors. If too strict, they could refuse materiel, thus damaging the contractors' profits; if too lax (or corrupt) they could do damage to the Union war effort. More important, delays in accepting the goods necessarily delayed payment. Donnelly maintained that the inspectors "never once failed to find [the P & G soap] up to the standard marked on each one of the boxes: 'Full Weight.'"[7]

Contractors also faced criticism from a public and press wary of profiteering from the war's first days. One newspaper declared that "cheating the government . . . is so common as to be presumed nearly universal." The paper also concluded that some businessmen—"men of fair repute"—purposely avoided government business to maintain their reputations, shrinking "from the imputation of contracting as though it were akin to forgery or theft." For its part, P & G did not inflate its prices, despite a competitive advantage in raw materials. In the March 1862 announcement of the soap and candle contracts in the *Gazette*, the awarding officer noted that the awards had "been given out at very low prices."[8]

To be sure, not all suppliers to the Union Army were as particular about the quality of their goods, and P & G's adherence to such high standards may have embittered other local manufacturers. One historian relates an anecdote in which a gang of hoodlums threw stones at the Procter home, breaking windows and hurling debris inside. A reporter explained that "both William Procter and James Gamble had been denouncing manufacturers who were cheating the government and the troops." Procter in particular had exposed a company which was supplying soldiers with supposedly woolen blankets actually made of mere rags. An unexplained fire in a wing of the P & G factory during the war might also have been due to sabotage.[9]

Some contractors not only faced the wrath of jealous local competitors, but also the prospect of concerted movements by the enemy or subterfuge by Rebel sympathizers; and the closer they were to the front, the greater the risk. Some company principals even had to take up arms to protect their property. P & G's great "military crisis" came in mid-August 1862, when Confederate Major General E. Kirby Smith launched an invasion of Kentucky. Beginning in eastern Tennessee, Smith moved through central Kentucky, and reached Lexington, only eighty miles from Cincinnati, in the first days of September.

Until then situated in friendly territory, and seemingly removed from the ravages of war, the citizens of Cincinnati now found themselves threatened by attack with no trained troops to shield them. Union Major General Horatio G. Wright, commander of the Department of the Ohio, acted quickly and gave Major General Lew Wallace responsibility for the defense of Cincinnati. Wallace promptly declared martial law, and on September 2, 1862, ordered that "all business must be suspended at nine o'clock to-day. Every business house must be closed." The employees of P & G had been working day and night for months to meet the demands of their contracts, and Donnelly remembered that P & G "was the only factory allowed to work at all during the reign of martial law."[10]

Meanwhile, Ohio Governor David Tod called for able-bodied men to come to the defense of Cincinnati until it could be garrisoned by regular infantry. Thousands of men answered Tod's plea. These farmers, woodsmen, and businessmen, armed with their own rifles and shotguns, and with little or no military training, were collectively called "squirrel hunt regiments." The founders of P & G were arguably too old to shoulder a weapon in defense of their city; however, the younger James Norris Gamble was a member of one of these homeguard units. Regular troops began to arrive and the alarm in Cincinnati subsided when it became clear that Kirby Smith's attention was actually focused elsewhere.

Contracting during the Civil War had its disadvantages, but businesses also reaped the benefits of an unprecedented and unforeseen economic force: wide distribution of their products and labels, and subsequent name recognition by large groups of customers. P & G delivered their supplies to Camp Dennison, Ohio, where they were further distributed by the Union Army. When the cases of soap and candles carrying the P & G name and their "moon and stars" trademark reached the camps, soldiers used every scrap of material. Donnelly recalled, "It was often said at the army camps that the only seats provided for them were the Procter & Gamble soap boxes, but they had plenty of them." After four years of this ersatz "advertising," P & G became one of the best known firms in the North.[11]

The reputation for quality, and name recognition, that P & G sowed during the Civil War produced a harvest of innovation and expansion that transformed it into one of the nation's largest and most familiar firms. To be sure, the saga of P & G in America's great conflict is fascinating; even more so because it strengthens our own sense of identity with the average soldier. But the company's experience is not singular: a host of other iconic names in American business—Brooks Brothers, Borden's, Tiffany's, *Scientific American*, du Pont, Squibb, American Express, and others—all had wartime experiences every bit as interesting. Here are their stories.

Figure 2. The sacking of Brooks Brothers during the New York draft riots
Source: *Harper's Weekly*

Figure 3. New York Zouaves wearing the North African-inspired uniforms.
Source: Library of Congress

CHAPTER ONE

An Army of Scarecrows

We know, Mr. Weller—we, who are men of the world—that a good uniform must work its way with the women, sooner or later. In fact, that's the only thing, between you and me, that makes the service worth entering into.

—*The Pickwick Papers*

MORE THAN FIFTY YEARS AFTER THE FACT, Eugene Ware still remembered how the militia companies in Burlington, Iowa—one composed mainly of Germans and the other of Irish—had attracted his attention. "They were both fiercely pugnacious," Ware wrote, "the Germans having a little more fight than the other . . . when there were festive occasions and these two military companies paraded, they paraded separately, and when the thing was over and military discipline at an end, there was liable to be a fight, and generally a fight that was stubborn."[1]

In the late 1850s, Ware got his chance to join. He bought his own uniform and, after some drilling, became quite proficient and proudly marched in the company's exhibitions in the city. As the unit matured, it grew more expert still, especially under the helm of an old, kind-hearted Swede who had fought in Europe and had been through the Mexican War. "Our Swedish captain wanted us to become Zouaves [a colorfully-adorned soldier popularized by the French wars in Africa]," Ware remembered, "so we all bought Zouave uniforms—leather leggings, red flannel baggy trousers, a light-blue woolen shirt, and a bob-tailed, dark-blue cloth jacket . . . with rows of round brass buttons. A little gold braid was put on and a jaunty cap with a gold band." Ware concluded that "a handsomer body of young men could not have been found."[2]

Ware's Zouaves constituted the larger part of another local military company: the "Wide Awakes," a pro-Union paramilitary organization that had chapters across the nation. The town's Democrats formed their own company, adopted a Scotch plaid uniform, and called themselves the "Douglas Clan" or the "Little Giants." With partisan tensions stirred, either the Wide Awakes or the Little Giants were promenading on the streets all the time, and—like the German and Irish companies he watched as a youngster—Ware was now party to fisticuffs of his own. "It was hard to have a political parade without a fight," he remembered.[3]

With the passing of Lincoln's election, it became apparent that war was likely. Even more men wanted to join Burlington's Zouaves, and Ware became a drillmaster of new recruits. By spring, the company had grown to 200 men. When news of the firing on Fort Sumter reached town, the unit immediately offered its services to Iowa's governor; but, with so many men prepared to go, Ware was not assured a spot.

"I went home that night with a very heavy heart," he remembered, "feeling that I was not going to get into the company and I was not going to get to see any of the trouble." A few nights later, at a local tavern, Ware encountered a Rebel sympathizer waxing poetic about how "one Southern man could beat five [Yankees] any time or any where." A fight ensued in which Ware came out on top; the victory won him accolades and—more important—a spot in the company.[4]

Only half the company had the Zouave uniforms, however, and local veterans of the Mexican War criticized the attire as unfit for the rigors of camp and battle. The state had no uniforms to give, so the girls in town organized themselves and made an outfit "the way they wanted it," Ware recalled, "with some art and some style put into it so that we would be adorned as well as uniformed." With bemusement, Ware described the homespun uniform in detail:

> The coat, as made, was a hunting-frock of the pioneer Daniel Boone type, fitting closely at the neck, cuff, and belt, but full of surplusage everywhere else. It was made of a fluffy, fuzzy, open-woven, azure-gray cloth, the like of which I had never seen before and have never seen since. The cuff, collar, and a band up and down the breast were flannel of a beautiful Venetian red, insuring a good target. Trowsers of a heavy buckskin type and color. Black felt hunting-hat, with a brilliant red-ribbon cockade.[5]

Now uniformed, Ware and his company joined hundreds of fellow statesmen in Keokuk, where they were mustered into the First Iowa Infantry in mid-May 1861 for three months' service. Few thought the war would last that long. The First left Iowa for Missouri in mid-June, marching from Macon City to Renick and then to Booneville in a week's time, as part of Brigadier General Nathaniel Lyon's "Army of the West."

"We now began looking for the foe," Ware remembered, "the 'foe' is what we were after." In Lyon's eye, the "foe" was the Missouri State Guard under Major General Sterling Price. Lyon had chased him from St. Louis to Booneville to Jefferson City and was now advancing toward Springfield.[6]

Ware had enlisted in April. It was now mid-July, and Lyon's campaign was wearing the men down. "Regarding the First Iowa, I may here say that they had begun to look tough," Ware wrote. "In the first place, no two companies were uniformed alike. Each company had a different shape of clothes and in different colors. . . . In addition to this, many uniforms had been completely worn out and the boys had bought what they could get, or had got new things from home already partially worn. It was a motley crew." Ware was right about the eclectic uniforms of his comrades. "[They] were a mixture of every shade and shape," one historian declared. "The jackets varied from dark blue to light bluish-gray, while two companies wore black and white tweed frock coats. The pants ranged from black with red stripes to pink satinet with light green stripes."[7]

It was all too much for Franc Wilkie, a reporter with the *Dubuque Herald* who was traveling with Ware's regiment. When he compared the condition of his fellow Iowans with a regiment of Missourians in "their clean, handsome blue uniforms and glittering rifles and sword bayonets with the dirty, travel-soiled appearance of our men, with their old-fashioned black muskets, I was ashamed of Iowa," he reported. He continued:

A State pretending to loyalty, sends a thousand men into service, looking like an army of scarecrows, while a secession state [Missouri] furnishes twice as many regiments, and gets them ready for service in a style unsurpassed by that of the best soldiers in the world. It was enough to make one curse in utter vexation to see our men as they trampled wearily through the sand—their rags fluttering like streamers—their whole appearance more like that of a crowd of vagabonds chased from civilization. If the children of Israel looked half as ragged and dirty and woe-begone, after their forty years tramp in the wilderness, as our men yesterday, they were a meaner looking set of men than one can well imagine.[8]

Wilkie needn't have been so critical of Iowa: the regiment that caught his attention was the exception to the rule in Lyon's army. Also, other Missourians were less well off; a soldier in the Third Missouri wrote that his regiment "resembled a rabble more than soldiers. Each one wore whatever clothes he chose to wear. They had become torn on the march. Some had no trousers anymore. In place of trousers they had slipped on sacks for head coverings." An officer in the First Kansas Infantry had "tinfoil shoulder straps sewed with black thread," and other Kansans had government-issued blouses and socks (if they were not barefooted) and headgear that ranged from "Jackson's white plug at Talladega to Scott's monstrosity at Cherubusco."9

Lyon and his "army of scarecrows"—about 6,000 strong—were camped at Springfield, Missouri. Confederate troops under the command of Brigadier General Benjamin McCulloch had joined Price's Missourians, making them about 12,000 strong. On August 9, both sides—each unbeknownst to the other—formulated plans to attack. At about five o'clock the following morning, Lyon, in two columns, attacked the Confederates on Wilson's Creek, about twelve miles southwest of Springfield.

The first major battle of the war west of the Mississippi was fierce; it was also confusing. The panoply of uniforms on both sides—Price and McCulloch's men wore a mix of blue, gray, and butternut themselves—led to several incidents of mistaken identity. At a critical point in the battle, Colonel Franz Sigel, commanding one of Lyon's two columns, saw a regiment in gray emerge from the smoke. The optimistic Sigel—who had pressed for the two-column approach—expected to link up with Lyon's forces at some time in the battle and, thinking that the approaching force was Ware's own gray-clad First Iowa, ordered his men to hold their fire.

In fact, the troops emerging from the haze were soldiers of the opposing Third Louisiana, and when they began firing it was a great surprise to Sigel and his men. Sigel, horrified at what he thought was tragic friendly fire, screamed in his native German, "*Sie haben gegen uns geschossen! Sie irrten sich!*" ("They [are] firing against us! They make a mistake!"). Some of the Union soldiers returned fire, but the Third Louisiana was largely unopposed and quickly routed Sigel's force from the field.[10]

The battle was going no better across the creek. Lyon had been killed leading the First Iowa in a charge; his column had faced three charges by Confederates up "Bloody Hill" and, low on ammunition, could scarcely face another. The Union force, now under Major Samuel Sturgis, retreated to Springfield.

As for Ware himself, he was justly proud of how his company and regiment fought in the battle and incredulous that they had left the field to the Confederates. Still, Ware drew two important lessons from his first of many actions in the war: "One thing which the battle . . . forever settled was that a 'mudsill' would fight," Ware decided. "And another thing was forever settled, that one Southern man could not whip five Northern men."[11]

Eugene Ware's experience with uniforms in the early part of the Civil War was not a singular one. In the hectic days following Fort Sumter, the federal government was hard pressed to supply uniforms for tens of thousands of volunteers, let alone impose standards for color, pattern, and quality. The states took responsibility—as best they could—for outfitting their regiments; a few governors were able to supply their men with durable uniforms that matched, but most relied on militia units—like Ware's Zouaves—to go to war in sometimes gaudy and often impractical attire until they could be properly outfitted.

In the early days of the Civil War, blue and gray had not yet taken on any partisan significance. On each side, soldiers wore both colors, even in the same regiments. This confusion due to the variety of uniforms made a great difference in the war's early days. The First Battle of Bull Run (a month before Ware's trial at Wilson's Creek) and the Battle of Cheat Mountain (a month after) witnessed "friendly fire" incidents caused by uncertainty about the uniforms of approaching parties.

In late September 1861, the War Department issued a circular to the governors, respectfully asking that "no troops hereafter furnished . . . be uniformed in gray, that being the color generally worn by the enemy," and requested instead that they adopt the blue uniform of the United States Army, as it was "readily distinguishable from that of the enemy." Nevertheless, as late as April 1862—just a few days before the Battle of Shiloh—Major General Ulysses S. Grant complained that some of his men were "still in the gray uniform, and owing to the bad quality of clothing on hand [were] reluctant to draw others" to replace them. It was the summer of 1862 before the Union ranks were rid of gray and the federal government assumed the full role of contracting and distributing uniforms.[12]

While the change resulted in improved quality and consistency of clothing, this did not make them any more comfortable. Most often, the uniforms just didn't fit: one Yankee soldier wrote that he "could never find . . . a blouse or pair of trousers small enough, nor an overcoat cast on my lines." Even when the clothes did fit, the heat in the South only made the wool more uncomfortable. One of the companies in the First Iowa, reporter Franc Wilkie wrote, was "uniformed in dark roundabout and pants, with a round cap of the same color. . . . Black is eminently respectable on all occasions, yet is not perhaps calculated for a summer dress beneath the broiling sun of the South."[13]

Regulations called for general officers to wear a double-breasted dark blue frock coat with an arrangement of buttons commensurate with rank (three sets of three for a major general, four sets of two for a brigadier, etc.), plain dark blue trousers, and a black felt hat. Still, they displayed variation in their dress, especially since officers were required to supply their own uniforms. George Armstrong Custer, for one, was famous for his showy dress—one officer exclaimed, "He looks like a circus rider gone mad!" Others, if less ostentatious, could still be very particular about their dress and often commissioned their personal tailors to make their coats. Gouverneur K. Warren wrote to his tailors at Richardson, Spence & Thomson with just pride:

> I have been promoted to Maj. Genl. Volunteers and wish if you have a piece of the cloth of which you made my last coat in June to have the breast of it and the shoulder straps changed . . . I might have the stars taken out of the straps and new ones put in if it can be done, or I could perhaps exchange them with you as the coat has never been worn except the day I was married, or I could give them away to some of my friends who have been promoted and order new ones.[14]

Another example of the fussiness (and investments) of Union general officers can be found in a letter from Major General John Pope to the same tailor:

> I enclose herewith a draft for $153, the amount of your bill. I am sorry to be obliged to tell you that the two uniform coats you made me are entirely useless to me. They were made out of the heaviest cloth, stuffed so full of padding and buckram, that it was an undertaking wearing them about on one's person and they would have fitted anybody else as well as me. I have spent nearly their whole cost in having them altered but without success. If I had not had them cut up so, I would send them back.[15]

The rank-and-file soldiers didn't have the luxury to be so fastidious about clothing. As a rule, they were content just to have enough. Still, even that was a tall order for a Quartermaster Department with the responsibility of outfitting each of its soldiers with an allowance of socks, shoes, hats, coats, jackets, shirts, trousers, and underwear. In four years, the department spent more than $300 million on clothing—twice as much as spent on weapons. The army had its own clothing establishments at various depots—each employing thousands of seamstresses at any one time—but they also depended on the large clothing industry in the United States.

One of the firms in that burgeoning industry was Brooks Brothers. Once the country's first "ready-to-wear" fashion emporium, it is now an American institution. Founded in 1818 and the oldest surviving men's clothier in the United States, Brooks Brothers had a Civil War far more interesting than its actual sales should have warranted: it has long been associated in literature—perhaps unfairly—with the war's early contracting scandals; it faced labor problems and a pitched battle within its very walls; it outfitted famous Union generals—Grant, Sherman, Sheridan, and Hooker—and crafted coats and suits for President Lincoln.

Henry Sands Brooks spent $15,250 for a building and property on the corner of Catharine and Cherry Streets in New York City, and he opened a clothing store there on April 7, 1818. Little is known of the founder himself; forty-six years old when he opened the store, Henry was the son of David Brooks, a physician and scion of a family that had come to America from England more than a century before Henry was born. In 1747, Dr. Brooks moved to Manhattan and established a private practice on the same corner where his son would open his clothing emporium.

Before going into business himself, Henry Brooks was employed as a "provisioner" supplying goods to seafarers, fur traders, and other trailblazers of sea and shore. The occupation made him a well-traveled and well-connected man, with a reputation as a dandy, leading him quite logically to his own enterprise. One company history states that Brooks was "known particularly for his colorful waistcoats. . . . Since the bulk of his trans-Atlantic luggage consisted of fulfilling requests for friends who wanted materials, coats, and waistcoats from abroad, it was a natural step to go into the business professionally."[16]

The Brooks family had something of a monopoly on the corner of Catharine and Cherry. Henry's business addresses were 80 and 116 Cherry; his residence was listed at 159 Cherry, his mother's at 97 Catherine, and his brother David's at 148 Cherry. But the corner had more than a family connection: it was the center of great commercial energy and an ideal location to start an enterprise. The city's principal shipyards were in the neighborhood, and the corner led straight to the Brooklyn ferry. By 1830, Cherry Street—from James to Market—was the center of a thriving clothing trade.

Henry's stated philosophy was to "make and deal only in merchandise of the best quality, to sell it at a fair profit only, and to deal only with people who seek and are capable of appreciating such merchandise." America had not yet developed its own sense of fashion and well-heeled gentleman of the era—those "capable of appreciating" Henry Brooks's goods—still looked to London for trends in dress. To fulfill his mission of "the best quality," then, Henry had to make clothes of British style *and* material. To that end, he built on his early trading relationships with British seaman and merchants so that he had ready access to products of their best mills.[17]

Before Brooks died in 1833 (apart from daily charge books, not much is known about the first decade-plus of the enterprise), he brought his sons—Daniel, John, Elisha, and Edward—into the business. The sons, ranging from their early teens to mid-twenties, carried on the business as their father had—the eponymous "H. & D. H. Brooks & Co." (Henry's brother David had been his partner for a time)—for nearly two decades before changing the name to "Brooks Brothers" in 1850. At about the same time, they established the "Golden Fleece" as the company's trademark. The icon—a sheep suspended in a ribbon—had a wide-ranging origin, from the mythical ram sought by Jason and the Argonauts to the emblem of an elite order of fifteenth-century knights. The brothers more likely took it from its long-time association as a symbol of the British wool trade.

By mid-century, the brothers had established their enterprise as one of the city's premier clothiers and themselves as rich men. Of the firm's reputation, a period walking guide for the city declared, "Commencing in a moderate way, upon a safe and sure foundation, the enterprise from time to time has been gradually enlarged, until, at present, it has reached a commanding position among similar establishments . . . In one word, it is a model establishment, and as such contrasts favorably with any in the country. Every variety of Clothing is kept constantly on hand for sale." In

1855, two of the brothers—Edward and Elisha—were listed in Moses Yales Beach's encyclopedia of the city's wealthiest citizens.[18]

The endorsement's closing line holds a clue to the reason behind the firm's success: ready-made clothing. Before the advent of the sewing machine, all clothing was made by hand. The rich depended on tailors, the poor on homespun. Iowan Eugene Ware remembered that, when he was a boy, "The clothes were made by old women, as a rule. There were widows and others who, as seamstresses, would go around to the houses and make clothes for the children. There were a couple of old ladies who always came to our house and whom my mother employed to make clothes, and my mother frequently did the cutting-out of the clothes herself. They were not scientifically fashioned, but I never found any trouble with them."[19]

Likewise, clothing expert Jenna Wessman Joselit declared that for the average nineteenth-century American, "assembling and maintaining a wardrobe was by no means easy. A drain on their finances and their energies, it took some doing. . . . The practice of having [stylish] clothes made . . . demanded patience and ready-cash, both of which were in short supply among everyone but the well-to-do." Neither Henry Brooks nor any of his sons knew how to cut or sew, but they were expert at selling off-the-rack outfits of high quality at a nominal cost. For more discriminating gentlemen, Brooks also maintained a department of tailors.[20]

By the 1850s, the city's professionals and upper classes were leaving the environs of lower Manhattan and moving north and west. To stay close to their customers (and their money), the brothers opened another store at the corner of Grand and Broadway in 1857. *Valentine's Manual*—the city's annual gazette and almanac—described the new multi-story store "as the largest establishment of its kind in the world." The directory continued:

> This magnificent warehouse, is one of the most substantially built, elegantly furnished, and conspicuous architectural ornaments on Broadway. The whole area comprised in its five floors is 100,000 square feet. . . . Nearly all the walls and lofty ceilings are frescoed in a style of consummate elegance. . . . [On the first floor] some twenty strong and ornate pillars support the lofty frescoed ceiling, and along the walls at intervals rise immense mirrors, six by twelve feet in dimensions, framed in elaborately carved black walnut . . . the chandeliers and gas-fixtures are of the richest and heaviest description. . . . [On the second floor] rises

17

a pagoda, fifteen feet in diameter by thirty feet in height. The dome is surmounted by a Globe Clock, with four dials, which in the evening is illuminated from the inside by gas-light, thus showing the time to all points throughout the floor."[21]

The Brooks were doing well on the eve of the Civil War, indeed; but the conflict would bring to their door a new clientele of thousands that would stretch the principals—and their principles—to the limit.

Brooks Brothers had a long and happy association with area militia units, many of which looked to the clothier to provide their uniforms before and at the outset of the Civil War. For example, the 55th New York Militia—a French-American unit that styled itself "The Lafayette Guard"—retained the colorful uniform of its Gallic heritage and contracted with Brooks Brothers for "60 French Imported Scarlet Fez Caps at $1.25 each" as well as brown drilling pants until sufficient cloth could be had for their traditional red trousers. Likewise, on April 19, 1861—less than a week after the firing at Fort Sumter—Wilson H. Smith, recording secretary of Company C of the 2nd Connecticut Militia, noted in his minutes two resolutions: first, that the unit adopt the hat of the state uniform, and second: "That we telegraph to Brooks Brothers to send a cutter up to measure the Company."[22]

While the "Garde de Lafayette" had secured its own uniforms, the state of New York was anxious to outfit thousands of volunteers as quickly as possible so that they could be sent to Washington. To that end, within days of the beginning of the war, the state's military board placed advertisements for complete uniforms for 12,000 men: "a jacket of dark Army blue cloth . . . the coat to be buttoned with eight buttons . . . ; trowsers . . . of light Army blue, cut full in the leg and large around the foot; an overcoat of light army blue; and a fatigue cap of dark blue, with a waterproof cover, to be made with a cape which will fall to the shoulder." The coat, trousers, and overcoats were to be made in four sizes. An important proviso was that the uniforms should be "well and properly cut and made . . . strongly and thoroughly sewed and stitched, and all materials shall be of the best quality of their respective kinds."[23]

The contracts were open to competitive bidding, but given the nature of the national emergency, potential suppliers were given only twenty-four hours to prepare and submit bids and samples. The contract was awarded to

Brooks Brothers at $19.50 per uniform, with 2,000 to be delivered each week. Other firms made bids based on conditional availability of the correct cloth, whereas Robert Freeman—a longtime Brooks Brothers employee—represented that *only* his firm could positively furnish the necessary material. Within days it became clear not only that Brooks Brothers itself did not have enough material to make the uniforms, but also that there wasn't even enough material to be had on the local market to complete the order.

Brooks Brothers asked permission to substitute gray cloth of equal quality for some of the uniforms. The state was in a quandary: the military depots were filling quickly with volunteers (all without uniforms), and the danger to the capital city called for them to be outfitted as quickly as possible. William A. Jackson—the state's inspector general—telegraphed to New York urgently asking for permission to amend the contract. Philip Dorsheimer—the state's treasurer, acting on behalf of (but apparently not in concert with) the Military Board—agreed to the substitution.

Unfortunately for the soldiers—and for Brooks Brothers' reputation—some of the substitute cloth was lower-grade material known in the garment industry as "shoddy"—and the uniforms began to fall apart within weeks. The historian of the 19th New York remembered the uniforms with acrimony: "Stripes of dark gray ran through them, with streaks of butternut intermingled. Patches of green, spots of brown, and splashes of other colors, dotted their surface, and no less than eighteen different hues were counted in them by an inquiring volunteer. Shabby in color, uncomfortable from the gritty dust in them, flabby to texture, they were also ungainly in cut." Another soldier who wore the jackets described the cloth as a "coarse, fluffy, flimsy material." At the slightest provocation it began to fall apart "irritating the skin and covering the floor with refuse."[24]

The workmanship of many of the uniforms was also dubious and showed signs of haste and carelessness in their making; the *New York Times* reported that "some were without buttons; some with button-holes not worked; some with seams unsewed." Fingers were pointed in all directions. Brooks Brothers declared that the uniforms had been duly certified by a board of inspectors, and the inspectors insinuated that the Military Board allowed a change in the contract out of corrupt motive. The board—infuriated at the charge—declared the inspectors incompetent and inattentive. The papers censured the Military Board, first for not acting fast enough to outfit the state's volunteers—charging it with parsimony, want of zeal and patriotism, and undue attention to forms and procedures (they called it "red-tapeism")—and then later for the scandal, which the board could fairly say was actually due to too-quick attention to the volunteers.[25]

The scandal—compounded by similar outrages in Philadelphia and Washington—led to widespread interest in Congressman Charles Van Wyck's investigating committee, which was charged to look into the contracts made during the war. Van Wyck went from city to city (a dozen in all) looking into irregularities in contracts for steamships, cattle hides and beef tallow, and other goods—irregularities alleged, supposed, or real. "Plenty of swindling has been discovered," the *Janesville* (Wisconsin) *Daily Gazette* declared, but it mentioned only *one* firm by name: "Brooks Brothers of New York made a clear $100,000 by their clothing operation with the state."[26]

In New York, the members of the Military Board and each of the brothers Brooks were deposed on four questions: the terms of the original contract as they understood it; the circumstances that led to a change in the contract; whether they had any personal interest—direct or indirect—in the contract; and whether they had "any knowledge of any money or other valuable thing being paid, promised, or given to any person for aiding [the] Brooks Brothers to obtain an acceptance of their proposals" or the change in the contract.[27]

As a rule, all the men were in accord on the terms of the original contract and the circumstances that led to the change in the bid. There was less agreement on matters of personal gain. Robert Freeman—the Brooks Brothers agent who, purposely or unwittingly, misrepresented his firm's ability to fulfill the contract—faced most of the fire. Authorities accused him of obtaining early notice of the pending contract and improperly using it to his advantage. He was also charged with gifting Treasurer Dorsheimer's wife with a new dress on behalf of Brooks Brothers. When interrogated, one board member recalled that "Elisha Brooks . . . informed me that they 'had designed to do something handsome for Robert Freeman,'" but didn't know if Freeman was aware of the pending gift.[28]

Likewise, William Jackson—who had left his office as the state's inspector general to take command of the 18th New York Volunteer Infantry—faced allegations that he used his influence to award the contract to Brooks Brothers. Jackson and the 18th performed admirably at the Battle of First Bull Run, but a combination of the unhealthy southern climate and the privations of service in the field conspired to make him ill, and he died in Washington, unable to clear his name personally.

Certainly, of all the parties involved, the Brooks stood to gain the most. It may seem hackneyed, but had they stuck to their father's principles—to make clothes of the best quality at a fair profit—they might well have avoided recrimination. In addition, the contract allowed Brooks Brothers to divide the large order among other clothiers, an act which would have quickened the outfitting of the volunteers, lessened haste and carelessness in the cutting and sewing, and most importantly, minimized jealousy among their disappointed rivals (who probably pushed for the investigations). But instead, the brothers kept the contract for themselves. Future contracts were purposely divided among several clothiers.

Few argued that the Brooks's winning bid was unfair; the contract even allowed for an increase in price if the great demand for the necessary articles created an increase in their market value. The Brooks's mistake was failing to reduce the price when they substituted the cheaper grade of fabric. When a New York legislator pressed Elisha Brooks as to how much money he made or saved by changing the cloth, he answered, "I cannot answer how much; I have never made the calculation." Unsatisfied with Brooks's "plausible deniability," the lawmaker pressed again, but Brooks demurred, replying "I think I can't ascertain the difference without spending more time than I can now devote to the purpose." In the end, Brooks Brothers replaced about 2,300 uniforms at a cost to the company of more than $45,000.[29]

The fact that any ready-made clothier felt confident enough to meet the demand for thousands of uniforms in short order was due to two important factors: the scale of the garment industry and the efficiencies gained from technologies such as the sewing machine. Brooks Brothers serves as an excellent example of both. James W. Miller—a foreman with the firm—indicated the magnitude of the clothing industry when he told reporters in 1860 that his "house alone [does] a business of over $1,000,000 annually." As impressive as his own sales were, though, Miller added "that the house of Brooks Brothers does not make 1-100th part of the machine-made clothing manufactured in New York," putting the business in that city alone at $100 million annually. The Brooks Brothers store on Broadway employed more than 200 salespeople to meet that demand.[30]

The increase in the amount of clothing that could be made—and then sold—was due in no small part to new technologies, especially the sewing machine. The first patent went to Elias Howe, Jr., in 1846, but he failed to successfully launch his product in the American market. He tried again in England but failed there also and returned to the States only to find that other machines were on the market. The new contraptions had original features but still infringed on Howe's patent, causing him to launch a legal battle that continued into the mid-1850s.

Isaac Singer, an erstwhile actor, mechanic, and sometime inventor, introduced a more perfect and practical machine in 1850. He began selling it and—like others before him—found himself a combatant in the "sewing machine wars." In 1856, a number of machine manufacturers—Singer among them—each accusing the others of infringement, met in Albany, New York, to pursue their suits. An able attorney representing one of the parties proposed that they "pool" their patents rather than waste earnings on countersuits. Once they secured Howe's cooperation, the men formed a combine, and terms were arranged so that royalties were split until the patents expired.

While the $125 price tag on a new Singer machine was prohibitive for the average housewife who did the family sewing, the nation's clothiers were early and eager adopters. Miller stated that Brooks Brothers used dozens of sewing machines in their stores, and "patronize those that others use, and do about three-fourths of all their sewing by machines, and pay annually for sewing labor about $200,000." One historian wrote of a young girl's impressions of the massive operation at Brooks Brothers: when Sally Shephard visited the highly appointed Broadway store with her father in 1861, she was "no less impressed by the four hundred persons cutting and sewing on the premises as she was by the bronze pillars and the painted rotunda."[31]

With many hundreds of his machines turning out tens of millions of dollars in ready-made clothing—and then an equal value in uniforms—Singer could be rightly proud of his invention's role in the war. His reputation for flamboyance and promotion was on full display at a large parade held in early March 1865 in New York to celebrate Lincoln's second inauguration and a string of Union successes on the battlefield. A reporter attached to the *Dubuque Democratic Herald* wrote, "One of the most imposing displays in the procession [was] that of the Singer Sewing Machine Manufacturing Company, with their six-horse teams, splendidly decorated, drawing trucks, upon which are erected magnificent pavilions filled with young ladies operating the Singer machines, in the manufacture of army clothing. On the sides of the pavilions was inscribed 'We clothe the Union armies while Grant is dressing the rebels.'" The "float" was escorted by a full band and a thousand men, all employees of the company.[32]

Because uniforms were the single most expensive class of goods produced for the Union armies during the Civil War, the potential financial rewards were huge for the private garment industry, including firms such as Brooks Brothers. But they didn't have the contract pie all to themselves. The firms competed with another class of workers: the thousands of seamstresses and tailors employed in the government's own arsenals, turning out tens of millions of dollars in uniforms. These colliding private and public interests led to battles over wages and job security and forced the Quartermaster Department into a difficult balancing act with very high stakes: what historian Mark Wilson has called the "make or buy" decision.[33]

For their part, the seamstresses at the government-run clothing halls guarded their fraction of the war economy jealously and pressured authorities for a bigger part still, at the expense of private industry. Certainly, the early uniforms scandals—in which Brooks Brothers played its unfortunate part—didn't help the contractors' cause, and the army seamstresses used the stain of profiteering to their advantage. When Sarah Jacobs—a seamstress at the St. Louis arsenal—was in danger of being downsized, she wrote President Lincoln with the entreaty that he "open again the workrooms [and] furnish through your quartermaster materials to these women, which can be wrought by their hands . . . into clothing, better than it is being made through the mediumship of private contractors, whose only care is to make the most profit—by the least work."[34]

Not only did the government garment workers champion for a greater share of the work to be done, they also pressed for higher wages for the work they were already doing. They organized themselves into groups (for example, the Sewing Women's Protective and Benevolent Association) to wield economic and political power; these collectives in turn put pressure on the private firms to raise their rates as well. At a rally of army seamstresses in Philadelphia, labor activist Martha Yeager railed against the aristocrats "who would live off the labor of others and then grow rich at their expense." Brooks Brothers was not immune to these wage pressures and activism.[35]

During the summer of 1861—in the wake of the contract scandal—Brooks Brothers dropped its rates by nearly twenty percent, on the grounds that business was dull and the firm could not afford to pay its usual wages. By fall, though, the firm had secured additional state contracts, and its workers—especially the firm's German tailors—felt justified in asking for their former prices. After some discussion among themselves, the tailors appointed a committee to call upon the principals, presenting a petition outlining their grievances and requesting an advance to their former rates. The committee "met with a cold reception from Mr. Dan Brooks," reported the *New York Times*. Brooks referred the men to foreman James Miller, whom, he said, "would adjust the difficulties and arrange a bill of prices satisfactory to all parties."[36]

The committee was not satisfied with Dan Brooks's curt dismissal and persisted that the brothers Brooks—and not Miller—"were the proper persons for them to consult." The Brookses deigned to an interview with the committee on a Saturday morning and agreed to give the former wages, with a few exceptions. The workers were still not satisfied, and about 100 of them met that evening "for the purpose of remonstrating against the reduced prices." The meeting was "regularly organized," reported the *Times*, "and much earnestness was manifested on the part of all present." They concluded to "work another week for the proposed prices, compare books, and decide on the course to be pursued by them hereafter."[37]

No more was reported on the Brooks Brothers' labor problems, but their wartime trials were far from over. In the summer of 1863, a confluence of events set New York City ablaze—literally and figuratively—and found the war not just at the doorstep of Brooks Brothers but within its very walls.

The problems actually started the previous spring when, on March 3, 1863, Congress—facing a shortage in military manpower—passed the country's first conscription act. The National Enrollment Act authorized the president to draft citizens between the ages of eighteen and thirty-five into military service. "Peace Democrats" were particularly upset (both on principle and on rhetoric) at provisions that allowed drafted men to either pay a $300 commutation fee or procure a substitute.

In fact, the act was crafted to spur voluntary enlistments, and liberal "bounties"—as high as $500 in some localities—encouraged recruitment (and the sorry practice of bounty jumping) and filled quotas without conscription.

Still, some politicians (notably New York's Governor Horatio Seymour) openly condemned the law, declared it unconstitutional, suggested that it was enforced along partisan lines (Seymour claimed that Democrats were drafted at a greater rate than Republicans), and used the symbolic argument of "a rich man's war and a poor man's fight." At the same time, the Tammany Hall political machine—the city's base of Democratic power, led by William "Boss' Tweed—was engaged in enrolling Irish immigrants as citizens so they could vote in local elections. Many discovered they now had to fight for their new country.

The draft lottery started quietly enough on Saturday, July 11, 1863, at the Ninth District Office on 3rd Avenue and 46th Street. Using the "wheel of misfortune," fully half of the state's 2,500-man quota had been selected without incident when the doors closed for the day. On Monday, July 13, the draft resumed peacefully, or so it seemed; the city's "Black Joke Engine Company 33," still rankled that one of its brethren had been called up (firemen were traditionally exempt from militia duty), had decided over the weekend to "rough up" the lottery office on Monday.

By late morning, the crowd of onlookers that gathered to witness the Jokers's "mussing up" had turned into an angry mob. It didn't help that Sunday's city newspapers carried both the names of Saturday's draftees and a roll of the dead and wounded from the Battle of Gettysburg; the Union victory had come at a terrible cost, and not a few of the fallen had Irish surnames. The draft office was guarded by a skeleton force of sixty uneasy policeman, led by G. T. Porter, captain of the city's 19th Precinct. Most of the city's militia—which might have been used to keep the peace—were still in Pennsylvania, having been called there to meet the emergency at Gettysburg. Apart from the police, the only other force available in the city was a small number of troops garrisoned at the harbor and a few soldiers of the "Invalid Corps"—disabled veterans fit enough only for guard duty.

A pistol shot triggered a volley of stones from the mob. Porter's men held off the mob long enough for the draft officials to escape but then retreated. The crowd stormed inside, and within minutes the office was in flames. The arson was the first act of nearly four days of unabated violence that targeted the city's armories, newspaper offices, institutions for free blacks, homes, and shops. Just as the Battle of Gettysburg had immortalized many smaller actions by name—Little Round Top, the Wheatfield, the Peach Orchard, Devil's Den, and others—so the Draft Riots had their own: the Battle of

Bleecker and Broadway, the Defense of the Tribune, the West Side Riots, the Attack on the Colored Sailors Home, and the Sacking of Brooks Brothers.

"From the first of the riot clothing appeared to be a great desideratum among the roughs composing the mob," *Harper's Weekly* declared a few weeks after, "a large number of marauders paid a visit to the extensive clothing-store of Messrs. Brooks Brothers, at the corner of Catharine and Cherry Streets. Here they helped themselves to such articles as they wanted, after which they might be seen dispersing in all directions, laden with their ill-gotten booty." The nation's other popular weekly—*Frank Leslie's Illustrated*—mentioned among other victims that "Brooks's clothing-store [was] plundered." The blandly factual summaries don't do justice to the violence within the store's walls.[38]

The store was attacked on the night of July 14, the second day of rioting. The most detailed report of the battle at Brooks Brothers can be found in the official police account. First on the scene, the police were also the first to publish a record of their heroics (indeed, before the year closed). Thirty police from the city's First Precinct were sent to the store's defense. The street lamps and lights in nearby homes were extinguished. "The night was very dark," reads the account; still, the Brooks Brothers store "was lighted up by the rioters so as to enable them to select and carry off the most valuable of goods." The police charged and were met by a "volley of musketry, stones, bricks, and etc, from all directions."[39]

The First's Sergeant Matthew, stationed in front of the building, charged into the store to repel the rioters. "Then commenced a scene which is indescribable," the police account continued. "The thieves attempted to rush through the police and escape. Some fell upon their knees before the uplifted clubs, shrieking for mercy, while the others wildly rushed in search of ways for a safe exit. On the second story, however, the rioters showed fight; but the police, making a determined charge, soon drove them into the rear building, where the majority of them, with most of their spoils, were kept and ultimately secured."[40]

The police account indicates that their appearance was "hailed with terror by most of the lawless." Some of the mob jumped downstairs and, once outside, were confronted by reinforcements from the Third and Fourth Precincts, "who drove them with terrible punishment, down Catharine and through Cherry Streets." "Upwards of a hundred shots were fired by the rioters" in the melee at Brooks Brothers, claimed the police record, which also detailed some of the close calls: Officer Van Ranst, of the First, received a pistol ball in his cap ("had he been but a little taller the bullet would have pierced his brain," the record stated grimly); Sergeant Finney, of the Third, was wounded in the face; and Sergeant Delany, of the Fourth, "was fired at by a man who was only about four feet from him, the wadding of the pistol knocking the Sergeant's cap off."[41]

The police spent the night and some of the rest of the week hunting up goods stolen from Brooks Brothers; they recovered $5,000 worth hidden in different homes in the ward. For the balance of Tuesday night and some days after, the police and Brooks Brothers employees kept guard at both stores (including thirteen-year-old Francis Lloyd at Broadway and Grand, who would one day become president of the company). Heroic as the police might have been, they were badly outnumbered and beleaguered, and control of the city was not reestablished until federal troops arrived (after a forced march from Maryland). The riot had largely subsided by the morning of Thursday, July 16. A period account places the toll at about 100 civilians killed, with another 300 injured. Property damage was more than a million dollars. (Brooks Brothers themselves recorded losses of $70,000).

For their part, the rioters never explained why they targeted Brooks Brothers. To be sure, the city's working-class Irish—who made up the bulk of the rioters—were incensed that summer: wartime inflation had eroded what little spending power they had, and in a few instances when they had gone on strike to protest low wages, employers had replaced them with black workers. Brooks Brothers' own labor problems a year earlier had not been with the Irish, however, but with their mostly German tailors (who also suffered at the hands of the rioters). Perhaps the rioters saw the clothier as a symbol of the city's elite, or maybe they remembered the uniform scandal. More likely it was a simple matter of the store being in the wrong place at the wrong time.

A year later, the editors of *Valentine's Manual* were still incredulous as to why the mob attacked the Catharine Street Store, stating (with not a little naiveté) that "the Messrs. Brooks are fair, upright gentlemen, of mild manners and such simplicity of deportment as to allay and conciliate rather than excite ill feeling in any with whom they come into intercourse."[42]

Brooks Brothers continued to deliver uniforms to New York troops throughout the war; in October 1861, Brigadier General Chester A. Arthur—then the state's quartermaster general and later the country's twenty-first president—accepted the firm's offer "to furnish overcoats for the 21st Regiment New York Volunteers (three hundred at eight & seven eighths dollars each) according to sample sent." Others contracts followed: 650 overcoats for the 12th New York State Militia in 1863 and 800 jackets and trousers for the 7th at war's end. Still, Brooks Brothers never became one of the prime contractors to the Union Army, no doubt because of its early war problems.[43]

The firm did do a steady business in outfitting some of the war's more famous Union generals, including Sherman, Grant, Sheridan, and Hooker. It's curious that some of these notable customers—especially Sherman and Grant—hailed from west of the Mississippi rather than the presumably more stylish east. On the other hand, perhaps that was the *very* reason they looked to Brooks Brothers to clothe them. As one historian suggests, some people "have an odd way of getting themselves into what they somehow think is modish dress when they come to New York."[44]

In June 1865, Ulysses S. Grant—fresh from his victory over Robert E. Lee—and his wife, Julia, traveled to New York to make a ceremonial return to his alma mater, West Point, and to attend a rally at the city's Cooper Union in a show of support for President Andrew Johnson. The newspapers celebrated Grant's visit with great fanfare: "The Adored Hero, the Admired Soldier, the Honored Guest," declared the *New York Times* in its headline. Of the crowd gathered at a morning reception at the Astor House, the *Times* reported the following:

> Looking for the Lieutenant-General commanding the armies of the United States, they expected to see an imposing figure, a full-breasted, elaborately-buttoned coat, gold tinsel on his legs, epaulettes on his arms, and sword and pistol by his side. There was no such there. Standing square in front of the fire-place . . . a medium-sized, well-built man . . . clad in a brown sack-coat, with light-checked trowsers; and patent leather pumps. . . . So looked Grant, the soldier they admired.[45]

Grant biographer William S. McFeely wrote that Grant's outfit may have been "exactly what a newly successful businessman in Galena or St. Louis might have worn" but was certainly out of place in more stylish cities such as New York, and that he "must have looked strange indeed at the end of the day, at the Union League Club." McFeely added that Grant's big-city friends soon got him to Brooks Brothers, and for the rest of his days he dressed "correctly, in quiet clothes."[46]

William Sherman also had a reputation for carelessness in his attire. An officer who served under him wrote that during wartime, Sherman appeared "to have an aversion to new clothes," adding that he "seldom or never buttons his coat either across his breast or around his waist. His vest is always buttoned by the lower button only . . . It is doubtful if at this time any one can be found, except the General's tailor, who can tell when his coat was new. . . . One would readily imagine, judging by its appearance, that he purchased his uniform second-hand."[47]

Sherman's reputation, though, was somewhat unearned: he may not have been a dandy, but he *was* particular. Even as a poor lieutenant on the frontier, Sherman ordered clothes from John Fraser, a venerable New York City tailor. His personal correspondence shows that Brooks Brothers had Sherman's measurements in 1860 and that the clothier supplied his uniforms during the Civil War. As his biographer Lee Kennet wrote, Sherman's coat "might be wrinkled and soiled, but it was a gentleman's coat, made by a gentleman's tailor."[48]

Another westerner—President Abraham Lincoln—also carried a reputation as a careless dresser. "He may have been honest," one biographer wrote of Lincoln's early career as a lawyer, "but he wasn't much to look at. His blue pants floated a good inch above his socks." His homespun wear was typical of the frontier, but, because Lincoln was so tall, his clothes fit worse than most. (His trousers—four feet in length—would have reached the underarms of an average man.) In 1855, when Lincoln arrived in Cincinnati to help defend a client in an important patent case, his fellow counselors (including his future secretary of war Edwin Stanton) described Lincoln as "awkward and ungainly in appearance, his clothing utterly devoid of the tailor's art, ill-fitting and in no wise suited to his angular frame . . . his appearance was that of the average western farmer of the period."[49]

Others insisted that Lincoln "wasn't sloven and wasn't a buffoon." Judith Bradner—a Bloomington socialite who had once entertained Lincoln in her home—recalled that he "was not so careless about how his clothes looked as some people say." She admitted that Lincoln's clothes "did not fit him well," but added "the material was of the best. His linen was always fresh and clean."[50]

As president, Lincoln at least had plenty of clothes to choose from. From the time he was nominated, gifts poured in, many in the form of wearing apparel—such as hats, socks, shoes, and full suits (including a bullet proof coat of chain mail). One gentleman, who carried a handsome silk hat to the president-elect in January 1861 (the gift of a New York milliner), recalled that in receiving the hat, Lincoln laughed heartily over the gifts of clothing and remarked to Mrs. Lincoln, "Well, wife, if nothing else comes out of this scrape, we are going to have some new clothes, are we not?"[51]

Brooks Brothers tailored many of President Lincoln's suits (as they have for many chief executives since); on the occasion of his second inauguration, the clothier presented him with a handsome overcoat (a "great coat" as they were known then) as a gift. The coat was truly one of a kind. Its workmanship was exquisite: made of wool finer than cashmere, the coat was pieced and sewn with intricate stitching. The most appealing aspect was the coat's lining. A talented New Jersey seamstress spent several weeks hand-stitching an elaborate pattern, repeated on each side: at the center of the design was an American bald eagle, wings spread; in its beak, a ribbon bearing a patriotic inscription; shields—filled with stars and stripes—were above and below the eagle; the field was surrounded with scallops and other rich ornaments.[52]

The coat was a favorite of Lincoln's, and he wore it on special occasions, including the night he was assassinated, April 14, 1865—ironically one of the happiest days of his life. He dressed for the theater in the style of the day: black broadcloth frock coat and matching pants, white shirt, bow tie (Lincoln preferred the pre-formed bows), and his favored Brooks Brothers overcoat.

Few extant firms from the Civil War era continue to take a beating in the literature as does Brooks Brothers. Historian Stuart Brandes, an expert on war profiteering in American history, admits there were numerous problems with the early Brooks Brothers uniform contracts but justly concludes that, while they caused "much embarrassment to New Yorkers," they did "no significant damage to the war effort." He adds that "the matter hardly deserved the notoriety it received."[53]

Like shoe factories in Gettysburg and other Civil War myths, the illusion of Brooks Brothers as the archetypal Civil War profiteer endures: one recent biographer of Boss Tweed and his Tammany Hall machine states matter-of-factly (and incorrectly) that "none less than Brooks Brothers supplied twelve thousand sets of uniforms early in the war using 'shoddy'—ground up rags—that fell apart after a few days." Perhaps the illusion endures because Brooks Brothers itself endures, but if it does it is for lack of facts, perspective, and historical context.[54]

The fact is that only a fraction of the uniforms that Brooks Brothers supplied were made from (admittedly) substandard material and had to be replaced (at Brooks Brothers' expense). In terms of perspective, Brooks Brothers can hardly be thought of as a chronic profiteer: apart from a few more contracts to supply the New York militia, it never became one of the premier suppliers to the Union Army. The historical context is also important. In the years between the world wars, the Army's quartermasters still complained of the vagaries of supplying a large army with uniforms and pointed to the very problems that had plagued Brooks Brothers in the Civil War: securing large lots of uniform cloth of uniform color of durable fabric suitable for the rigors of campaign.[55]

One thing that has endured—as legend and as relic—is Lincoln's Brooks Brothers overcoat. Soon after his death, rumors and myth surrounded the late President's assassination clothes. One story had the suit being displayed in the window of a Brooks Brothers store on lower Broadway as a promotion. As the legend goes, an angry crowd—appalled at the crassness of such a marketing campaign—smashed the window and trashed the store. Another persistent (but false) legend has Brooks Brothers never making a black suit again, in deference to the suit worn by Lincoln that night.

The coat, now on display at Ford's Theatre National Historic Site in Washington, D.C., had a long and indirect trip in getting there. Mrs. Lincoln gave the assassination clothes to White House doorkeeper Alphonso Donn (who remained as doorman through the administration of Grover Cleveland). Donn cherished the garments and refused many offers to buy the clothes, including a $20,000 offer from P. T. Barnum. From the time Donn received the coat, it became the victim of souvenir hunters, who snipped pieces when his back was turned. Upon Alphonso's death, the coat was passed down through his family.

Late in 1915, a Massachusetts congressman introduced "A Bill . . . Providing for the purchase of the suit of clothes worn by President Lincoln at the time of his assassination." The legislation authorized the sum of $7,500 "from any unexpended moneys of the amount set aside for the construction and expenses of the Lincoln Memorial." The bill did not pass. In 1924, the latest of the Donn owners—in need of funds—placed the clothes at auction, but they were returned to her by a mysterious stranger who bid a few thousand dollars to protect the interests of the family. The clothes were then willed to Dorothy Donn, granddaughter of the original owner, who placed the items in a series of bank vaults for safekeeping.[56]

The granddaughter (now Mrs. J. Marvin Smith) tried to sell the Brooks Brothers coat in the 1930s, with hopes it could be properly conserved and displayed, but her asking price of $50,000 found no takers among the museums and historical societies she contacted (not even from Brooks Brothers, another story has it). In 1967, Mrs. Smith renewed her efforts by placing an advertisement in the *New York Times*. (The paper would call it "the most famous and expensive Brooks Brothers suit of all time.") The coincident reopening of Ford's Theatre as a National Historic Site afforded an ideal opportunity to acquire the clothes. Another congressman—Iowan Fred Schwengel—secured a generous gift from American trucking interests and bought the artifacts from Mrs. Smith. The coat, since cleaned and restored, is now on exhibit at the theater.[57]

After the battle at Wilson's Creek, the First Iowa left Springfield and marched to Rolla, where they were put on flatcars and boxcars and delivered to the arsenal at St. Louis in late August "in the presence of a vast crowd that yelled and cheered as if they could not make noise enough," Ware recalled. The men got up at 4 a.m. the following day. ("We had got into the habit of getting up early," Ware wrote, "and could not sleep in the morning.") Roll was called, breakfast was had, and mail was delivered. "Then we all went down into the Mississippi River," Ware remembered, "and had fun in the water."[58]

On return to the arsenal from their day at the beach, the men had a great surprise waiting for them: boxes of uniforms sent by the state. "These State uniforms were very neat," Ware wrote. They included a black hat, light-blue trousers, and a dress coat buttoning up the chin made of fine cadet gray cloth with a light-blue collar and cuff trimmings. "I got a uniform that fitted me as if a tailor had made it," Ware remembered with satisfaction (and humor: "I looked like a Confederate officer," he added). The men struck out for baths and barbers and threw away everything they had worn till then. Shaved and bathed, the Iowans made a good impression at the evening's dress parade: "Nobody would have known the regiment," Ware concluded.[59]

The reception given by the city heartened Ware and his comrades considerably. Museums, theaters, restaurants, and other establishments were open to them *gratis*. "I never put my head out of [my] hotel but that—having on my First Iowa uniform," Ware recalled, "the first German who saw me took me by the arm to the nearest beer saloon, and after introducing me to everyone he knew in the room, said 'You fights *mit* Sigel—you drinks *mit* me.'"[60]

When it returned home to Iowa, the First was greeted with equal aplomb. The regiment—then finished with its three-months' service (and more)—disbanded, but Ware reenlisted in the cavalry. And why not? Like Dickens' "gentleman in blue" who addressed Mr. Weller in the *Pickwick Papers*, Ware's uniform did "work its way with the women." "The girls had been praising us so that we felt it incumbent on us to prove we could do it over again if we wanted—and we did," Ware wrote. "Without the inspiration of women there could be no armies, no great battles, and but little of what we call 'history,'" he concluded.[61]

"Clothes make the man," or so the truism goes; but do they? Grant was unfashionable, Sherman-unbuttoned, Lincoln-ungainly; and Eugene Ware un-uniformed—but each did his part to save the Union without the benefit of his Sunday best. In the end, perhaps a simple seamstress made the best fashion statement of all in the Civil War years: on the carefully sewn festoons held in the mouth of the eagle on the dark silk lining of Lincoln's Brooks Brothers coat, she stitched a fitting sentiment: "One Country, One Destiny."

Figure 4. Noncommissioned officers' mess of Co. D, 93rd New York Infantry Source: Library of Congress

Figure 5. Facsimile of a wartime Borden condensed milk label Source: Sullivan Press

CHAPTER TWO

Consecrated Milk

The soldiers' fare is very rough, the bread is hard, the beef is tough;
If they can stand it, it will be, through love of God, a mystery.

—*A wartime poem*

October 3, 1861

My Dear Wife,

Instead of your husband this week I am afraid that you will have to be satisfied with a letter. When I last wrote you, I had no doubts that this would be my last week in the service but things are in a very unsettled condition and there is no telling now when we will get off. . . . If the U.S. ever gets me into the service again it will be when it is in more desperate straits than at present. . . . I am well with the exception of depressed spirits consequent of our situation but brighter days are ahead. . . .

Accept much love from your affectionate Husband,

Charles[1]

October 19, 1861

My Dear, Dear Husband,

I cannot tell you how happy I was receiving your letter this afternoon for I had missed you so much and was longing to hear from you. . . . I feel that I can now say go where duty calls and God be with you to bless and protect you. . . . Peace shall again spread her angel wings over the land. . . . I expect I shall have some sad and lonesome hours as I have already felt the loss of your company. . . . I am like the Dove that has lost its mate, wandering around from place to place looking for something, I hardly know what . . . but it will all be right by and by if I can only hear often from you.

Your loving wife,

Kate[2]

October 19, 1861

My Dear Wife,

According to promise, I commence to write you another letter. . . . We received our horns and uniforms yesterday. . . . Our cook is just setting the table for dinner. I am writing on the dining table, part of which is a door, laid up on some forked sticks. . . . The 37th Regiment have a colonel that they captured the day before we landed. The scouts bring in Prisoners every day . . . Dinner is about ready and after it we will have to go out and practice. We are all well and are enjoying ourselves finely. . . . Write soon as possible for I am anxious to hear from you.

Your Husband,

Charlie[3]

October 20, 1861

My darling Husband,

This has been a beautiful pleasant day. Oh! I do feel so much like resting awhile on my love's lap tonight. . . . Mother is going with me for dinner. We have our knitting with us as we are making socks for the Soldiers. It would be a good plan for you to wear cotton ones under the woolen ones. . . . O how time flies. Tomorrow you will be gone two weeks but I am anxious the time should pass around so I can again see my husband. . . . You do not know how I miss you at night to keep me warm. . . . I will adopt for my motto, 'hope on, hope ever,' and with a goodbye kiss I close for this time.

Your ever loving wife,

Kate[4]

October 24, 1861

Dear Kate,

Having a few moments of leisure I thought I would drop you a few more lines. . . . Yesterday afternoon [we] crossed the river went up it about two miles and bought some apples . . . Had all the cider we could drink . . . For supper we had pork, rice, potatoes and coffee. We do not starve here though our eatables are not gotten up in such style as the most of us are used to at home. I have had a first rate appetite ever since I left home and can eat the hard crackers with a gusto. . . . Give my love to all. How I would like to be at home this evening.

I remain as ever your affectionate husband,

Charlie

P.S. I am anxiously awaiting a letter from you.[5]

November 9, 1861,

My Darling Husband,

Another lonely Sabbath has passed away. . . . Need I tell you where my thoughts were?! On my dear husband—wishing him with me just there—for you do not know how lonesome I am at times for you. . . . I want to go this evening to hear Mr. Clokey once again. . . . I only wish my love was here to go with me when I see other wives with their husbands. You don't know how I feel. . . . Earl wrote if he had not enlisted he never would again. He has not a cent yet and has been sick and his mother is needy . . . Do you know how much you are to get a month? Did you pay for your horn or is it to be taken out of your month's pay?

Now my darling, I must have another kiss and say good night . . .

Kate[6]

November 11, 1861

Raining as usual . . . and as usual I take advantage of the day to write. . . . I know you must have enjoyed your visit to the country and hope you remembered me when you was partaking of the many good things for here we only have them mentioned as things that are in existence in some parts of the world yet we have plenty of what we have though I must confess we have some huge pigs in the band. . . . It is wonderful what hogs some men make of themselves.

Charles[7]

November 16, 1861

I received a good letter from Sister Mollie today with a piece of poetry cut from some paper about 'My Charlie has gone to war' . . .

> My life is so weary, so full of sad pain;
>
> Each day brings its shadows, Its mist and its rain;
>
> There's no say of sunshine, My pathway to cheer;
>
> But sorrow would vanish if my Charlie were here.

Won't Hez and Will laugh when you tell them they are Uncles and you Pa. . . . Han and I did not iron today but busied ourselves making you and Hez night caps of red cruel. . . . I thought you would appreciate anything that I made with my own fingers. . . . You can wear this at anytime or at night. . . . Adieu my dear Ducky.

Kate[8]

November 19, 1861

My own Darling Wife,

I thought that I would drop you a line this afternoon. . . . I often read your letters over especially when I go a week or so without hearing from you. . . . Jno. Hawkin's wife sent him two nice large cakes and some nice fresh butter. He divided with the members of the band and we had a regular feast for dinner. . . . We are getting so that we play very well and are highly praised by the officers for the progress we have made yet there are some in the band that will never make players . . . I believe I have nothing more to write about at present. Remember me to all the folks. Much love to your own dear self . . .

From your Husband,

Charlie[9]

Charles Ramsay—a musician in the 44th Ohio Volunteer Infantry—and his wife, Kate—pregnant at home with their first child—were faithful, frequent, and loving correspondents during the Civil War. Their early wartime letters give witness to what dominated their lives: for Kate, it was the longing for a husband that had gone to war and hopes of a happy future as a family; for Charles, it was his duty as a soldier and, more often, food. In this he was not alone. Civil War soldiers—like those in armies many years before and after—found their rations wanting in taste, quantity, and dependability. "No wonder," one historian wrote, "every soldier's letters and diary commented more on the awfulness of his diet than on anything else."[10]

Napoleon's maxim that an army "travels on its stomach" proved no less true during the Civil War, and generals on both sides gave attention to—and were frustrated by—the need to feed their armies. Union General Ulysses S. Grant reportedly wired the War Department in late 1864, declaring "I will not move my army without onions!" In a letter to his son, Confederate General Robert E. Lee complained, "'I have been up to see the Congress and they do not seem to be able to do anything except to eat peanuts and chew tobacco, while my army is starving." A Connecticut soldier put the truism even better than Napoleon, writing, "An army is a big thing, and it takes a great many eatables and not a few drinkables to carry it along."[11]

For Union soldiers, the regulation daily "eatables and drinkables" for the greater part of the war included a pound of "hard tack" crackers or the equivalent in bread or flour, a pound and a quarter of fresh or salt beef or three quarters of a pound of bacon, as well as servings of beans or peas, rice or hominy, coffee, tea, sugar, vinegar, salt, pepper, potatoes, and molasses. On paper, the Union ration was generous enough that an esteemed wartime professor could boast, "No government ever provided more liberally for the wants [of] its soldiers in respect to food." Indeed, the Union ration stood well when compared to the other great standing armies of the world. But regulation did not always correspond to reality, and the quantity of food that actually made it to troops in the field varied considerably. As one soldier wrote, "Some days we live first rate, and the next we don't have half enough."[12]

Even when there was food-a-plenty, the soldiers—heretofore accustomed to meals by the good graces of their mothers and wives—were not prepared to cook it. At best, the distribution of culinary arts in the ranks, North and South, was very uneven. While one reporter boasted that some Rhode Island infantrymen "have been making money cooking for other regiments," another—stationed with Confederates in Alabama—wrote that "the process of cooking is as much a source of amusement to the troops as it was to myself." Recipe books ("receipts" they were called then) were quite popular in American households, but they were not easily adapted to the rigors of camp life. Eventually, books such as *Camp Fires and Cooking* provided "culinary hints for the soldiers" (as the subtitle promised). Others gained newfound confidence in their kitchen skills; "I am thinking seriously of writing a cookbook when I get home," one soldier wrote.[13]

Although the ration was ample, the lack of nutritional value combined with the dearth of talent in the kitchen had serious health consequences for the soldiers. The most persistent problem was a deficiency in fruits and vegetables, which could result in scurvy. Also, the food that was available was often fried in copious amounts of pork fat, and the resulting gastric disturbances added more numbers to the sick list. One worried surgeon feared the soldiers in his care would succumb to "death from the frying pan."[14]

What the ration lacked in nutrition it made up for in monotony. Variety may be the "spice of life," but it is also the sworn enemy of the commissary department, which depended on a simple ration to ensure that they could fill the needs of a million men. To supplement the ration, soldiers counted on the camp sutlers who provided something of a traveling "general store" and were compelled by army regulations to provide "good and wholesome provisions at the market price." To be sure, the soldiers argued that the prices weren't fair, and surgeons declared the sutlers' wares an "unmitigated curse," but apart from foraging and the occasional package from home, there were few alternatives.[15]

Advances in food preservation—especially canning—made it possible for sutlers to feed a million soldiers with luxuries such as sardines, salmon, and sauces. Like so many other technologies, canning was born of military necessity. In 1800, Napoleon Bonaparte offered a substantial reward to anyone who could devise a food preservation method in order to keep his armies adequately supplied while on campaign. Nicolas Appert—a French confectioner—won the prize for his invention of sealing food in glass jars. Soon after, Englishman Peter Durand perfected Appert's idea, replacing the fragile glass with tin cans. At first, the process was laborious as only five or six cans could be made per hour. What's more, the cans were hard to open: French and British soldiers had to cut the cans open with bayonets (or rifle fire) or pound them open with rocks.

Still, with advances in pressing tin (and the first can openers), canned goods became very popular in America in the antebellum years; the popularity was only accelerated by the Civil War, with the industry growing from a prewar production of five million cans a year to more than thirty million by war's end. Though canned goods were too heavy to become part of the regular army ration, every soldier still received them: in packages from home, as welcome treats from the various Sanitary Commissions, or from the camp sutler. One historian deemed food technology and production so important that he named one canning pioneer—condensed milk inventor Gail Borden—among the most influential people of the Civil War.[16]

Gail Borden was born on his father Gail's farm in Norwich, New York, a scion of seven generations of Bordens who had first settled in America in 1638. Borden's youth was typical of any local farmer's son, with chores, romps in the woods, hunting, and contact with the local Oneida Indians. When Borden was fourteen, his parents moved to what is now Covington, Kentucky, where Borden apprenticed to his father as a surveyor.

Within a year they moved again, this time to Indiana Territory. Here Borden obtained his only formal schooling, totaling less than two years. Once a young man in his late teens, Borden took on various odd jobs as a surveyor, flatboat operator, and—despite his lack of education—a

Figure 6: Gail Borden

schoolteacher. A crack rifleman, he also rose to the rank of Captain in the local militia company. Despite an active life, Borden had long suffered from a persistent cough, and it was made worse by the cold winters. In hopes of improving his health, Gail and his brother Tom set out for the South in 1822, first to New Orleans, and eventually to Mississippi.

Once settled in Amite County, Borden again became a schoolmaster. His health improved and so did his standing in the community. A few years later, he was nominated to take office as the county surveyor, and then as deputy federal surveyor. In 1828, Borden married sixteen year-old Penelope Mercer; meanwhile, Borden's brother had moved to Texas, and Tom's enthusiasm for the territory and its seemingly infinite prospects had prompted their parents to move there as well. In 1829, Borden and his pregnant wife moved there also.

Borden's first employment in Texas was farming and raising stock. Owing to his experience, he was the natural choice when Stephen F. Austin needed someone to supervise the official surveys of the colonies. Borden also represented his home district at the 1833 convention to seek separation from Mexico. During the Texas War of Independence, several of the Borden brothers fought with Austin's army. Gail became editor of the rebel newspaper—the *Telegraph and Texas Register*—and published two of the future republic's most famous stories: the declaration of independence from Mexico and the rallying cry, "Remember the Alamo!"

With independence won and a republic founded, Borden settled in Galveston. Then just an outpost, Galveston was home to little more than alligators, snakes, and turtles. Borden compiled the first topographical map of the island, made surveys, and eventually laid out the city. By the graces of Sam Houston, Borden also secured the important and influential position of customs collector. For a dozen years, from 1839 to 1851, Borden was agent for the Galveston City Company, a real estate corporation which owned large tracts on which the city would be built.

At nearly fifty years old, an ordinary man would have been content to live out his life with a reputation as one of the Lone Star State's pioneers, but Borden was anything but ordinary, and he spent the next quarter century devoted to a new line of work: invention. When he noticed that the threat of yellow fever lessened after Galveston's first frost, he built a large refrigerator with the idea of housing the locals to freeze the fever out of existence. He invented a portable bathhouse so that the island's females could bathe in private. Borden then devoted himself to his "terraqueous machine," a wagon with a sail meant for travel on land or water. None of the ideas came to fruition, but Borden was undeterred; "I never drop an idea except for a better one," he once said.[17]

In Borden's new train of ideas, the "better one" would be a concentrated food of dehydrated meat and flour that he called the "meat biscuit." As opposed to his previous ideas, the value of the meat biscuit was quickly recognized. An influential scientific paper called it "an invention of the first importance, both to our own country, and . . . the whole human race." Borden secured a patent for the invention and won one of only five gold medals awarded to Americans at the Great Council Exhibition in London in 1851. Borden had high hopes of securing army contracts and invested all that he had in a plant to manufacture the meat biscuit, but the business never materialized.[18]

Indeed, even before the meat biscuit enterprise was officially dead, he was already on to another; "I am greatly encouraged to embark in the Milk business," he wrote a friend in 1854. Indeed, if there was a supposed market for the meat biscuit, the market—and societal need—for a reliable and portable supply of milk was undoubted. No one knows for sure what inspired Borden to pursue his hallmark invention of condensed milk. One story attributes it to Borden's sympathy for the plight of the immigrant children who were without wholesome milk on his return from the London Exhibition. An admirer attributed it to the fact that his friend Borden was "so full of the milk of human kindness."[19]

Whatever the reason, Borden began experimenting with condensed milk in earnest at his home, now in New York, until he developed a process which yielded a milk of good flavor and keeping. He applied for a patent in May 1853, but the Patent Office questioned the novelty of the process for three years. Borden, with the help of some influential scientists, was able to prove that vacuum protected the milk from the air and kept it clean while it was being condensed. On August 19, 1856, Borden received Patent No. 15,553 for an "Improvement in the Concentration of Milk." Still, his meat biscuit patent had never guaranteed his success, and for some time he failed to secure enough money to build a plant to produce the milk.

After a chance meeting on a train, Borden formed a partnership in 1858 with Jeremiah Milbank, an experienced businessman and financier who had the foresight to trust in Borden's eventual success. The men styled their new enterprise the "New York Condensed Milk Company," and began to do business in earnest. With Milbank's financial backing, local sales grew quickly, especially after New York newspapers published scathing articles exposing the unsanitary conditions of the city's dairies. Given Borden's record of lackluster commercial success, though one could still wonder whether condensed milk would have an appeal beyond his neighbors.

Though Borden's failed meat biscuit endeavor took place nearly a decade before the Civil War, it informed his eventual wartime activities because in doing so, Borden established ties with the government—especially the army—and acquired a business sense that would eventually suit him well. Borden's dealings with the government are all the more interesting because they include correspondence between and among soldiers in the antebellum army that would become household names—on both sides—during the Civil War.

In 1850, Edwin V. "Bull" Sumner, then a brevet colonel of the First Dragoons on the frontier at Fort Leavenworth, Kansas, espoused the virtues of Borden's meat biscuit in a letter to Amos B. Eaton, a major in the army's Commissary of Subsistence. "I have tried the 'Meat Biscuit,' and find it all, and more than the inventor thinks it is," Sumner wrote Eaton. "I am convinced that I could live upon it for months, and retain my health and strength," Sumner continued, adding, "In my judgment, this is a very great discovery, and must lead to important results."[20]

Like Borden, and others of his supporters, Sumner saw the advantage in the "compression of wholesome food into a smaller compass," as he put it. "Think of a regiment of 500 men, cutting loose from all magazines for two months," Sumner continued with enthusiasm. He admitted that changes would need to be made before the meat biscuit could be used on the scale he envisioned, but concluded that "we ought to commence using it in the army at once," adding that "[Borden] had better send me a dozen of these canisters before I march upon the plains this summer."[21]

One of the army's chief surgeons, Dr. J. J. B. Wright, M.D., also penned a testimonial. "I have examined and tried the meat biscuit . . . have used it in the hospital and at our private table; and have no hesitation in bearing testimony to its excellence as an article of diet," he wrote Surgeon General Thomas Lawson, adding, "I think it admirably adapted for the use of troops on long marches or campaigns." Wright also testified to the hardiness of

Borden's invention, writing that a friend of his had leftover powder that was well over a year old, but was "now in as good condition . . . as when it was first prepared."[22]

Likewise, Captain John G. Tod wrote the Secretary of War from his post in Texas that if the War Department would order 100,000 pounds of meat biscuit powder, the entire cost would be saved in the difference in freight charges alone. Other officers—including James Longstreet, then a brevet major on the frontier, but soon to be one of the foremost Confederate generals—added their own endorsements. Their testimonials compelled the Quartermaster Department to convene a board of six officers to act on Sumner's suggestion of a prolonged biscuit trial.

Unfortunately, their findings were not in Borden's favor. Borden had thought six ounces of meat biscuit more than sufficient as a ration (Sumner had written that he "could not use four ounces a day"), but the board disagreed; even when increased to a twelve ounce ration, the board thought the meat biscuit insufficient to "sustain life in health and vigor whilst on active duty." Their report also declared that Borden's invention failed to "appease the craving of hunger" or sustain "much mental or bodily labor." In the end, the board felt "reluctantly compelled to report unanimously" against adopting Borden's meat biscuit.[23]

Perhaps the board's most stinging conclusion was that Borden's biscuit was "unpalatable." Others put it more cruelly; the famous journalist Frederick Law Olmsted recalled a bivouac on his journey through Texas when his party's dinner choice was watery potatoes or Borden's meat biscuit; they prepared a substantial dish of it—according to directions—but after trying it, turned to the watery potatoes. "It may answer to support life, no doubt, where even cornmeal is not to be had," Olmsted wrote of the meat biscuit, "but I should decidedly undergo a very near approach to the traveler's last bourne, before having recourse to it." For his part, Borden always thought that no one prepared it as well as he did.[24]

Borden was appalled at the army's report and denounced it as "villainous"; he also concluded—in a fit of paranoia—that the board's conclusions were "a plot" influenced by meat producers who had a cozy relationship with the Quartermaster and saw danger in his invention. As his Galveston factory continued to make the meat biscuit tins, Borden considered putting pressure on Congressmen assigned to the powerful military appropriations committees, but was dissuaded by his brother. He did, however, continue to court sailors, hospitals, and physicians, and anyone else he could strong-arm to at least try the biscuit. On seeing Florence Nightingale's reports from the battlefields in Europe, Borden thought he could capture another military market—if not his own country's—and wrote a friend, "how much I would like to take a ton or two of the MB to the Crimea."[25]

In the end, the meat biscuit never found the large market Borden had gambled on. Despite the ultimate failure, the experience provided him with contacts among leading military officials that would prove a boon to Borden when the Civil War started a few years later. Many of the military correspondents mentioned above—Sumner (Borden's most ardent champion), Lawson, Tod, and Wright—played an important role in the war. Eaton—the most influential—was appointed a lieutenant colonel and assistant commissary general in 1861 and given the important task of distributing provisions to the troops. The army became Borden's best customer, as he had always hoped; however, it would be his condensed milk—not the meat biscuit—that would secure his fame.

On the eve of the Civil War, Borden's New York Condensed Milk Company was doing well. To be sure, neither Borden—nor his patron, Milbank—were enjoying a fortune, but Borden was characteristically optimistic about the future and Milbank was satisfied that he had made a good investment. The war solidified that satisfaction; from the first shots to the final surrender, Borden's challenge was to meet an immense demand. In three months in 1862, Borden—at capacity—sold nearly 50,000 quarts of milk from his plant in Wassaic, New York; a year later he was able to send out an equivalent amount in a few days.

Still, Borden could complain, "we do not meet half the orders." To that end, he opened more facilities in Pennsylvania, Maine, Connecticut, and his eventual flagship factory at Brewster, New York, which alone could produce 20,000 quarts of condensed milk daily. Borden's milk was never part of the *official* army ration, but—as Union General William T. Sherman recalled—the commissary often supplied his soldiers with "all manner of patent compounds," including "desecrated vegetables and consecrated milk."[26]

A reporter for the New York *Observer* visited Borden's Wassaic factory during the Civil War and marveled at the "interesting and impressive" operation, and concluded that he had never seen a factory where "so much order, cleanliness, and comfort were combined" in any like production. The entire process—from receiving milk from the farmers to sending it off in boxes was done at the factory, all "with such scrupulous regard to cleanliness, that the result is irreproachable," the reporter wrote. A tin shop was at work constantly, producing eight thousand cans each day; the workers were all young women aged eighteen to twenty, who earned "more than a dollar a day easily." The reporter noted that the chief market for Borden's milk was "in the army, where it is a great blessing as you will readily believe."[27]

"Borden's condensed milk in cans was one of the luxuries invented at this time for our delectation and comfort," wrote a Massachusetts colonel, who—like many Union soldiers—mentioned the "great blessing" by name in their letters and memoirs. The soldiers either asked that the milk be sent from home, received it by the graces of the Sanitary Commission, or—most often—bought it from the sutler. At fifty to eighty cents a can (a good day's wages for a private soldier), however, it was a rare indulgence. "Only a recruit with a big bounty, or an old vet the child of wealthy parents, or a re-enlisted man did much in that way," one soldier recalled. A New York soldier garrisoned at Fort Pulaski, Georgia, which was off limits to sutlers, remembered a comrade-turned-tradesman who would "pass through the casemates calling out 'Borden's condensed milk?'" Reportedly civilian sales also got a boost when word got out that First Lady Mary Todd Lincoln served Borden's milk at the White House.[28]

Though Borden's condensed milk was not an official ration item, it was in the Union army's official list of medical supplies (as was his extract of beef). Surgeon General William A. Hammond declared that the milk was "in extensive use in our armies and hospitals," and "proved most serviceable on the battlefield as a source of nutriment for the wounded." In the hospitals, a favorite concoction was "milk punch," a combination of condensed milk and brandy or whiskey, which Hammond declared an unmatched remedy for the low fevers which plagued the army. Even when Borden's milk wasn't being used for its intended purpose, it was still a valuable commodity. One nurse, determined to secure some fresh pork for dinner with her fellow matrons, remembered, "I took a can of condensed milk . . . and soon made a trade." Another nurse, responsible for cooking for hundreds of sick soldiers on floating hospitals, recalled that when the food stores were exhausted, they broke up hard-tack into buckets full of sweetened milk and water. "Oh, that precious condensed milk," she exclaimed, "more precious to us at that moment than beef essence!"[29]

Confederate soldiers were also treated to Borden's milk, especially when they captured Union supplies. Henry Kyd Douglas, a staff officer to the famous "Stonewall" Jackson, remembered a memorable winter dessert of canned peaches into which he poured a can of condensed milk, all stirred with the point of his sword. "Peaches and cream in January, and furnished by the enemy, too!" he exclaimed. "I well remember the first time I went down and saw the spread table—with genuine coffee and condensed milk—my first acquaintance with it," Howard McHenry—a Confederate soldier from Maryland—remembered of his inaugural meal as a prisoner at Fort Delaware. By war's end, though, the treat of sweetened milk was too much for starving Rebels. "[We] shared our food until every haversack was empty," a Pennsylvania volunteer remembered of the surrender scene at Appomattox. "The sweet aroma of real coffee staggered the Confederates," he added, "[and] condensed milk and sugar appalled them."[30]

For Gail Borden, the Civil War was more than business; it was quite personal, indeed—for himself and for his family. Texas—a Confederate state—might have wondered how it lost Borden to the North, but it did not forget its favorite son. The *Houston Tri-Weekly* telegraph, an unapologetic Rebel newspaper, reported that Borden's condensed milk was a "Texas institution [which] the war has not abolished . . . it is a successful and valuable invention."[31]

Yankees might have been forgiven for being equally curious—if not suspicious—as to the leanings of the Texan. Was he an unrepentant Rebel who stayed in the North only to reap the economic benefits of the war? Any questions as to Borden's loyalty were laid aside at the outset. When a less-than-patriotic citizen treated the crowd waiting outside the *Herald* newspaper office in Winstead, Connecticut, to a tirade against Lincoln's call for volunteers, Borden interrupted and stated—in a firm voice—"My father [is] in Texas, my brothers are in Texas, my children are in Texas, and the bulk of my earthly possessions are in Texas. But we must have a government. I did not vote for Mr. Lincoln, but I would vote for him today—aye, and fight for him, too."[32]

If that declaration wasn't enough, he added an exclamation point of sorts less than two weeks later when the *Times* of Amenia, New York, published

Borden's public statement. "I have 'run up my colors,'" he wrote. "My best possessions are in Texas, that misguided State where I had hoped to spend my last days; yet I love my whole country and government more, and wish to do what I can to sustain them."[33]

Later in the war, Horace Greeley—fire-breathing editor of the thoroughly-unrepentant abolitionist newspaper, the *New York Tribune*—devoted a full page to Borden and expounded on the dairyman's Union bona fides (though, as Borden's principal biographer warns, Greeley would not have hesitated to publish opinions—even manufactured ones—which coincided with his own):

> Those who now hear Mr. Borden express his willingness . . . to give his last dollar and his life, with his gray hairs to put down the Rebellion and crush out its cause, would not suppose that he was once a large land-owner and slaveholder in Texas. . . . His father has just died, unable to escape from Rebeldom. His brothers, he believes are Union men, though obliged to appear to be Rebels. To all rebels, Gail Borden is opposed, heart and soul, and his greatest anxiety appears to be to live to work for the Union army. He thanks God fervently every day that he is able to work in this cause. He knows that products of his manufactory are directly aiding the good cause.[34]

For the Borden clan, the Civil War was quite literally a "war between brothers." Gail Borden's two sons, John Gail and Henry Lee, took up arms on opposite sides; John with the Union and Henry with the Confederacy. Little is known of Henry Lee Borden's service, except that he enlisted with the 35th Texas Cavalry ("Brown's Cavalry") in April 1862 and mustered out at war's end. One biographer has Henry Lee spending most of the war at the Dance Brothers and Park gun manufactory in Columbia, Texas.

John had been born in Galveston, but moved to New York with his father as a teenager. He attended schools in Brooklyn and Connecticut and was enrolled at Eastman College in Poughkeepsie, New York, when the war broke out. Born and reared in Texas, John—as one biographer wrote—"had shown a decided sympathy for the Southern side of the controversy." Nevertheless, owing to the "tolerance and nice sensibility he had inherited from his father," the biographer declared, John was able to "disregard the sentiments influenced by the memory of boyhood associations."[35]

Inspired by his attendance at a mass Union rally in Poughkeepsie, John—at age eighteen—enlisted in the 150th New York Volunteer Infantry, where he mustered in as a sergeant. The 150th New York had a distinguished record during the Civil War; after duty in Baltimore in early 1863, the 150th joined the Army of the Potomac's XII Corps at Gettysburg in July 1863, then the Army of the Cumberland for the Atlanta Campaign, Sherman's March to the Sea, and finally the Carolinas, until Johnston's surrender in 1865. John missed out on a good part of the excitement, though, spending most of his time in federal hospitals with chronic diarrhea. After a sea voyage taken to restore his health, John re-enlisted in August 1863, this time with the 47th New York Infantry with an officer's commission. Less than a year later—still plagued with sickness—he was compelled to retire, securing a disability discharge.

Although his condensed milk was an unqualified success, Borden was constantly striving to advance the process. Three times during the Civil War, Borden secured re-issued patents for further improvements. Nor did Borden limit himself to milk. In 1862, he secured a patent for improvements in concentrating and preserving cider and other fruit juices, and he applied the same process to coffee. Records show that during the war, Borden purchased thousands of dollars worth of coffee beans and tens of thousands of bushels of apples. The concentrated juice met with great acclaim by soldiers and civilians alike. More than forty years later, a Nevada woman wrote the company, "During the Civil War . . . I boarded at Earles hotel on Canal St. . . . and Mr. Gail Borden sat next to me at the table. [His] Condensed Cider was most delicious—Is this cider manufactured now? If not, why not?"[36]

Likewise, Union Major General William T. Sherman benefited from the fruit juice. Sherman realized the importance of fruits and vegetables as anti-dotes to scurvy, a disease that could debilitate a malnourished army. "I have known the skirmish-line, without orders, to fight a respectable battle for the possession of some old fields that were full of blackberries," he remembered. Therefore, when Borden heard that Sherman's supply lines in Georgia were stretched thin, he was equal to the emergency. At the conclusion of one Sunday's services at his Connecticut church, Borden raised his hand to stay the clergyman and parishioners from departing. He then asked them to "Dress appropriately and devote your afternoon to picking blackberries

and I will prepare them and forward them to the soldiers." The congrega-
tion's labors yielded three hundred bushels, which Borden's factory hands
turned into juice and jelly and sent to Sherman's headquarters. Reportedly,
Sherman wrote Borden in thanks for stopping the potential epidemic.[37]

The war also witnessed the possible resurrection of Borden's failed meat
biscuit. As early as 1861, a body of military surgeons declared that "Borden's
meat biscuit may be a valuable article of diet when fresh meat cannot be
obtained." In 1864, Eben Norton Horsford—a former Harvard professor
and influential American scientist (known as the "father of American food
technology")—published *The Army Ration*. The pamphlet was a detailed
scientific study of the army's ration, with recommendations on how to
"Diminish its Weight and Bulk, Secure Economy in its Administration,
Avoid Waste, and Increase the Comfort, Efficiency, and Mobility of Troops."
One of Horsford's recommendations was to concentrate animal food,
specifically to make fresh meat into sausages for armies on the march and
beef concentrates for hospital use. In doing so, he referred to "Mr. Borden's
long continued labors in this field, crowned with distinguished success" as
"proof of the practicability of his plan." Later that year, a Wisconsin newspaper stated matter-of-factly that "Borden, the condensed milk man, is going
to make meat biscuits for the federal troops."[38]

Despite the immense popularity of his product, Borden—like many other
businessmen—faced the postwar consequences of overexpansion. After
consulting with Milbank, his sons, and especially the farmers with whom
he had contracts, Borden was able to stem production and thus the crisis.
The popularity of condensed milk also witnessed the genesis of nearly a
dozen other producers, some under license with Borden and others as inde-
pendent factories. One competitor went so far as to hijack Borden's label. In
response, Borden renamed his product "Eagle Brand" in early 1866, a name
that stands to this day. He left no answer as to why he chose the name;
his principal biographer offered a number of possibilities: the Texas eagle
which Borden had hunted or Eagle Cove in Galveston, home to the island's
Indians. As good as any explanation, and the one most often cited, is a rush
of postwar patriotism.

At sixty-five, Borden could be forgiven for being tired, and so he moved
back to Texas, to a community in Colorado County that would eventually
be called "Borden." Over time, he concerned himself less and less with the

day-to-day operations of the factories and more with his grandchildren and other visitors. In 1873, Borden attended the Texas Veterans Association meeting in Houston, where talk centered more on the Civil War than of the old-timers' epic fight for independence. When someone asked Borden's opinion on the "Late Unpleasantness," he answered, "When will the war be over? Eight years ago Lee surrendered and yet we are in turmoil, when will peace be restored between the North and South? When will the radicals of both sections permit us to return to our former relations? The South has been conquered. That was bad enough. . . . I doubted the wisdom of secession [but] that is ancient history. . . . We have all suffered from that mistake but the dregs are getting bitter now."[39]

Borden died a few months later, on January 11, 1874, after a short bout with pneumonia. Borden's body traveled from Texas to New York on a private rail car. At his funeral, the presiding pastor eulogized Borden based on a fitting passage from *Romans*: "Not slothful in business; fervent in spirit." Borden himself had picked a site on a hill overlooking the Woodlawn Cemetery grounds in White Plains, and had marked it with a granite milk can. After his burial, a handsome monument replaced the can, with the apt inscription, "I tried and failed, I tried again and again, and succeeded."[40]

After Borden's death, his youngest son—Union veteran John Gail Borden—took over the helm of the firm and the New York Condensed Milk Company continued to prosper under his direction. John Gail was forced to retire in 1885 due to frail health, at which point he handed over control to his brother, former Confederate cavalryman Henry Lee Borden, who—though divorced and in New York to pursue an affair with a soprano many years his junior—successfully shepherded the firm's operations. Finally, in 1899, control of the company was given to someone other than a Milbank or Borden.

In the end, a full stomach can only take a soldier—far from home and lonely—so far, and few things provided more "nutrition" than a letter from loved ones. One need not guess at the joy that both Charles and Kate Ramsay experienced in exchanging their next letters from home and camp:

December 5, 1861,

My Dear Husband,

O My Dear Darling, rejoice with me for all is over. Our little soldier boy is 3 hours old. You may know I feel pretty well in bed to be able to write while laying. O but I did suffer! It was born 4 1/2 o'clock this morning but I am tired and must stop. If my breasts do not trouble me, I will get along. I think the lode weighs 10 pounds, it is so big!

Your Wife,

P.S., Mother R says she never saw such a brave soldier as I was while in pain.[41]

December 14, 1861,

My Darling Wife,

You cannot imagine my joy upon receiving your letter this morning. I had heard through a letter from Howard John to brother Hez that our boy had been born but he did not say how you were getting along or anything about your condition . . . when I received your letter this morning with the postscripts written by your own dear self so soon after our darling was born, I could not help but rejoice for I could not but conclude from that that you were getting along finely . . . when I came back to quarters they all knew it and I was goaded on all sides by 'How are you Pap?' . . . Write to me often and let me know how you and the rest of the family, our family, get along. You know that I will have a greater interest on hearing often from home. . . . Kiss our darling for me.

Charlie[42]

PRESENTATION SWORDS,
REGIMENTAL COLORS, Etc
TIFFANY & CO.,
550 & 552 Broadway, New York.
DEPOT OF GENERAL EQUIPMENT,
Comprising everything pertaining to the PERSONNEL or CAMP FURNITURE OF THE SOLDIER. Officers studying the necessities of active service, or the perfection of uniform and material, will do well to examine this large collection of Foreign and Domestic Arms, Uniforms and Miscellaneous Trappings.

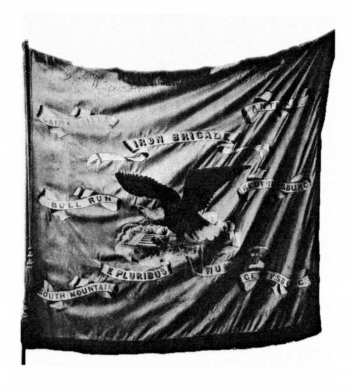

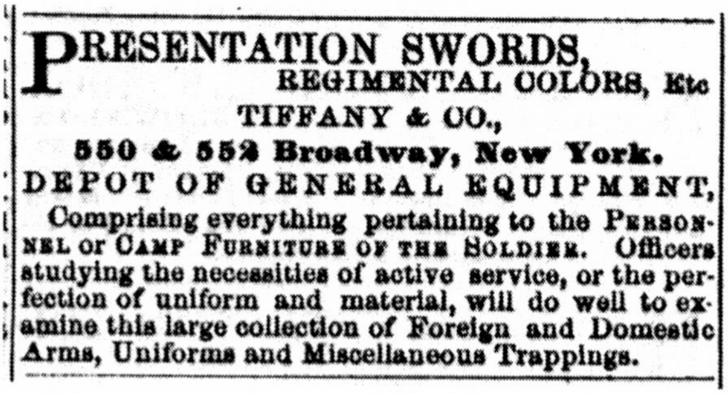

Figure 7. Matthew Brady's photograph of the Tiffany & Co. colors presented to the Iron Brigade in 1863.

Source: Wisconsin Historical Society (WHS 25598)

Figure 8. Typical wartime (1864) Tiffany advertisement.

Source: *Army-Navy Journal* (Courtesy of Guy Hasegawa)

CHAPTER THREE

Gold Braid and Cutlery

That flag now rent and tattered,
by shell and bullet shattered,
Is sacred in our eyes;
For when the Captain found it,
five brave ones were lying around it,
Who fell to save the prize.
— D. Bethune Duffield

ON APRIL 15, 1861, President Abraham Lincoln called for 75,000 militia to put down the Southern rebellion in answer to the important question of whether the Union and its liberties might be preserved for later generations. Of that number, the president asked Wisconsin for only a single regiment of a thousand men; ten pre-war militia companies gathered at the fair grounds in Milwaukee and quickly filled the state's quota to become the "First Wisconsin Active Militia." Such was the patriotic fervor and enthusiasm in the Badger State, though, that many more companies offered their services.

Governor Alexander Randall organized the surplus of volunteers into a second regiment and called them to Madison. The men that made up the Second Wisconsin came from cities and towns across the state—Milwaukee, Madison, Racine, Oshkosh, Portage, and others. The companies arrived by turn in Madison with a colorful mix of nicknames—"Belle City Rifles," "Grant County Grays," and the "Fond du lac Badgers"—and bivouacked at the appropriately named "Camp Randall." Before the soldiers left for the capital city, many of their hometowns—in ceremonies practiced across the Union—had presented the companies with flags. Though not crafted to Army specifications, the banners were sincere tokens of esteem and patriotism, and the soldiers swore oaths to bring them back unsullied by rebel hands.[1]

The Portage Light Guards arrived in Madison in gray uniforms and with handsome silk national colors; the men from La Crosse also in gray and a company flag of white silk and blue fringe with the inscription "Presented by the Ladies of La Crosse." The "Miners Guard" arrived partly uniformed with a "handsome merino United States flag." The "Janesville Volunteers" arrived without uniforms at all, but did bring a "superb national flag of silk." In special ceremonies, the young ladies of Racine had bestowed the "Belle City Rifles" with an impressive flag of dark blue silk and silver fringe. On one side was painted a shield inscribed "Racine, 1861" with a national flag draped on either side and surmounted by an eagle holding the bolts of Jove. The motto "Remember Sumter" was over the shield, and on scrolls near the center were the sentiments "For Freedom" and "For God."[2]

The Second Wisconsin's commander and officers were all leading men in the state: Colonel S. Park Coon had helped secure Wisconsin's place in the Union and had been attorney general; others had attended West Point or were prominent businessmen. As for the men in the ranks—if period accounts are to be believed, anyway—their character and reputation were less stellar than the officer corps; at the very least, it was uneven. As they gathered at Camp Randall, local newspapers reported that the boys "stayed quietly in their tents, read their Testaments, looked at the pictures of their loved ones, and tried to keep comfortable." Other accounts had the men roaming the streets at night, raiding breweries, and "lack[ing] the restraint which a wholesome discipline would impose."[3]

The men were not long at Camp Randall. Having arrived in late May, they were dispatched to the now-styled "seat of war" before June was out. They left Madison with a stirring address from the governor: "This rebellion must be put down in blood, and treason punished by blood." They were greeted with equal aplomb in Chicago, Toledo, and Cleveland—where "hundreds and hundreds of the most beautiful women" lined the parade route—and Baltimore. They camped in the suburbs of Washington for a month, until mid-July, when—as the war began in earnest—they began to establish a reputation for hard fighting and dedication to their flag that belied their status as "rough, vulgar blackguards."[4]

At the Battle of Bull Run—where they were assigned to a brigade led by Brigadier General William T. Sherman—the Second Wisconsin made several charges up Henry House Hill under heavy fire, which they returned in kind. Wearing gray, they were also fired on from their rear by New Yorkers in their own brigade. The regiment rallied near a hospital, but as they tried to reform in order, an officer rode by and ordered the men to retreat to Washington as soon as possible and the best way they could. In the ensuing panic—compounded by a charge of enemy cavalry—a member of the color guard was wounded, and the color bearer left the Second's new national flag in the care of Private Robert S. Stephenson. Stephenson—in danger of losing the flag to the charging cavalry—saved the colors with the help of two regimental musicians who threw away their instruments and picked up rifles to stave off the charge.

While recovering from their losses at Bull Run, the regiment received a handsome flag. Made of two layers of dark blue silk, it was bound on three sides with heavy gold fringe. One side bore the Great Seal of the United States, painted in golds and browns; the regiment's name was painted in white letters in a gold scroll, edged with crimson, below the seal. On the reverse, the state seal of Wisconsin was painted in an arced panel edged in gold. The state motto—"FORWARD!"—was painted in crimson letters in a gold scroll above the seal. Governor Randall traveled from Wisconsin and delivered the flag to the regiment in person.[5]

By late summer 1862, the Second Wisconsin—along with the Sixth and Seventh Wisconsin regiments, and the Nineteenth Indiana—had earned the sobriquet "The Iron Brigade" for the soldiers' hard fighting in the Second Battle of Bull Run and the Battle of South Mountain. The reputation was solidified at the Battle of Antietam on September 17, 1862. In the storm of that battle—one soldier in the brigade thought that "in the intensity and energy of the fight and the roar of the firearms" his other engagements "were but skirmishes in comparison"—the Wisconsin flags were the targets of inordinate enemy fire. "The flag of the Sixth received four bullets in the flag staff, and some fifteen in the fly," he continued, adding that another of the brigade's flags had received "three bullets in the staff and more than twenty in the fly."[6]

On the eve of the battle, Stephenson, who—by virtue of his heroics at First Bull Run—had been promoted to color bearer in the Second Wisconsin, was sick in a field hospital. When he heard the skirmishing on the morning of the 17th, he left his bed and pushed on alone to find his regiment. When he found the Second Wisconsin—already under fire—he reported to his Captain and declared his unyielding fidelity, saying "Captain, I am with you to the last." Stephenson took the colors and held them until he was shot down, pierced with seven bullets. Corporal George W. Holloway—also a color bearer—fell, mortally wounded. "When found, after the battle," a brigade historian chronicled at war's end, "their bodies were lying with their heads resting on their knapsacks."[7]

Flags—such as those bravely carried by the Wisconsin color guards at Antietam—along with swords, heraldic symbols, and medals, constitute a special group of objects in the annals of military history. As objects they have both form and function. In form, many of them are beautiful objects of art and craftsmanship with iconography that is both ceremonial and documentary. In function, their purpose can be practical—that is, a means to distinguish among formations or to give signals on a battlefield—and symbolic, fostering intangible concepts of *esprit de corps*, morale, chivalry, and glory. For Americans, the Civil War marked a turning point in the use of these objects: after the war, swords and flags became less important (at least in function), while heraldry and medals were institutionalized.

Edged weapons can be traced back to prehistoric times. First made of flint, their manufacture and strength were perfected over millennia such that they were often the decisive weapon until firearms replaced them as the fighting implements of choice. During the Civil War, swords were issued to sergeants, musicians, and some artillerymen in the ranks, and were purchased by officers; they were designed for fighting, but rarely used for such, and—especially for officers—were more ornament than weapon, serving mainly as a symbol of rank. The cavalry still carried sabers, which were used to great effect during spectacular charges throughout the war.

While the sword may have been in decline as a weapon, the Civil War marked the zenith in American-made "presentation" swords. Weapons have been considered appropriate as gifts to warriors and heroes since ancient times (Achilles and Ajax exchange arms in Homer's *Iliad*); during the Middle Ages and the Renaissance—indeed, even in modern times—monarchs and other heads-of-state exchanged arms as symbols of mutual respect or national pride. The sword is a favorite presentation weapon as its every part—blade, guard, grip, pommel, and scabbard—represents a "canvas" on which the jeweler, silversmith, and engraver can practice their art. During—and especially after—the Civil War, grateful citizens and subordinates gave specially commissioned swords as tokens of esteem.

Flags, or objects with the same purpose, have also been with us for thousands of years. The Egyptians distinguished military formations by effigies of animals; an Old Testament story tells of the Israelites encamped, each of the Twelve Tribes by the standards and ensigns of their fathers. The Romans had their *vexillum*, a cloth bearing the number of their century, cohort, and legion (the formal study of flags, "vexillology," takes its name from the Roman standard). In the Middle Ages, military flags often included religious symbols or were saints' relics themselves. The sixteenth and seventeenth centuries witnessed the evolution of a number of military flags—banners, pennons, guidons, jacks, standards, streamers, pendants, and pennants—each with a special meaning or purpose. In all cases, the flags became icons of unit solidarity and tradition.

At the outset of the Civil War army regulations were specific about the number and dimensions of the colors that infantry, artillery, and cavalry could carry into battle. The flags were large—nearly six feet square—and with good reason: on a smoke-choked battlefield, the regimental colors might be the only visible trace of a unit on the field. Flags drew enemy fire, and casualties were often worst around the colors. No wonder that the regulations called for a large color guard—from six to nine men—chosen for their precision *and* character. The regulations were also specific about the design of the flags, but patriotic locals and professional makers often put icons on the flags to reflect regional or ethnic pride.

The Civil War also marked the beginning of formal unit "heraldry" in American arms. As with flags, heraldry has important functions: first, to distinguish combatants on the battlefield; second, to tell a story (one historian dubbed heraldry the "shorthand of history"). Heraldry—in the form of "coats of arms"—was first practiced to distinguish among knights covered in armor. Changes in tactics and technology may have made plate armor obsolete, but the practical need to distinguish soldiers of different units in the same army is timeless, as is the desire to be "bedecked with symbolic figures representative of ideals, achievements, and exploits," as one American officer put it.[8]

The tradition of heraldry in the United States Army is usually attributed to Major General Joseph Hooker, commanding the Union's Army of the Potomac, who, in 1863, established a system of corps badges to boost *esprit de corps* and to aid in identifying units on the field. Although Hooker's order was the first systematic plan of heraldry among the Union armies, the genesis is better traced to Union Major General Philip Kearney, who, a year earlier, angrily mistook some officers for stragglers in his own command, and thereafter ordered his officers to wear a round patch of red cloth on their caps. Soldiers in the ranks, eager to identify themselves with Kearney's command, adopted the practice. The first badges were relatively simple designs: circles, crescents, trefoils, and stars; over time, other corps adopted symbols that, in the spirit of good heraldry, told a story.

Like swords, flags, and heraldry, medals, and other honors and awards, have been a part of military history since antiquity. At their best, they encourage a desire among soldiers to emulate the feats of others and provide an opportunity for the citizenry to recognize selfless sacrifice. At their worst, they are given to curry political support or are divorced from deeds on the battlefield and thus lose their meaning. In the Roman Republic, decorations—javelins, decorative swords, silver and gold cups—were given on merit without regard to rank, but in the Empire they were reserved for officers of high rank. Likewise, the medieval orders of chivalry were first shared by a small fellowship of warriors; later they were bestowed on servants of the state and lost their martial character. The nineteenth century saw the rebirth of awards recognizing courageous acts: the Prussian Iron Cross, the British Victoria Cross, and the French *Croix de guerre*.

Decorations for valor also became part of the American fabric during the Civil War. The Founding Fathers, sharing distaste for what they considered to be the trappings of European royalty, were reluctant to bestow honors on its officers and private soldiers. Still, the American Revolution witnessed the first of America's official military decorations, including General George Washington's "Badge of Military Merit"—a heart in purple cloth, edged with narrow lace or binding—that had the purpose, as his orders stated, to "cherish virtuous ambition . . . as well as to foster and encourage every species of Military Merit." Most important, the award was not limited to the higher ranks; "The road to glory in a patriot army and free country is thus open to all," Washington wrote.[9]

After the Revolutionary War, the badge fell into disuse (although never officially abolished), and the Civil War found the Union with no official medal to honor gallantry. In early 1862, Congress established the "Medal of Honor" for the army (following the pattern of a similar award approved for the Navy a few months earlier) to recognize deeds of valor. The Act authorized the president to present the medal in the name of Congress to soldiers who "shall most distinguish themselves by their gallantry in action, and other soldier-like qualities during the present insurrection." The medal was the only authorized honor during the war (which led to some unfortunate and frivolous decorations), but commanders, states, and civil bodies also commissioned awards of their own.[10]

To craft swords, flags, badges, and medals of style and substance worthy of the deeds they recognized, public and private concerns in the Civil War era looked to the same source as realms, republics, and the rich had for twenty years before and for more than a century since: Tiffany & Co. From souvenirs and jewelry to mark President Lincoln's inauguration, to a variety of military goods during the war itself, to awards for gray-bearded veterans years after, Tiffany's talented "army" of jewelers, craftsmen, and silversmiths supplied a variety of goods to the Union war effort, many of which remain as valued objects of art—and meaning—to this day.

The scion of Squire Humphrey Tiffany of England and several generations of New Englanders, Charles Lewis Tiffany was born in Killingly, Connecticut, in 1812. His father, Comfort Tiffany, left his native Massachusetts and settled in Connecticut where he engaged in making cotton goods. Charles was raised in Killingly, attended the local schoolhouse, then studied at the Plainfield Academy, about ten miles from his home. Tiffany's father expanded his cotton goods business and placed Charles, then only fifteen, in charge of an adjoining general store. Charles managed the business successfully for a year, keeping the books and buying supplies, then finished his education in Brooklyn.

In 1837, Charles Tiffany joined friend and schoolmate John Young in New York City where Young was employed in a stationery and "fancy goods" store. With a thousand dollars borrowed from Comfort Tiffany, the young men opened their own store, the aptly named "Tiffany & Young," at 259 Broadway in New York City in September. It was a risky time to start a business as some of the city's established entrepreneurs had already failed in the "Panic of 1837," and some thought the uptown address a poor location. Indeed, the first few days sale totaled less than ten dollars, but the inauspicious start was soon followed by a profitable holiday: almost $700 on New Year's Eve alone (gifts were exchanged on New Year's Day at that time).

Tiffany had already acquired a taste for fine and unique things—"an instinctive avoidance of beaten paths," one historian called it—and the store was filled with an array of goods: bric-a-brac and *papier mache* from the Orient (like Henry Brooks, founder of Brooks Brothers, Tiffany courted the ship captains who returned from their ocean travels with novelties to sell), umbrellas and walking sticks, furniture and fans, and other curiosities. The store was robbed on New Year's day 1839—a loss of nearly $4000 in those "fancy goods" (Tiffany and his partner had wisely emptied the cash drawer, though)—but they recovered, and as the ensuing prosperity required an expansion, they purchased the neighboring storefront.[11]

In 1841, the men took on a new partner, J. L. Ellis, and the firm became known as "Tiffany, Young & Ellis." Ellis brought badly-needed cash to the expanding firm; more importantly, he brought experience in the European jewelry market, and he became the company's chief overseas buyer. By 1844, the store was importing expensive and quality Italian and English jewelry; indeed, so popular were the imports that the partners discontinued selling their once-fashionable baubles and concentrated on the more costly items. A few years later the store was crafting and selling its own silverware and gold jewelry. In 1852, Charles bought out the interests of Young and Ellis (on friendly terms), and the store became "Tiffany and Co."

A number of enduring hallmarks were established during the early days of the company. The characteristic shade of robin's egg blue—known as "Tiffany Blue" (itself a registered trademark)—was chosen in the first few years and has since become a symbol of elegance and exclusivity. Likewise, Tiffany's "Catalogue of Useful and Fancy Articles," now known as the "Blue Book," was first published in 1845. In 1853, Tiffany installed the store's famous nine-foot-tall wood-carved figure of Atlas bearing a clock (the works crafted by Tiffany's jewelers). An 1860s story and engraving in a national weekly told how clerks and message boys, unable to afford their own watches, depended on Atlas for accurate time.

Money poured into Tiffany's stores both far and wide. New York was heavy in ore from the Gold Rush, and ladies were dressing "with more magnificence than ever . . . thus do they support the luxury stores," the press reported, adding—with sympathy for the husbands -- "it takes a Croesus to maintain a woman of fashion." Tiffany had also opened a store in Paris, headed by Gideon F. T. Reed, late of a leading jeweler in Boston. The European royals and the traveling American rich patronized the store, and it grew as rapidly and prosperously as the headquarters store in New York, which had moved again to grander premises at 550 Broadway.[12]

Charles Tiffany, dubbed the "King of Diamonds" by the press, justly acquired a reputation as an excellent promoter, in no small part due to his friendship with Phineas T. Barnum, whose museum of spectacles and freaks was only blocks away. In 1850, when Barnum brought the noted opera singer Jenny Lind to America, her first stop was at Tiffany's, where she commissioned a handsome silver tankard for the captain of her ship. When one of Barnum's circus elephants was sentenced to death for trampling and killing ten men, Tiffany bought the carcass, displayed the hide, and advertised that fine leather articles could be made from the late "Mr. Forepaugh." In 1858, with the Atlantic cable successfully laid, Tiffany bought the remaining length of telegraph line and fashioned a variety of souvenirs—paperweights, bracelets, and cane handles—that proved so popular that police were required to maintain order at the store.

The publicity would have been for nought were it not for Tiffany's growing reputation for excellence. He engaged the services of leading craftsmen and insisted on the highest practical quality in all his productions. Up to that time, most silver work had been done with melted vintage Spanish or Mexican coins whose purity varied widely. Tiffany instructed his silversmiths to use as pure silver as possible—925 parts of 1,000- equivalent to English sterling. Tiffany contracted with John C. Moore, the leading silver craftsman of the day, to supply Tiffany's exclusively. Lind's presentation tankard was typical of the firm's beautiful (and restrained, unlike some of the rococo pieces of the era) work: the handle was a mermaid rising from the sea; Triton emerged from the cover; a rainbow, reminiscent of an incident on her trip, was carved on the sides.

When the Civil War broke out, Charles Tiffany, a true Connecticut Yankee, wasted no time in taking the side of the Union. He bought the property next door, expanded his store, and pushed the diamonds and brooches aside to make room for an increasing inventory of military goods that could be "forwarded to all parts of the Loyal States," as a typical Tiffany advertisement declared early on in the war.[13]

With his connections in Europe, especially Paris, Charles Tiffany ordered models of an array of the best of army equipment on the continent (Solingenin, in Germany, and Klingenthal, in the French Alsace, had been the leading sword-making centers for some time), and produced a catalog for the Quartermaster General with a promise to make or order anything needed. Soon, orders began to pour in to Tiffany's for all manner of materiel: passants, cap ornaments, Navy lace, surgical equipment, buckles, grenades, badges, flags, and Derringer pistols.

Not surprisingly, given the firm's reputation for finery, the catalog also included "campaign luxuries," including a patent camp chest, available exclusively through Tiffany's, and complete with imported silver-plated tableware. No wonder, then, that a wartime Tiffany salesman noted in his diary, "Business in the diamond department is very slow, but we are very busy in gold braid and cutlery."[14]

Indeed, it was with "cutlery," in the form of swords, that Tiffany's made a significant contribution during the Civil War. From the start, the company was steeped in requests from the likes of Union Major General John C. Fremont, who telegraphed Tiffany's with urgency from his St. Louis headquarters: "Continue sending swords same as sixteen forwarded today. Send rapidly as possible and advise by telegraph of each shipment." Tiffany contracted with the federal government for more than 9,000 swords in the first year of the war alone, and more than 20,000 by war's end.[15]

Ever the promoter, Tiffany targeted officers directly; advertisements in the *Army and Navy Journal* advised that "Officers studying the necessities of active service . . . will do well to examine this large collection of Foreign and Domestic Arms, Uniforms, and Miscellaneous Trappings." Another, in *Harper's Weekly,* proudly declared: "[we] have in store, and are receiving by every steamer, SWORDS, 'warranted to cut wrought iron.'"[16]

When Tiffany wasn't promoting the store's martial cutlery himself, the press did it for him. "Few persons would suspect that the white marble building on Broadway, tenanted by [Tiffany & Co.], is in fact a first-class armory," one newspaper declared, adding:

> It is true that no blunderbusses, arquebusses, matchlocks, or other murderous engines are fabricated there; but the springy, elastic, faithful sword is made in large numbers, of unvarying excellence, and superb finish from scabbard to guard. If any zealot in his mad career should draw a sword and throw away some of the scabbards we saw . . . we should like to have them cast our direction. We have seen the process of forging the blades and grinding them, and the excellent temper bestowed upon them imparts a higher character as trusty weapons than mere external gilding.[17]

To be sure, thousands of the swords that Tiffany produced during the Civil War were worn and employed on the battlefield, but the firm became famous for another kind of arm: the presentation sword. From the war's start to end, Tiffany turned out hundreds of the swords as testimonials, many of them set with precious stones and costing from a few hundred to

thousands of dollars. "Eulogium cannot express the elaborate and exquisite cunning manifest in every line of the delicate tracery that covers the
blade, or the strength and beauty of the figures which adorn the hilt and
guard," one paper declared. "Some presentations swords have been made
here which cost as high as $2,400 . . . although we may remark that the
designs of the ornamentation are chaste and in the best taste," the report
concluded in words that Charles Tiffany would have been proud to have
written himself.[18]

Officers were honored by cities, states, and admiring subordinates with
presentation swords: Major General Henry Halleck by the "ladies of St.
Louis," Major General Ambrose Burnside by his home state of Rhode
Island, Brigadier General J. J. Stevens by the non-commissioned officers
and privates of the "79th Highland Guard," and many others. Perhaps the
most famous swords made by Tiffany's during the war were the two offered
at the great Metropolitan Fair, held as a benefit for the United States
Sanitary Commission in New York City, on April 4, 1864. The elaborate
pieces, valued at several thousand dollars each, were to be given to two
Union heroes, one each from the army and navy. "Books were opened and
subscriptions were received from one dollar upwards . . . each subscriber
registering his name for whomsoever he or she might prefer," one paper
reported, adding that the "spirited competition" was "carried on between
the friends of Lieutenant General Grant and Major General McClellan."[19]

Leslie's Weekly described the army sword in detail, giving testament to
the careful attention—and expense—that the Tiffany designers, jewelers,
silversmiths, and engravers bestowed on every part of the piece, the whole
of which was steeped in military iconography from the ancients to America
itself:

> The grip of oxidized silver: on the obverse side, in low relief, a head of Mars,
> surrounded by a trophy composed of military insignia and weapons of the
> past and present times; on the reverse side, a figure of Victory with laurel
> wreath in her uplifted hands, the joyous sounding cornets at her feet, and
> over her head a diadem of stars. The guard, slender at each end, swells into
> a rich medallion, upon which is sculptured the wrathful Medusa; at the
> back of the grip is the head of a ram, identical with that familiar ornament
> of the sacrificial altar of the Greeks. The shell of the guard . . . is filled with
> a fine relief representing the combat between Hercules and the Nemean

lion. The whole is surmounted by a spirited piece of solid sculpture . . . the helmeted head of America. Set in the helmet are rubies, diamonds and sapphires, representing the national colors. The scabbard is sterling silver, the tips in richly carved relief, laurel leaves etched in gold. The inscription: 'Upon Your Sword Sits Laurelled Victory.'[20]

Nearly 45,000 votes were cast in the army contest alone: more than 30,000 to Grant; 14,500 to McClellan; and the balance to an assortment of minor favorites. Admiral David G. Farragut was declared the winner in the naval contest (the Navy sword was less ornate, and the Union League presented Farragut with another Tiffany sword; Farragut saw fit to have the firm make a brooch for his wife, patterned after the diamonds in the hilt). "Thus ended the sword controversy," one paper declared. More important, generous gifts, including $10,000 from the "Loyal Men of New York" and $3,000 from one "Loyal New Englander," added to proceeds from thousands of subscriptions, yielded more than $100,000 for the fair.[21]

Tiffany's connection with the Civil War started with no less a seminal event than a pre-inauguration visit by Abraham Lincoln. Lincoln is known to have made some personal trips to the store during visits to New York City. Though Honest Abe may have been simple and plainspoken, his wife, Mary Todd, was not (her expensive wardrobe and penchant for spending elicited nasty comments in Washington society), and the President made several purchases for her at Tiffany's. In 1861, as President-elect, Lincoln spent $530 for a seed-pearl parure comprising earrings, a necklace, a brooch, and two bracelets. Lincoln gave the set to his wife, who wore it at the inaugural ball in March 1861 (Mathew Brady took a now-famous photograph of the First Lady wearing the set). Tiffany's also presented him with a silver presentation pitcher to mark the occasion.

The diamonds, brooches, and attention to high society might have been set aside, but they were not entirely forgotten. Indeed, at the same time that Tiffany was advertising swords to soldiers and sailors, he was still marketing to the civilian population. "[Tiffany & Co.] would respectfully inform their Patrons and the general Public, that they have recently re-arranged and considerably extended the STATIONERY DEPARTMENT of their FANCY GOODS ESTABLISHMENT," one ad declared. "[We] have now unequalled facilities for furnishing the latest styles of Correspondence and Wedding

Stationery; Cards of all sizes and shapes, engraved upon the premises with punctuality and dispatch," it continued.[22]

Fittingly, Tiffany's was involved in two of the nation's most notable wartime weddings: one, between a "General" and his fair lady, was in keeping with Charles Tiffany's penchant for self-promotion and association with P.T. Barnum, and the other was a match of powerful political interests. For years, Barnum's most celebrated attraction had been a trio of midgets: Charles Sherwood Stratton, George Washington Morisson Nutt, and Lavinia Warren Bump. Under Barnum, they took on the stage names "General Tom Thumb," "Commodore Nutt," and "Mercy Lavinia Bumpus." Stratton—the most famous—started life as a large baby, weighing more than nine pounds at birth. He developed normally for the first few months, growing to two-feet in height and fifteen pounds, but then he stopped. At four years, he hadn't grown an inch or gained a pound.

Barnum heard about Stratton and—after reassuring his parents (who became business partners)—he taught the boy how to sing, dance, impersonate, and perform. At only five years old, "Tom Thumb" made his first tour of America, which became a huge success. A year later, Barnum took young Stratton on a tour of Europe making him an international celebrity. A few years later, Barnum trumped up a fierce rivalry between Stratton and Nutt for the hand of Warren, finally announcing Stratton as the lucky suitor. The wedding—which took place on February 10, 1863, at Grace Episcopal Church—was front page news. Tiffany's gift for the little couple—a silver horse carriage—was capital among all the presents, and was displayed in the store's window for weeks before the ceremony.

Abraham Lincoln did not attend the Thumb nuptials (although he did receive the couple in the White House), but—later that year—he did witness another well-publicized wedding: that of Miss Kate Chase, the eldest daughter of Secretary of the Treasury (and later Chief Justice) Salmon P. Chase to then-Senator and former Governor William Sprague of Rhode Island. Lincoln, Secretary of State Seward, and other members of the cabinet attended the November 12th wedding, which took place late in the evening at Secretary Chase's residence.

Tiffany's provided the bride's splendid wedding jewels—tiara, bracelet, and earrings—made from pearls, diamonds, and gold "so delicately wrought that the eye [caught] little else, at a cursory view, than [the] precious jewels." The jewelry was featured in a handsome engraving in the following week's issue of *Harper's Weekly*, accompanied by an equally- handsome story on the nuptials and the ornament. The *Harper's* writer was especially enamored with the ingenious crafting of the tiara (which had "a curiously-achieved adaptedness") with pieces that could be removed at the wearer's will ("with the word presto it is detached") to serve as necklace, hair-pins, or brooch.[23]

A few months earlier the war *nearly* came to Charles L. Tiffany's front door—as it *actually* had at Brooks Brothers—such that he might have had cause to use his own warranted swords. During the draft riots, Tiffany received word that the mob was moving down Broadway, intent on storming and destroying businesses in that area, including his own. Tiffany barred the windows, shuttered the doors, and, as company lore has it, passed out rifles to his employees while they charged hand grenades with powder and took strategic positions around the store. Thus equipped, Tiffany's "army" stood ready until police stalled the rioters before they reached the storefront. The danger having passed, the wary employees turned to the delicate task of disarming their grenades. "No," Tiffany told them in one account, "You don't know how. I'll do it myself."[24]

Unlike other contractors, Charles Tiffany was never criticized for profiteering or dealing in poor goods. Still, the war's nouveau rich—the "Sybarites of Shoddy" they were called—made their way to the store. Tiffany happily took their money, for which he was chastised, though more gently than Brooks Brothers. "The papers say that every body is growing rich out of this war," *Harper's Weekly* declared in an editorial at mid-war, adding "Certainly the display of wealth has never been equaled in this country." Prices of luxury items had increased several times over; still, clothiers had never sold so many silk dresses and lace, cartwrights never so many carriages, upholsterers never so much furniture, and as the paper declared (contrary to the bemused salesman's diary entry of the war's first days), "Tiffany never sold so much diamonds and so much jewelry as this season."[25]

Meanwhile, as Kate Chase was planning her nuptials, the Iron Brigade was getting ready for a ceremony of its own, and—like the bride's—Tiffany & Co. was involved.

As if the bloodletting at Antietam wasn't enough, the Iron Brigade, and its flags, faced other trials of fire in the following months, including the battles at Fredericksburg in December 1862 and at Chancellorsville the following spring. At Gettysburg, the brigade suffered terribly, especially amongst their colors. The Second Wisconsin lost its entire color guard killed or wounded in its fight against Archer's Brigade at Willoughby Run; the Sixth Wisconsin and Nineteenth Indiana, likewise, as they supported other fights. Sergeant Daniel McDermott, color bearer of the Seventh Wisconsin, was wounded just as his regiment retreated through the town, a blast of Confederate grape and canister "shivering the flag staff into a number of pieces." McDermott, who had carried the colors in all of the regiment's engagements, was placed on a caisson "still hanging to the tattered banner, which he waved in defiance at the foe."[26]

The 24th Michigan, which had joined the brigade before the Battle of Fredericksburg, had the highest total loss of all of the many Union regiments at Gettysburg, with casualties of eighty per cent. The regiment carried a single flag at Gettysburg: beautifully appointed national colors made by Tiffany and Co., whose embroidered flags were among the most desirable (and expensive) honors a regiment could hope for. The Twenty-fourth's Tiffany banner, a gift of F. Buhl & Co. of Detroit, was presented to the regiment before it left its home state in August 1862. In a speech, a local dignitary hoped that "in the smoke and din of battle," the flag's "beautiful folds [would] ever be seen." The regiment's commander, Colonel Henry Morrow, noted that locals had issued a check to the color bearer, Sergeant Abel G. Peck, with an additional $100 promised if the flag was returned. It was a reward that Peck would never receive.[27]

Peck was killed early on the morning of July 1st at Gettysburg, carrying the Tiffany flag. In turn, two others, Corporal Charles Bellore and Private August Earnest, took the flag off the ground and bore it until they too fell dead. First Sergeant Everard B. Welton reached forward, picked up the banner, and held it until Col. Morrow took the flag from his hands. Morrow handed it to Corporal Andrew Wagner, the last of the color guard, who fell wounded. Morrow again took the flag to rally what was left of the regiment. "Private William Kelly . . . took the colors from my hands," Morrow remembered, "remarking as he did so 'The colonel of the Twenty-fourth shall never carry the flag while I am alive.'" Kelly was killed instantly. Morrow turned the flag over to Private Lilburn A. Spaulding, then took it again to rally the regiment in their retreat, until he too was wounded. Blind and bleeding, Morrow was forced to leave the field, but not until he bestowed the flag on an anonymous soldier who, badly wounded, bore the banner back, then fell dead.[28]

If the Iron Brigade's flags were in poor shape even before the Battle of Gettysburg—and they were—then they were in tatters afterwards. Wisconsin's governor had already authorized new flags for his state's regiments that spring—beautiful national colors with the units' battle honors stitched into the stripes and blue regimental standards with the state seal—but they did not arrive until August. Still, the soldiers were loathe to part with their battle-worn banners. Lieutenant Colonel Rufus Dawes, commanding the Sixth Wisconsin, wrote that they had "sent their old flag away yesterday, and were sorry to see it go." The new flag was a "very handsome silk color," he added, but he wished that they could "keep our old color lance, which has three bullet holes through it, and two other marks."[29]

The men sent their flags back to Wisconsin reluctantly; in spite of their condition—or rather, because of it—the state was equally reluctant to retire or dispose of them. Instead, they were lent to the Great Northwestern Soldier's Fair held in Chicago that fall. For an admission of fifty cents, visitors to the fair could enter the "relic room" of war trophies and see the tattered flags of the Second and Sixth Wisconsin. Thousands of people visited the displays, and the fair netted nearly $90,000 in relief funds. "More attractive than aught else," reported one observer, "were the battle torn flags . . . though rent in shreds . . . they lent a lustre to the walls."[30]

Meanwhile, a group of Washingtonians—all citizens of Wisconsin, Indiana, and Michigan—concluded to recognize the heroic conduct of the Iron Brigade at Gettysburg with a special presentation flag from Tiffany & Co. Made of the finest blue silk, the banner cost over one thousand dollars. Its "colors, lights, shades, and contrasts were very brilliant" and the embroidery "in a degree of perfection unsurpassed," remembered a soldier in the Twenty-fourth Michigan. In the center was an eagle "which fairly seems to fly, so true to nature is the skillful . . . work," he added. In bold Gothic letters, the names of the five regiments were stitched along with the chief battles in which they had participated. The whole was unfurled from a "lance of the finest wood," and—in true Tiffany style—"fastened by a silver rod and socket, from which hangs a richness of scarlet and tassels." The flag—also in true Tiffany style—was exhibited in the store for all to see and admire.[31]

The committee chose September 17, 1863—the anniversary of the Battle of Antietam—as a fitting occasion to present the Tiffany-crafted colors. A large evergreen arch with the words "Iron Brigade" overhead and "Welcome Guests" underneath was erected. Notable guests were invited and speeches prepared for the ceremonies. Unfortunately, Major General George Meade ordered the army on a march to Culpeper, Virginia, where a representative met the brigade to bestow the flag, if only with less pomp. "The victuals are here, and the liquors, but no splendid bower and no distinguished guests," Dawes wrote. Still, the "flag program came off according to program," he recorded, but added that it was an "affair that conferred little honor on the brigade as gentlemen," the officers, generals, and staff being "almost unanimously drunk."[32]

The brigade flag was not suited (nor allowed by regulations) for the rigors of campaign and therefore sent to Madison, Wisconsin, for safekeeping, until it was needed again to "rally the troops," though the time would be long in coming: well after the war was over and for reasons less sublime.

At the Battle of Fredericksburg, the Army of the Potomac's Irish Brigade—absent its own handsome Tiffany-crafted flags of rich green silk, embroidered with Gaelic allegory (harps, shamrocks, and a heavenly sunburst)—wore sprigs of boxwood in their caps for identification. Thus, while unit heraldry in the American army can properly be traced to the Civil War, its origins were as simple and primitive as those of the ancients. Likewise, the corps insignia that generals Kearney and Hooker prescribed were simply cut from colored cloth. In time, though, officers adopted (or prescribed) more elaborate devices and commissioned jewelers—sometimes Tiffany & Co.—to craft them to the commanders' tastes in design and materials, from bone to coin metals to solid gold.

In the fall of 1863, two corps from the east—the Eleventh and Twelfth under Hooker (he had since been replaced as commander of the Army of the Potomac)—were sent west to aid in the relief of Chattanooga. A western soldier in the Fifteenth Corps had never seen a corps badge, and when he observed the Twelfth's star emblem on everything from wagons to tents to hats, he asked—in good humor—if everyone in the corps was a brigadier general. In turn, the wag was asked what his corps badge was. "Why, forty rounds in a cartridge box and twenty in the pocket!" he replied. Shortly thereafter, Major General John A. Logan, commanding the Fifteenth, heard the story and issued orders prescribing a corps badge (made by Tiffany's): a miniature cartridge box, and—above the box—the inscription "Forty Rounds."[33]

In April 1864, Major General Ambrose Burnside, commanding the Army of the Potomac's Ninth Corps, ordered a new badge for the unit: "a shield with the figure 9 in the center, crossed with a foul anchor and cannon, to be worn on the top of the cap or the front of the hat." Those who so desired (and could afford it), could also wear a medal of the same design—in gold, gilt, silver, white metal, copper, or bronze—attached to the coat as a pin or suspended from a red, white, and blue ribbon. "The designs for this badge are now in the hands of Messrs. Tiffany & Co., New York," Burnside's order continued, "and samples will be had at headquarters about the 27th."[34]

Kearney, who first instituted the corps badges, was also the inspiration for two early decorations during the Civil War. In November 1862, officers in the First Division of the Army of the Potomac's Third Corps adopted a medal in his honor (he had been killed at the Battle of Chantilly that September), to be awarded to officers who had served in battle under Kearney and whose "military record is without stain." The medal, constructed of gold, bore the motto *"Dulce el Decorum est Pro Patria Mori"* ("Sweet and fitting it is to die for one's country."). The following spring, Brigadier General David Birney, who had succeeded Kearney as commander of the Third, provided for a "cross of valor" to be awarded to non-commissioned officers and privates who "had most distinguished themselves in battle."[35]

Other decorations followed, including the Gillmore Medal (for gallant and meritorious conduct during the operations before Charleston) and the Butler Medal (to honor the gallantry of African-American troops late in the war). The Grant Medal, issued to its namesake by a grateful Congress, was made of gold and engraved with a bewildering amount of allegory; one wag declared that the medal was "three pounds in weight, on one side a bad like-ness of Grant; on the reverse, a goddess in an impossible position."[36]

Tiffany & Co. delivered medals to states that wanted to decorate their citizen-soldiers and to officers who, like Birney and Butler, wished to recog-nize the bravery of men in their command. Ohio spent nearly $16,000 for thousands of medals to be given to its soldiers "as a slight testimonial of the high appreciation by the State of . . . devoted patriotism in entering upon a second term of enlistment . . . actuated only by the purest love of coun-try." Tiffany's crafted the medals, made of bronze and one-and-a-half inches in diameter, in accord with the Resolution of the state's Assembly, which insisted that "its artistic features . . . be equal to the 'Crimean Medal,'" (given to British soldiers and sailors who fought in the Crimean War, noted for its very ornate clasps and suspenders). Tiffany's also struck medals to commemorate the 1862 battle between the ironclads *Monitor* and *Virginia*, and another presented to Major General George H. Thomas, "The Rock of Chickamauga," on behalf of the State of Tennessee; it bore his famous words, "I will hold the town till we starve."[37]

In 1864, then-Brigadier General George Armstrong Custer commissioned Tiffany & Co. to craft one of the rare medals of the war—on his own design and at his own expense—which he presented to fellow Michiganders in his cavalry brigade. He designed the medal while he camped with the brigade in Virginia during the previous winter. He sketched the award in his personal journal and headed each of his report entries with a drawing of the medal; many years later, a loose colored-pencil sketch was found in the journal, which historians believe may have been a model he created for Tiffany's.

The medal was constructed of gold with blue enamel trim; the body, a gold star with a Maltese cross, with the name "Custer" cast into the center of the cross. At the bottom was the Latin word *"Tuebor,"* meaning "I will defend," borrowed from the Michigan state seal. Plain on the reverse, the medal was attached to a yellow-orange ribbon with a pin of crossed sabers at the top with a T-bar attachment pin.[38]

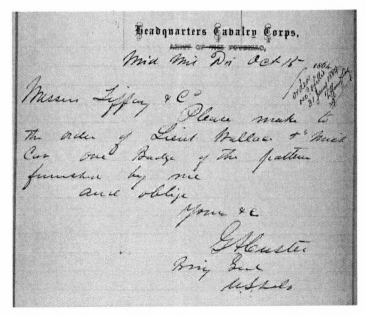

Figure 9. 1864 letter from Brigadier General George A. Custer to Tiffany & Co. to make one of the "Custer Medals." Source: Terry Reilly

As the medals were awarded only at Custer's behest, they were received and worn with great pride. After receiving his medal, Col. James H. Kidd of the 6th Michigan Cavalry, remarked with gratitude: "The gold in this badge is not more precious, it is not rarer, than the frankness, the generosity, the want of distrust which has always characterized your intercourse with me. The associations—the Michigan Brigade of Cavalry, its leader, Custer, his deeds and theirs, are enough to make your gift one of inestimable value always."[39]

Company legend has it that the great Atlas clock above Tiffany's stopped at the exact hour of Lincoln's death. True or not, one thing is certain: many years after Appomattox and the assassination, the firm continued to do a brisk business in war-related items, as towns across the country presented their favorite officers with testimonials. "It was a small and poor town that did not present its favorite officer with a [Tiffany] sword," one historian declared.[40]

The last of these notable war testimonials were elaborate solid silver services associated with claims against the Confederate raider *Alabama*. The United States brought a lawsuit against Great Britain, in which it accused the defendant of building and selling warships to the Confederate government. Known as the "Alabama Claims," the suit sought compensation for insurance losses, the pursuit and destruction of Union ships, and prolonging the war. Arbitrators from Brazil, Italy, and Switzerland met in Geneva, Switzerland, during the winter of 1871-72; there, they found Great Britain legally at fault, and ordered reparations in the order of $15 million.

In 1873, the United States government commissioned Tiffany's to craft three identical five-piece sets to present to the arbitrators "as a mark of appreciation"—as the inscription stated on each—"of the dignity, learning and ability and impartiality" with which they discharged their various duties. The iconography on the pieces represented ancient Greek themes: on the handles of the punch bowl was Dionysus, the god of wine, and the figures holding the candle cups included Ariadne, wife of Dionysus. The wine coolers featured Demeter holding a sheaf of wheat and a plowshare, and a personification of commerce holding a globe. Before presenting the suites, Tiffany & Co. exhibited them at their store, where they were greeted approvingly by the press.[41]

Like her husband's Brooks Brothers overcoat, Mary Todd Lincoln's Tiffany pearls took an interesting (but more direct) journey to becoming a national treasure. Walter Hoving—head of Tiffany & Co. from 1955 to 1980—kept on a shelf of his office window a framed copy of Brady's photograph of the First Lady wearing her pearls. The photo "was a nagging reminder . . . of a gap in the Tiffany legend," wrote one Tiffany historian, as Hoving thought the pearls were lost to history. In 1970, on Lincoln's birthday, Tiffany's ran an ad showing the Brady photograph in Hoving's office. Soon after, the firm received a phone call from a woman in Connecticut who believed she had the Lincoln parure.[42]

The firm—always interested in tracking down historic pieces—asked the woman, Mrs. Melvin Dichter, to bring the necklace to the store so it could be authenticated. She brought the pearls and an interesting tale: she had inherited the jewelry from her great-grandfather, who had bought what he believed to be the Lincoln pearls at auction. The necklace was too tight around his wife's neck, and he had the matching earrings set into the string of pearls to lengthen it for a better fit. An expert at Tiffany's examined Mrs. Dichter's jewels (which had the Tiffany mark), compared them with the Brady photo, and concluded they were indeed the Lincoln pearls. He was wrong; Lincoln's granddaughter, Mary Lincoln Isham, had donated the pearls—along with other family heirlooms—to the Library of Congress many years before.

The combination of craftsmanship, scale, and historical significance make many of the Tiffany items made during the Civil War—especially swords, medals, and other presentation pieces—valuable pieces of art in private collections and museums. The most ornate swords have brought well over a million dollars at auction, and the Art Institute of Chicago's *Alabama* silver set is considered among the most important presentation silver suites produced by any American firm in the nineteenth century. Still, in terms of lasting *meaning*, the flags have the most interesting legacy.

So successful was the display of the Iron Brigade flags—tattered as they were after the Battle of Gettysburg—at the Soldier's Fair in Chicago in late 1863, they were displayed at other fairs until the war's end. In donating the flags, Wisconsin's Quartermaster General, Nathaniel F. Lund, urged that they be used and displayed with great care, for they were "kept . . . as sacredly as a trust committed to her by her sons who have suffered for the life of the nation." Another state official reminded fair organizers that the battle flags had "a value to the people . . . which cannot be estimated."[43]

When the flags weren't being used to raise money, they were being used to raise more volunteers for the Union army. In January 1864, Brigadier General Edward S. Bragg, a Fond du Lac native who had risen to command of the Iron Brigade, led veterans of the Sixth Wisconsin through the streets of Milwaukee en route to a reception in their honor. There, Bragg and the veterans joined Brigadier General Lucius Fairchild, a Madison native who had lost his left arm fighting with the Iron Brigade at Gettysburg. Fairchild was now Wisconsin's Secretary of State, and had brought with him one of the flags of the Sixth to greet his comrades and to challenge young men to enlist.

Less than two years later, Fairchild was governor and began organizing Wisconsin veterans into a powerful political force. In doing so, he was not afraid to use the state's battle flags as props in what became known as "Bloody Shirt Campaigns"—the emotional practice of inspiring antipathy against the South and the Democratic Party by equating them with treason and appealing to the public's resentment over the late war. In July 1866, Fairchild organized an immense ceremony in Madison, ostensibly to commemorate the end of the war but with the added benefit of featuring the potential political strength of organized veterans. The Iron Brigade colors were featured prominently in the procession. The "Bloody Shirt" demagoguery—perfected by Fairchild, a born orator—worked wonders in the first few post-war elections.

As time passed though, the public, and even the veterans, became weary of the post-war enmity. When Fairchild sent nearly two dozen battle flags, including one from each of the Iron Brigade regiments, for display at an 1871 political rally (billed as a soldier's reunion) for Wisconsin gubernatorial candidate, and former Major General, Cadwallader C. Washburn, the reception was lukewarm. Alfred E. Haven, associate editor of a state paper and an Iron Brigade veteran himself, lambasted Fairchild ("a political blood sucker") and his tactic. Real peace would never come as long as the Bloody Shirt politicians "delight in bringing in view scenes of the late war," Haven wrote, adding, "It needs no display of tattered flags."[44]

Washburn carried the election, but, as if in answer to Haven's appeal, the flags were trotted out less and less. After appearing at a rally in Madison in 1872, it was another four years before the flags were displayed again in public. By the mid-1870s, the political pendulum had swung such that Democrats secured majorities in Wisconsin and in Washington, DC. The new Wisconsin legislature passed an act to preserve the battle flags; by decree the banners were not to be removed from their cases unless required for their conservation. A year later, the law was amended to allow their use at reunions; they were displayed at the first reunion of the Iron Brigade Association in 1882, where the teenaged daughter of a wartime newspaper boy attached to the brigade had her photograph taken with the Tiffany colors.

More than fifty years after the surrender at Appomattox—on Flag Day, June 14, 1918—surviving veterans and other dignitaries gathered in Madison at the new state capital building. They were there to dedicate an even newer hall where the state's battle flags were to be properly displayed. Jerome Watrous, an Iron Brigade veteran, delivered an address entitled "Looking Over Our Old Battle Flags." Of all the artifacts of the war, Watrous concluded that the battle flags—"Those . . . old, faded, torn emblems of our great, strong nation," as he called them—would serve as the best reminders of the country's great fight to preserve the Union. And as for the soldiers' affection for those banners, he declared they "had been woven into the colors."[45]

A WEEKLY JOURNAL OF PRACTICAL INFORMATION IN ART, SCIENCE, MECHANICS, CHEMISTRY AND MANUFACTURES

VOL. VI.---NO. 10. NEW YORK, MARCH 8, 1862. NEW SERIES.

New Mode of Mounting Cannon.

The accompanying engraving illustrates a mode of mounting cannon, by which the guns may be loaded while the men are perfectly protected, even in operating heavy barbette guns.

A circular platform, A, is pivoted at the center to a solid base below, and fitted to revolve on friction rollers. Upon this platform is secured the vibrating frame, B, which sustains the gun carriages, C C. The frame, B, is made of great strength, and it supported by the uprights, D D, by means of a massive shaft,

to bring the other gun into position ; the wheel, G, at the same time being turned to oscillate the frame, B, and bring down the discharged gun and carry the loaded one up over the level of the parapet. As the gun comes into position, a man steps upon the platform, H, for an instant, to direct the aim ; and it is only for this instant that the gunner or any one of the garrison is exposed to the enemy's fire.

The recoil of the guns is taken up by heavy india-rubber straps, carried around the breech of the gun, as shown.

1861, and further information in relation to it may be obtained by addressing the inventor, Obadiah Hopkins, at No. 420 Sixth avenue, New York city.

To Render Ivory Flexible.

In reply to a correspondent, the editor of the *Amer. Drug. Circ.* says that to " to render ivory flexible, it should be immersed in a solution of pure phosphoric acid of sp. gr. 1.130, and left there until it ceases to be opaque. It should be then taken out, washed with water, and dried with a soft cloth. It is now so

HOPKINS'S IMPROVED MODE OF MOUNTING CANNON.

E, in such manner that it may oscillate on this shaft.

The gun carriages, C C, are supported at the ends of the frame, B, on shafts, so that they also may oscillate in relation to the frame, though they are maintained in a horizontal position by means of chains. These chains, F F, are attached to both ends of the gun carriages, and carried around the shaft, E, to which they are secured, so that they may wind up and unwind equally and together, thus keeping the gun carriages always in a horizontal position.

The shaft, E, is turned to wind the chains upon it, and thus oscillate the frame, B, by means of the hand wheel, G.

As soon as the elevated gun has been discharged the platform, A, is turned upon its central pivot, in order

By this mode of mounting, the gun is exposed to the enemy's fire only for a brief space, while in position, and the men are not exposed at all, with the exception of the brief and partial exposure of the man who directs the aim.

In casemates there is the advantage of having two guns to fire alternately from one embrasure ; one being in a safe position to be loaded, while the other is brought to bear upon the enemy's ships or troops and discharged.

In mounting cannon in this manner for naval purposes, there may be the advantage of not having openings in the bulwarks, as the gun can be turned to any point, elevated and fired over the bulwark.

The patent for this invention was granted Dec. 17,

flexible that it may be bent like leather. On exposure to dry air it returns to its original hardness, but it becomes flexible again by treating it with hot water. There is no difficulty in giving to ivory various colors —black, blue, green, red violet, &c. The process is simply one of dyeing. You are mistaken in supposing that ivory is composed chiefly of carbonate of lime. Like the substance of all teeth, it is mainly phosphate of lime, with a little carbonate, and a large quantity, equal to about one-fourth of the whole, of gelatinous matter or cartilage.''

A six horse power steam engine drives one set of cards with all its attendent machinery in a woolen mill.

Figure 10. Typical wartime front page of *Scientific American.*

78

CHAPTER FOUR

A Regiment of Inventors

> In the arts of life man invents nothing; but in the arts of death he
> outdoes Nature herself, and produces by chemistry and machinery all
> the slaughter of plague, pestilence, and famine.
>
> —George Bernard Shaw

"BE IT KNOWN," the aspiring inventor's application began, "that I have invented a new and improved manner of combining adjustable buoyant air chambers with a steamboat or other vessel for the purpose of enabling their draught of water to be readily lessened to enable them to pass over bars, or through shallow water, without discharging their cargoes." Three drawings, illustrating various aspects of a ship combined with the novel chambers, accompanied nearly two pages of detailed specifications and claims. Simply put (for specifications in letters patent are rarely simply put), he had devised a contraption to lift boats over shoals.[1]

Like many inventions, his was born of frustration and personal experience: not once but twice in the span of two decades he had found himself stuck in a boat that had become stranded on sandbar or other shallow. The first occurred in 1831, when he was a young man of twenty-two. He, his second cousin John Hanks, and his stepbrother John Johnston, hired themselves to local trader Denton Offutt to take a flatboat loaded with goods down the nearby Sangamon River, then on to the Illinois, and finally down the Mississippi to New Orleans. In March, after the snow had melted, the young men found their patron at the appointed meeting place; but Offutt—characterized by one writer as "a hard drinker, a hustler . . . easy with promises"—had not brought the boat.[2]

Facing a long walk back across the muddy prairie to their homes, the men instead offered to construct the craft themselves from local timber. The boat was built, launched, and loaded with Offutt's wares, but it soon became stranded on a milldam. The vessel took on water, which threatened to sink the boat and its cargo. The future inventor leapt into action. After hailing curious onlookers to send a boat, he unloaded part of the cargo to right the craft. He secured an auger from the village and drilled a hole in the bow of the sinking craft to let the water run out. With the hole plugged, he helped move the boat over the dam and proceeded to New Orleans with his crew.

Seventeen years later, now a successful lawyer and a freshman congressman on his way home after his first term, his boat became stranded after running aground on a sandbar. He told his law partner William Herndon how the captain had "ordered the hands to collect all the loose planks, empty barrels and boxes and force them under the sides of the boat. These empty casks were used to buoy it up. After forcing enough of them under the vessel she lifted gradually and at last swung clear of the opposing sand bar."[3]

The congressman watched this activity intently. Surely it carried him back to the day when he and his small company freed their homemade flatboat from the gristmill dam on the Sangamon. Herndon recalled that "continual thinking on the subject of lifting vessels over sand bars and other obstructions in the water suggested to him the idea of inventing an apparatus for this purpose." The inventor, true to his nature, put it more simply: "I am never easy when I am handling a thought," he said, "till I have bounded it north, bounded it south, bounded it east, and bounded it west."[4]

Back at his law office, he set to work demonstrating the feasibility of his idea. The patent law at that time required that all applications be accompanied by a model of the invention. Walter Davis, a local mechanic who had a shop near the office, lent his tools and assisted in making the model. Herndon later wrote of his partner, "Occasionally he would bring the model in the office, and while whittling on it would descant on its merits and the revolution it was destined to work in steamboat navigation." Herndon confessed that he though the idea impracticable but said nothing out of respect for his friend's reputation as a boatman.[5]

On a return visit to Washington early the next year, the aspiring inventor took his model and idea to Z. C. Robbins, a patent attorney in the capital city. Robbins remembered, "He walked into my office one morning with a model of a western steamboat under his arm. After a friendly greeting he placed his model on my office table and proceeded to explain the principles embodied therein and what he believed to be his own invention, and which if new, he desired to secure by Letters Patent."[6]

Robbins had become thoroughly familiar with the construction and equipment of flat-bottomed steamboats while living in St. Louis, and he informed the new client that his improvement was indeed novel. "Thereupon he instructed me to prepare the necessary drawings and papers and prosecute

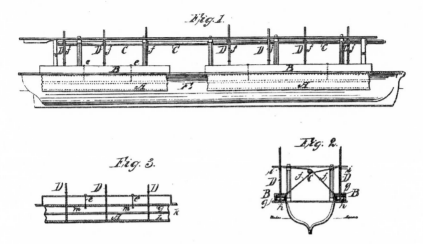

Figure 11: Drawing of Lincoln's flatboat lift patent.
Source: United States Patent and Trademark Office

an application for a patent for his invention at the United States Patent Office," Robbins later wrote. With his client's thirty dollars in gold in hand to pay the application fee, Robbins filed the necessary paperwork.[7]

In April, Robbins wrote his client, "It affords me much pleasure to inform you that I have obtained a favorable decision on your application for a patent," promising that it would issued in about a month. Weeks later, the *Scientific American*, in its weekly list, noted the following about patent number 6,469, one of twenty issued from the United States Patent Office during the week of May 22, 1849: "To A. Lincoln, of Springfield, Ills., for improved method of lifting vessels over shoals."[8]

Throughout his life, Abraham Lincoln was intrigued by inventions and admired inventors. One biographer wrote of Lincoln having "a streak that had more in it of Eli Whitney than of David Thoreau." Another of Lincoln's law partners commented that Lincoln had "an inventive faculty" and was "always studying into the nature of things." While the accident of his birth in the wilderness supported his rough and popular "rail splitter" image, Lincoln was actually adept at mathematics and engineering, having worked for several months as a surveyor. As a lawyer, patent cases were his bread and butter. In 1858 he had a (very) short career as a paid lecturer and gave his speech "Discoveries and Inventions" to local young men's and ladies' groups.[9]

Lincoln's invention came at a time when American technology was still the domain of amateur inventors. "Shade tree mechanics" could secure a patent, and perhaps even wealth, without immense venture capital, formal schooling, or the imprimatur of professional associations. All that was required was an original idea and some tools. Indeed, by their nature, inventors—as opposed to the increasingly professionalized scientific community—relied more on empirical evidence than on esoteric theory: they needed only a device to work as they had imagined it would.

The fledgling country's inventive spirit had a definite Yankee flavor. Of nineteen other inventors who received patents the same week that Lincoln did, only two lived in slave states. The pattern held for at least another decade: in 1859, the United States Patent Office issued almost 4,500 patents to citizens of the United States. More than a quarter of those were issued to New Yorkers. New England contributed another thousand. What would become the eleven Confederate states contributed fewer than three hundred; Virginia led the pack with sixty-five patents, twenty fewer than tiny Rhode Island.

The American Civil War has been called the "first modern war" because of the technologies that were employed: railroads, telegraphs, ironclad warships, machine guns, and mines were all used effectively for the first time in a major conflict. Yet these innovations had actually been developed before the war. The *real* demand was for improvements. To that end, "Yankee ingenuity" was wielded as a weapon itself during the war, with inventors plying their trade in the "arts of death," as Shaw put it. One newspaper, noting that the "inventive faculty of the country is in the Northern States," put out the call for improvements more colorfully:

> Our countrymen at large should be encouraged by the government to direct their attention forthwith to the improvement of all sorts of instrumentalities. . . . Let our Yankees go to work, and we doubt not but that they will soon be able to turn out some unheard of and undreamed of implement or missile which will sweep our enemies from the face of the earth. Take our word for it, these geniuses will yet produce some patent Secession-Excavator, some Traitor-Annihilator, some Rebel-Thrasher, some Confederate State Milling Machine, which will grind through, shell

out, or slice up this war, as if it were a bushel of wheat or an ear of corn or a big apple.[10]

The key to the paper's entreaty and promise was the phrase, "should be encouraged by the government." Fortunately, Lincoln brought his own "inventive faculty" and technological competence to the White House. During the war years, he took a great personal interest in the development and testing of new weapons. As president, one of Lincoln's favorite haunts was the Navy Yard where the intelligent and able Commander John A. Dahlgren headed the Navy's ordnance department. Lincoln also witnessed weapons trials—or what one officer cynically referred to as "champagne experiments"—at the Washington Arsenal, often for ideas that Lincoln himself had championed.

However, inventors were more often than not rebuffed by overworked, uninterested, or overly conservative personnel in the Army's Ordnance Bureau. Some inventors wrote directly to Lincoln with their ideas, but even the president's indulgent secretaries could only let so many through. What inventors needed was a cheerleader: an organ that would foster, cajole, debunk, advise, and put pressure on the government to accept innovation.

Inventors and mechanics found that advocate in the *Scientific American*. As America's oldest continuously published magazine, it has delivered opinion and news about developments in technology for more than 150 years. Founded as a weekly broadsheet by Rufus Porter in 1845, the magazine has attracted the attention of inventors and scientists both famous—legend has it that, as a boy, Thomas Edison walked three miles each week to get his copy—and obscure and now boasts more than a million readers around the globe.

The *Scientific American* of the nineteenth century was targeted primarily toward inventors and machinists—more like today's *Popular Mechanics* than its own modern counterpart, which reports on the cutting edge of theoretical science. During the Civil War, *Scientific American* played an important role by fostering and reporting on innovations that had an impact on the battlefields and waters, while weathering wartime crises of its own.

Born in Boxford, Massachusetts, Rufus Porter was, according to his principal biographer, a "Yankee Da Vinci" with a "grasshopperish interest." With minimal formal schooling, Porter was by turns an apprentice shoemaker, itinerant musician, accomplished painter, schoolmaster, and prolific inventor. He concocted dozens of devices, including a camera, revolving almanac, fire alarm, steam carriage, and washing machine. Porter never sought patents for his ideas; instead, as soon as he developed an invention he would sell it for a small sum. Such it was for Porter's "revolving rifle," which he sold to Samuel Colt for one hundred dollars.[11]

Porter's interests eventually turned to journalism. In 1840, while living in New York, he bought an interest in a weekly newspaper. In 1841, he began a new series of the paper, which he dubbed the *New York Mechanic* and billed in the subtitle as "The Advocate of Industry and Enterprise, and Journal of Mechanical and Other Scientific Improvements." Despite early success for the *Mechanic*, within months, Porter—true to his nature—had found a new interest in electroplating. He sold the paper, though he remained editor for a few months of what the new owners had named the less provincial and more ambitious *American Mechanic*.

In 1845, while working as an electroplater in New York, Porter invested one hundred dollars to start a new weekly. He called it the *Scientific American* and borrowed the subtitle from his *New York Mechanic*. Porter began the first issue—a five-column, four-page folio published on August 28, 1845—with an engaging overture:

> [W]e have made arrangements to furnish the intelligent and liberal working man and those who delight in the development of the beauties of Nature, which consist of the laws of Mechanics, Chemistry, and other branches of Natural Philosophy—with a paper that will instruct while it diverts and amuses them, and will retain its excellence and value, when political and other newspapers are thrown aside and forgotten.[12]

In addition to the auspicious subtitle, the *Scientific American* also shared the format of the earlier *Mechanic*. For a subscription fee of two dollars a year, Porter delivered a front-page engraving of an invention (usually his own), news on other recent inventions (often his own), essays on moral subjects, and even some music and poetry. Porter wrote almost all the articles himself, a departure from the contemporary practice of reprinting material exchanged with other newspapers and journals. Despite the originality and breadth of content, Porter's new journal failed to attract a significant audience.

The enterprise was also the victim of bad fortune: on October 20, 1845, a fire completely destroyed the *Scientific American*'s printing plant, interrupting publication for three weeks. Porter established a new plant in the Sun building, but soon became bored and sold the paper, less than a year after he had started it, to Orson Desaix Munn and Alfred Ely Beach.

Munn was born in Monson, Massachusetts, attended school at the Monson Academy, and decided to pursue a career in business. At nineteen, he began work as a clerk in a Springfield bookstore. Two years later, Munn was managing a general store when Beach, a friend and Monson classmate, persuaded him to join in purchasing the *Scientific American*. Beach's father was owner of the *New York Sun*, to whose offices Porter had moved his plant after the fire. On July 23, 1846, Munn, Beach, and a third associate, Salem H. Wales, bought Porter's interest and his 200-name subscription list for $800.

The men established the firm of Munn & Co. and secured an office in New York City. Porter stayed on as editor for nearly a year while he taught Munn the intricacies of publishing. Munn published the *Scientific American* as a paper chiefly devoted to the interests of the American inventor (discarding Porter's moral essays, music, and poetry) and published a weekly list of all patents, with associated claims, issued by the Patent Office. Indeed, the popularity and reputation of Munn's *Scientific American* soon made its offices a gathering place for inventors.

At the time, there was a paucity of expertise in patent law, except in the largest cities, and would-be inventors flooded the magazine with requests for advice. To meet the demand, Munn launched the Scientific American Patent Agency in 1847. The agency established a reputation for competence and honesty and became the foremost of its day. In 1860, with offices in New York City and Washington, D.C., Munn & Co. secured one-third of all patents issued by the U.S. Patent Office. One of its agents, Robert Washington Fenwick, had trained in the offices of Z. C. Robbins, the solicitor who had secured Lincoln's patent.

Despite the attacks of other journals—an editor of a rival publication, pointing out a mistake, wrote that "the *Scientific American* is an unfailing fountain of fun . . . it takes but a moment's reflection to discover that [it] is a goose"—the paper was the premier publication of its kind, outliving more than a dozen other technology and science journals launched at mid-century. On the eve of the Civil War, largely due to Munn's direction and head for business, Porter's quaint four-page broadsheet with only a few hundred subscribers had grown to sixteen pages and boasted a circulation of 30,000.[13]

From the beginning, the editorial policy of the *Scientific American* was decidedly nonpartisan. Porter set this tone in the inaugural issue, writing, "[W]e shall endeavor to avoid all expression of sentiment on sectional, sectarian or political party subjects." For Porter, the reasons for such a principle were philosophical: he felt that xsuch disagreements distracted the mechanic and inventor and threatened his creativity. For Munn, the policy was practical, allowing the magazine to avoid the sensitive issues of the day, the most sensitive being slavery. There is a noticeable absence of references to the South's "peculiar institution" in the *Scientific American's* antebellum pages.[14]

There was also an economic reason: *Scientific American* had a substantial circulation in the Southern states, and numerous inventors there did business with the patent agency. It made no sense for the editors to purposely infuriate their clientele, especially if the matters at hand were outside the realm of science and mechanics. While the policy may have been both practical and well-meaning, given the heated sentiment of the day, it was also naïve. In short, when it came to discussing what the editors called "the political troubles that are hanging like a black cloud over our country," the *Scientific American* was damned if it did and damned if it didn't.[15]

What the magazine dubbed "Our Secession Troubles" began soon after Lincoln's election. In an early December 1860 issue—just weeks after the polls closed—the editors featured an engraving and detailed description of the president-elect's 1849 invention, supposing "it would interest a vast number of our readers to see what sort of an invention emanated from the brain of so distinguished an official." They added, "The merits of this invention we are not disposed to discuss; but we hope the author of it will have better success in presiding as Chief Magistrate over the people of the entire Union than he has had as an inventor in introducing his invention upon the western waters, for which it was especially designed."[16]

The following April, the magazine reported with bemusement that a Northern subscriber accused them of "undertaking to cast a slur upon 'Honest Old Abe'" and guessed that the irritated reader "jumped at the conclusion that we had trumped it [Lincoln's invention] up for the purpose of casting ridicule upon his candidate." The matter did not end there.

Southern readers threatened to cancel their subscriptions (some actually did) and accused the *Scientific American* of rejoicing "over the election of a Black Republican rail-splitter." One Southern wag wrote in feigned indignation that the "publication of His Excellency's invention would enable the Northerners to ride into Charleston at low water, and thus reinforce Fort Sumter."[17]

The editors further complained that when it came to the "peculiar institution, about which there is so much strife, the public mind seems to have become so very touchy, that to state even ordinary scientific or mechanical facts bearing upon it, or to make an indirect allusion to it or its champions, *pro* or *con*, is sure to get somebody by the ears." As evidence, the editors pointed to two previous articles that had rankled readers on both sides of the issue.[18]

The first featured an engraving of an improved cotton picking machine with a "healthy looking negro" in the act of operating the machine, about which a Northern reader "wrote . . . in high dudgeon, charging that we were burlesquing the colored race, and cottoning to the South." The second article included a statement, published months earlier—"on the authority of someone who pretended to know all about it"—that the inhabitants of the South were more rawboned and lank than Northerners. Protesting their innocence at intending any offense, the editors told how "one of our readers in the South . . . immediately wrote us that he thought he discovered in it a concealed attack on the physical qualities of his people."[19]

While the magazine handled its first crisis of the war with humor, the second crisis was more serious because it directly challenged the probity of the *Scientific American* and the reputation for integrity that the proprietors of Munn & Co. had worked so hard to establish and maintain. In the summer of 1861, two Southern papers published a letter purported to be from the magazine's patent agency to an unnamed New Orleans entrepreneur. The letter, which was also printed by at least two New York City newspapers, included a proposal that the businessman conspire with Munn & Co. to secure control of existing patents so as to control a monopoly on invention and thereby "dictate our own terms to manufacturers and mechanics" when the Confederacy inevitably achieved its independence.[20]

The Southern papers rejoiced at the *Scientific American's* apparent assumption of a Rebel victory but denounced in an editorial the alleged proposal as the machinations of "rabid Black Republicans" with plans "to make money out of us [by] asking a Southern citizen to become a partner in [their] Yankee scheme." The editors of the *Scientific American* responded to the potentially scandalous charge in the August 17, 1861, issue of their paper. Printing the letter and the Southern editorial in full, they insisted that the letter was "an impudent forgery from beginning to end" and declared the author an "unmitigated scamp" who deserved "to be strung up within the coils of a hempen noose."[21]

The editors admitted being solicited by men from both the North and the South ("and probably by this scamp also") to enter into arrangements for securing patents in the Confederacy, but they maintained that to "connive in any way with those who are in arms against [the government's] authority" would be treasonable. They concluded by stating that if the independence of the Confederacy was ever recognized, they would be prepared to do business for inventors in those states as with any other foreign power.[22]

The third crisis, which started with the war and peaked at mid-war, was not unique to the *Scientific American*. The wartime editor of the *Knickerbocker* spoke for the *Scientific American* and most other contemporary publications when he wrote, "This is a bad time for newspaper and magazine owners." Having weathered the brief depression known as the "Panic of 1857," publishers found the Civil War a "bad time" of four long years, with decreased subscriptions, new taxes, and higher paper and printing costs.[23]

While newspaper circulation actually increased, no doubt due to a thirst for timely reporting from the battlefields, the war dealt a severe blow to magazines in lost subscriptions. The editor of the *Biblical Repertory and Princeton Review*, wrote, "We lost three hundred subscribers at one blow when hostilities commenced." Though partisan tempers resulted in a few lost subscriptions for the *Scientific American*, it was the break in communications and mail between the North and South that reduced circulation by large numbers. Just before the start of the war, the *Scientific American* boasted a circulation of nearly 30,000 copies per week. In the fall of 1862, Munn noted that the circulation had decreased to about 17,000 copies per week; by the spring of 1863, subscriptions had fallen further still.[24]

The hostilities also created a considerable shortage of newsprint with a corresponding increase in cost: more than forty percent by the end of 1862 and more than double at the height of the war. New taxes on newsprint and advertising also strained publishers' budgets. In a long editorial in late 1862, "An Important Crisis in the History of Newspaper Publishing," the editors of the *Scientific American* outlined the various business challenges they faced. Of the new taxes, they wrote, "We should cheerfully pay [them] as a moiety of our proportion of the war expenses." Cheerful though they may have been to pay their fair share in taxes, as a consequence of rising costs, the *Scientific American* raised its subscription fee in January 1863 from two to three dollars annually, a cost that remained unchanged for the rest of the nineteenth century.[25]

"In the midst of the great struggle that is now going on . . . we intend to devote a sufficient space in our paper to a record of the events of the war," the editors of the *Scientific American* promised in May 1861, adding:

> [W]e shall avoid the flying rumors . . . and shall endeavor to sift out from the conflicting reports only those statements which are fully authenti-cated. . . . The struggle will doubtless be one of the most gigantic and terrific that the world has ever seen. Both sides are amply provided with implements of destruction, they are each composed of millions of brave men, and they are bent upon their opposite purposes with the deepest and most determined earnestness. The great drama is already commenced, and its thrilling scenes, with their noble self sacrifice, sublime daring, heroic achievements, and grim horrors, are passing in swift succession before us.[26]

The editors seemed to anticipate what others didn't (or were afraid to admit): the war would *not* be over in ninety days, but would be a "gigan-tic and terrific affair," and through four years of sacrifice, daring, achieve-ments, and horrors, they kept their promise.

Soon after Munn & Co. purchased the magazine from Porter, the firm instituted what one historian called an "attractive orderliness" to its pages, to which he attributed the *Scientific American*'s wide appeal. The first page was always dominated by an engraving and description of a new or improved invention, a feature that originated with Porter's *New York Mechanic*. The following pages included articles on other new inventions and discoveries, editorials, an official list of patents and their claims issued the previous week, a column for queries, and an advertising page.[27]

Beginning with the May 11, 1861, issue, which featured a "Map of the Seat of War," dozens of issues during the Civil War featured front page engravings and reports on technological advances in weaponry, which the editors called "the grim enginery of war." The engravings included improvements in cannon (revolving, giant, and "war engines"), projectiles, rifles (breechloading, self-loading, repeating, and automatic), camp accoutrements (chests, tents, and bakeries), field fortifications, and shipbuilding (turrets, monitors, ironclads, floating batteries, and submarines).

Next, a full page on "Military and Naval Affairs" delivered up-to-date news from the front. On June 1, 1861, "with a view of presenting the latest intelligence from the seat of war," the publishers announced that the magazine would be mailed on Friday instead of Tuesday, so that "the *Scientific American* will have as late war news as any other weekly paper."[28]

While the "late war news" might have been directed towards civilian readers, the *Scientific American* did not ignore its soldier readers. It joined many other periodicals and newspapers early in the war by providing military instruction in its pages. Articles such as "Learning to Shoot," "Careful Loading of Rifles," "Purifying Water for Soldiers," and "*Scientific American's* Advice to Our Soldiers—Malaria and its Remedies," were all aimed at men who now found themselves in the army or navy.[29]

The *Scientific American* also did its part by getting copies of the paper into the hands of soldiers, reporting in May 1861, "We have been sending several hundred copies of the *Scientific American*, for a few weeks past, to the troops in the barracks opposite our office in the Park, and purpose to continue the practice" and promising also "to forward a number of copies to the several regiments located in Washington, and other portions of our country, every week as a gratuity." The magazine encouraged other publishers to do the same, writing, "After the drill duties of the day are over, the soldiers in camp are not only gratified to have something to read, but are morally and intellectually benefited in so doing."[30]

Soldiers returned the favor by writing from the field. A "valued correspondent from Missouri" wrote the *Scientific American* with a tongue-in-cheek suggestion of a "regiment of inventors, to be armed throughout with patent articles—patent rifles, patent tents, patent knapsacks, etc., for the purpose of defending the Patent Office, the repository of [our] genius." The correspondent, who had seen eight years service in the Austrian army, patriotically offered to serve in any capacity: "soldier, chaplain, or drummer, but would refuse the latter post unless supplied with a patent drum." The editors responded with a compliment to the country's soldier-inventors:

"Arm a regiment of sturdy inventors with the best which their ingenuity has yet devised, and they would conquer peace in a short time and compel Jeff Davis to go about his business."[31]

One of the truly unique features of *Scientific American* was a weekly section entitled "Notes and Queries." The magazine received more than a hundred pieces of mail each day. Many letters regarded mundane subscription matters or patent agency business, but most were questions from aspiring architects of destruction—the Union's true "regiment of inventors"—who trusted the magazine's staff to comment on the feasibility or originality of their ideas. During the Civil War, the *Scientific American* responded to hundreds of potential advances in military technology sent by readers, sometimes brutally and sometimes enthusiastically:

H.L., of N.Y.—Spectacles which would enable persons to see at night would be very useful, and, no doubt, very profitable to the discoverer. They would be of great advantage to night-scouting parties.

M.F., of Ill.—Your shell filled with chloroform and cayenne pepper would be a very harmless affair.

M.K., of Ill.—An arrangement of reflectors and lenses which would send a focus of light and heat two or three miles, without diminishing its intensity, so that it would set objects on fire with the same facility as an ordinary sunglass, would be novel.

N.E.B., of N.H.—The attachment to a projectile of wings to mow down the enemy is a very old thing, and we don't see anything valuable in your application of them.

A.S., of Ind.—Your submarine-gun port differs from all others we have seen and we think a patent might be obtained for it. Its simplicity is, we think, a great recommendation.

A.F.F, of Vt.—The attachment of knives to cannon balls in such manner as to be closed when the ball is placed in the gun, and thrown out when the ball is discharged is a very old idea. We do not know whether such balls have ever been used; we never heard of their use.[32]

Whether these specific suggestions attracted the attention of military decision makers is not known, and some would not come to fruition for decades. (Even rudimentary night vision goggles did not appear until World War II.) What is known is that influential officials—North and South—read the *Scientific American*. For example, on April 1, 1862, Confederate Secretary of the Navy Stephen R. Mallory wrote a letter to Flag Officer Josiah Tattnall, in which he discussed the expected renewal of engagements between Tattnall's flagship, the CSS *Virginia*, with the USS *Monitor*. Mallory wrote, "The *Scientific American*, in a recent number, publishes a neat wood cut of the vessel, and gives some data of her construction," and, based on his perception of the ship as published in the magazine, Mallory gave Tuttnall advice on strategies for assailing it.[33]

Two years later, Union Rear Admiral David G. Farragut, in a memo to the Navy's Bureau of Ordnance, wrote, "I perceive by the *Scientific American* that steel shot penetrates with great ease all the ironclad armor as yet presented for experiment." Writing as one who had the "momentous question of wood against iron to settle," Farragut clearly relied on the reputation of the magazine and its reporting in urging the bureau to secure steel shot for his use against Confederate ironclads.[34]

Generals also paid attention to the magazine. In a November 1863 letter written from Charleston, South Carolina, Confederate General P. G. T. Beauregard thanked General Joseph R. Anderson for sending "the slips of paper from the *Scientific American*." Presumably, the "slips of paper" were reports of the recent bombardment of Charleston with incendiary shells—purportedly containing the legendary "Greek Fire," which was written about widely in the Northern papers and copied in the *Scientific American*. The bombardment was unsuccessful, as most of the shells landing without exploding.[35]

Writing to Anderson, Beauregard poked fun at the inventive Yankee spirit: "What a nation of humbugs and humbuggers; and how incorrigible they are, always passing from one absurdity to another still worse! I sincerely hope we have parted company with them forever." But Beauregard concluded with a notion that one country's "humbug" is another's secret weapon, adding in a postscript (it is better if you imagine it in a whisper): "I am in possession of a 'liquid fire' which will make the Yanks open their eyes whenever I commence using it against their encampments."[36]

To say that the *Scientific American* was nonpartisan is not to say that it eschewed opinion. For all the years it was in print, the magazine was *all about* opinion. It defended lone, and often poor, inventors from vicious patent monopolies. It railed against incompetent and inconsistent personnel in the patent office, yet still defended the patent system against its detractors. It debunked frauds and humbug inventions—especially notions of "perpetual motion"—while championing innovations. And, along with offering opinions on specific suggestions from inquiring inventors, the *Scientific American* also offered opinions on public policy during the war.

Early in the war, the magazine pointed its finger at what it considered the Union's real obstacle to victory: "The only successes which we have yet achieved have been due to our superiority in the mechanic arts. With sadness, however, which we cannot express, we fear that the skill of our mechanics, the self-sacrifice of our people, and the devoted heroism of our troops in their efforts to save the country, will all be rendered futile by the utter incompetency which controls the war and navy departments of the Government."[37]

The *Scientific American* saved its most ardent criticism for the army's Ordnance Department, especially its intractable head, Brigadier General James W. Ripley. Ripley, a career soldier, was born in Connecticut in 1794, entered West Point in 1813, earned a commission as a second lieutenant of artillery a year later, and was promoted to first lieutenant in 1818. The next two decades found him in various recruiting posts. In 1841, as the new commanding officer at the national armory in Springfield, Massachusetts, he brought by-the-book discipline to the institution. Ripley was there for more than a dozen years, and he made improvements to the infrastructure and operations such that the by the end of his tenure the armory reportedly made more muskets at a lower cost than ever before.

Ripley was in Japan to present arms and stores to the Shogun when he heard of the Southern threats of secession in 1860. When a friend told Ripley that his country needed him, Ripley answered, "It can have me and every drop of blood in me." Ripley headed for Washington, where he was soon named Chief of Army Ordnance, replacing the patriotic but aging Colonel Henry Knox Craig. At sixty-six, Ripley was just four years younger than Craig, but he had a vigor and seniority—not to mention political allies—that recommended him to the post. Ripley brought the same sensibility of discipline, and quick temper, to the Ordnance Department that he had to the Springfield armory.[38]

Ripley also brought an almost ingrained distaste for inventors and new weapons. War Department regulations instituted in 1852 explained the policy that the Ordnance Department was to follow when approached by civilian inventors. If an aspiring inventor described the nature and advantages of the device to the department's satisfaction, it would order a test, for which the inventor had to furnish a prototype. Ripley's protocol was to almost universally refuse the opportunity for a test with the excuse that there was a lack of time; to be fair, his department *was* understaffed and overworked.

On June 11, 1861, then Colonel Ripley drafted a memorandum, "Notes on subject of contracting for small arms," that one historian felt deserved recognition as "one of the basic documents of the Civil War." With the first words of the memo, Ripley declared his view on military inventions, writing "A *great evil* [emphasis added] now specially prevalent in regard to arms for the military service is the vast array of the new inventions, each having, of course, its advocates insisting on the superiority of his favorite arm over all others and urging its adoption by the Government."[39]

To be sure, the flood of inventions could interfere with the efficient supply of uniform munitions, and some of the devices (and inventors) were humbugs. But Ripley seemed to delight in turning down the proposals that came his way. It was only for special pressure from Lincoln that a number of inventions were given a chance—a pressure that gave Ripley particular annoyance. The *Scientific American* published an anecdote on Ripley's distaste for Lincoln's lobbying:

> One persistent and worthy inventor, whom we have known for a long time, obtained a private audience with the Chief Magistrate, in reference to a long-range gun of peculiar construction that he has been experimenting on for years. Mr. Lincoln gave orders to the Ordnance Department that experiments on the weapon should proceed with dispatch; and on this being announced to some functionary concerned in the execution of the order, he exclaimed, 'What does Lincoln know about a gun? We're bothered to death with these inventors running here all the time.'[40]

If the rapport between Ripley and Lincoln was stormy, the relationship between the Ordnance Department and the inventors soon became what one historian labeled a "fog of mutual detestation . . . thick beyond dispelling." In early 1863, the *Scientific American* politely complained that "our inventors have been much discouraged in their efforts to bring forward their discoveries by the very persons who should, of all others, have aided them in so doing." They quoted an "astute official" as saying, "D— these new improvements!" Another editorial observed, "We do not think that any good end can be attained or the interests of the country subserved by snubbing our inventors and endeavoring to slight their productions; nothing is accomplished by this manner of treating them, nor will there ever be."[41]

The *Scientific American's* rhetorical gloves came off in September 1863 in a long editorial entitled "Impertinence of the Ordnance Department Toward Inventors." The piece accused Ripley and his staff of "rudeness and circumlocution of the rankest kind." The magazine lamented that things had "reached such a pass that inventors are shy of presenting plans that have to be experimented upon by Government before acceptance, and the consequence is that the country suffers." The editors acknowledged that not every man who presented himself was a "paragon of science and inventive talent," but this was no reason why he should not be given a fair hearing. The editorial ended with a satisfactory—and perhaps smug—conclusion: "Since the above was written, Gen. Ripley, Chief of the Ordnance Department, has been removed."[42]

The *Scientific American* took one last punch at the bureaucracy that had thrown so many roadblocks at the magazine's "regiment of inventors" in an article that accompanied the last wartime innovation featured on the front page. The editors took special delight in writing about an invention that had demonstrated a significant impact in spite of being ignored by military authorities.

The first page of the May 6, 1865, issue carried the headline "The Destruction of the Rebel Ram 'Albemarle.'" The Confederate navy's ironclad ram had dominated the Roanoke River and the approaches to Plymouth, North Carolina, through the summer of 1864, sinking and damaging a number of Union ships, until it was sunk in October 1864 by an intrepid party of thirteen men, led by Commander William B. Cushing. Cushing had rigged a "torpedo"—an explosive charge connected to a fourteen-foot spar—to a small craft, rammed the CSS *Albemarle*, and set off the charge. The design of the device had been attributed to Cushing and to William W. Wood, a navy engineer.[43]

In fact, the demise of the *Albemarle* was rather old news. The magazine had covered the story in its November 19, 1864, issue, pointing out that the destruction had been accomplished by "a method that has been frequently recommended in the *Scientific American*." The additional coverage several months after the sinking was warranted by information sent to the magazine by George V. Rutherford, who had suggested a similar contraption to the navy in the summer of 1862 but was turned away. The *Scientific American* article consisted primarily of incriminating "smoking guns": the correspondence Rutherford exchanged with the navy, in which the department had decided that "the present state of naval warfare precluded the possibility of adopting this style of invention."[44]

The editors opined with righteous indignation: "How their decision has been approved by the results of Cushing's bold experiment the country knows, rejoicingly, and recognizes in it another instance of that hasty official judgement which frowns upon invention as impertinent innovation, and which would keep the world forever running in the ruts of old fogyism, but for the persistence and courage of genius which overrides all obstacles, and often by a single daring action refutes the learned objections and doubts of erudite officials and fossilized philosophers."[45]

General William T. Sherman's 1864 holiday greeting to Lincoln—"I beg to present you as a Christmas gift the city of Savannah"—brought hope to a beleaguered man and a war-weary Union. A *Scientific American* correspondent, who was present at the New Year's Day reception at the White House, wrote a few weeks later of the President's mood, commenting that Lincoln seemed to maintain "a constant flow of genial mirth." The reporter added that the magazine's readers had a special friend in their Chief:

"I was much pleased to learn that in the midst of the many cares that press upon the President he is not indifferent to the claims of our inventors. Himself an inventor and patentee, he readily discerns the intrinsic value of all good inventions, not only to the public service, but also in their application to the industrial arts generally, and he will do all in his power to encourage and to promote the progress of these arts, by sanctioning all wise legislation in behalf of inventors."[46]

In April, on news of the surrender at Appomattox, the *Scientific American* shared the "profound joy which filled the hearts of the American people when the telegraph flashed the intelligence over the land that the central power of the rebellion was broken to pieces." And, while the editors had spent the war championing the ideas of the nation's inventors, in the end they thanked the "brave and devoted soldiers of our patriot army," many of whom the magazine counted as its readers, adding, "there has never before been marshalled in the ranks of war a body of men so high in all mental and moral attributes." The editors concluded with praise for the commander, General Ulysses S. Grant, extolling his many virtues and especially "the strongest element in his character . . . his inflexible tenacity of purpose."[47]

A week later, under the heading, "Our Calamity," the magazine wrote briefly and solemnly of Lincoln's assassination. The May 28, 1865, issue devoted space to a longer and more poignant eulogy to the president-inventor, recalling the December 1, 1860, engraving that precipitated the *Scientific American's* own "secession troubles", its gentle jibe in hoping that Lincoln would "have better success in presiding as Chief Magistrate over the people of the entire Union than he has had as an inventor", and the model of the boat Lincoln held under his arm in Z. C. Robbins's office:

> A model of a different kind; carved as one might imagine a retired rail-splitter would whittle, strongly but not smoothly. . . . The modest little model has reposed here [in the Patent Office] sixteen years—and since it found its resting place here on the shelf, the shrewd inventor has found it his task to guide the ship of state over shoals more perilous, and obstructions more obstinate than any prophet dreamed of when [he] wrote his bold autograph on the prow of this miniature steamer.
>
> The author's skill in buoying the great vessel of state over dangerous breakers has made his name honored throughout the whole civilized world.[48]

Figure 12. Vintage du Pont gunpowder label.
Source: Hagley Museum and Library

CHAPTER FIVE

Fire and Brimstone

The Saltpeter is the Soule, the Sulphur is the Life, and the Coales the Body of it.
— John Bate, *The Mysteryes of Nature and Art (1634)*

MID-MORNING ON JULY 3, 1863, having finished inspecting his guns on Culp's Hill and, in his words, "finding everything favorable," General Henry J. Hunt, the Army of the Potomac's chief of artillery, crossed over to Cemetery Ridge, to see what might be going on at other points on the Union line. He remembered the sight before him years later, "Here a magnificent display greeted my eyes. . . . Our whole front for two miles was covered by batteries already in line or going into position . . . Never before had such a sight been witnessed on this continent, and rarely, if ever, abroad."[1]

As he looked at the array of more than a hundred enemy cannon stretched over nearly a mile "in one unbroken mass," Hunt wondered what the sight might portend. It could be that the guns were a screen for supporting infantry that had left for another part of the Rebel line; or, they might simply be guarding against a potential counterattack by the Union army. Hunt thought otherwise. "It most probably meant an assault on our center," he wrote, "to be preceded by a cannonade in order to crush our batteries and shake our infantry." He guessed that the bombardment would be long and followed immediately by a frontal assault, with the enemy's whole army ready to exploit any success. Hunt was right.[2]

After colliding two days earlier, Confederate General Robert E. Lee's Army of Northern Virginia had fought Union General George G. Meade's Army of the Potomac outside, through, and then to the other side of the bucolic Pennsylvania town of Gettysburg. Having—in his mind—manhandled his opponent for two days running, and coming close to victory on both, Lee could not bring himself to leave the field. Despite evidence that frontal assaults were costly affairs with no guarantee of a result in his favor, Lee concluded that one last great thrust, directed at the Union center, would break the enemy's lines.

Lee determined that a massive artillery bombardment—to soften the opposing infantry and guns—was critical to the success of his plan. His chief lieutenant, General James Longstreet, gave his First Corps' chief artillerist, Colonel Edward Porter Alexander, responsibility for directing the fire. Despite the daunting nature of the task, Porter saw his orders as relatively simple, "First, to give the enemy the most effective cannonade possible . . . to try and cripple him—to tear him limbless, as it were, if possible."[3]

The early afternoon found Union soldiers in the center sweltering in nearly ninety-degree heat and high humidity. A skirmish over a barn between the lines escalated into a fierce fight but then fell quiet. Union General Carl Schurz felt the battlefield had "settled down into a tranquility like the peaceful and languid repose of a warm midsummer morning." Still, the "perfect stillness" made him uncomfortable; "there was something ominous, something uncanny, in these strange, unexpected hours of profound silence," he wrote, adding that they sharply contrasted with "the bloody horrors which had preceded, and which were sure to follow them."[4]

"Let the batteries open," Longstreet ordered, and at about one o'clock (an attentive mathematics professor, Michael Jacobs, recorded the time as exactly 1:07 p.m.) two guns of New Orleans's Washington Artillery fired their cue to signal the bombardment. Then, all along the mile of cannon, Confederate gunners unleashed a barrage of unprecedented fury. "We were not unfamiliar with artillery fire," one Union soldier would write, "but this proved to be something far beyond all previous experience, or conception, and the scene was terrific beyond description." Hunt thought the scene was "indescribably grand."[5]

Despite Alexander's hope that the cannonade would do more than "simply to make a noise," it was the din that soldiers and civilians remembered most. The continual roar of the guns—one indistinguishable from another—made many of the soldiers deaf for days after the battle. Sarah Broadhead, huddled in her cellar in town, remembered that it was "as if the heavens and earth were crashing together." Professor Jacobs wrote of the cannonade "producing such a continuous succession of crashing sounds as to make us feel if the very heavens had been rent asunder."[6]

The bombardment assaulted *all* of the senses. The explosions were not just heard; they were *felt*. Mississippian Lieutenant William Peel, crouched just behind one of the Confederate batteries, wrote that the bombardment "made the ground to tremble beneath its force." A Union artilleryman, returning fire, noticed how the concussion from his own gun sent waves rippling out across the grass to his front, "like gusts of wind."[7]

The smoke—which within minutes covered the field and limited visibility to just yards—was seen, smelled, *and* tasted. Albertus McCreary, a Gettysburg teenager, remembered that "the atmosphere was so full of smoke that we could taste the saltpeter." Sergeant Ben Hirst of the 14th Connecticut Infantry wrote his wife, "Turn your eyes which way you will the whole Heavens were filled with Shot and Shell, Fire and Smoke." Another soldier wrote that the "lazy air was now turned to a dark, wild and sulphurous atmosphere."[8]

But the din and intensity was for nought. To be sure, many of the Union guns in the center were damaged, but as smoke covered the battlefield it interfered with the aim of Confederate artillerists, whose rounds went high and far and landed in the Union rear. A foreign observer—Justus Scheibert of the Prussian Royal Engineers—summed up the effort as *"eine Pulververschwendung"*—"a waste of powder." The Rebel guns went silent and the second part of Lee's plan began; a brave, but failed assault—popularly known as Pickett's Charge—later immortalized as the "high water mark" of the Confederacy.[9]

If cannon and rifles were the "grim enginery of war," as the *Scientific American* had put it, then gunpowder was the fuel for those engines, and at Gettysburg and many other fields the fuel was employed to great effect—physically and psychologically—during the Civil War, as it had for centuries previously. When Francis Bacon declared that "Printing, gunpowder, and the magnet . . . these three have changed the whole face and state of things throughout the world," he gave testament to the fact that the influence of gunpowder in history cannot be underestimated.[10]

No one knows exactly when gunpowder was invented; one author suggested that anyone looking into its origins "is soon entangled in a web of mistakes, misinterpretations and misrepresentations." Its origins have been traced to Egypt, Persia, India, and Arabia, but most recent scholarship suggests that its birth occurred in China in the mid-ninth century A.D. Gunpowder was first used in fireworks, but it did not take long to see it used in simple ordnance. As elusive as the invention's provenance is its transfer to the West (an early work, attributed to "Mark the Greek," had the recipe and a perverse title: *Book of Fires for the Burning of Enemies*).[11]

However it was revealed, the recipe—which did not change for centuries—is actually quite simple and is the combination of three ingredients:

saltpeter, sulfur, and charcoal in a ratio of approximately 75, 10, and 15%, respectively (although early samples contained much smaller amounts of saltpeter), finely powdered and mixed well. Given the immense amount of gunpowder used during any large scale conflict, securing the "Soule, Life, and Body" was, not unexpectedly, an important consideration for the authorities of both belligerents during the American Civil War.

Charcoal has been used as a fuel for fires for millennia and would seem to be the least worrisome of the ingredients in terms of supply. In fact, the selection of woods required great care; it had been recognized for centuries that certain coals were poor because they yielded a smaller volume of gas and attracted moisture. Still, the willows and alders best suited for powdered charcoal were readily obtained in the North, and in the South, the more plentiful cottonwood proved reliable.

Sulfur, or brimstone, had long given gunpowder its association with Hell. At the time of the Civil War, sulfur was almost entirely imported, primarily from Sicily, where it was found in the island's volcanic regions. The Confederacy had a ready supply in the tons of sulphur in New Orleans used for refining sugar. Supplies could also be obtained near mineral springs in Mexico and in Texas.

Saltpeter, also known as niter (chemically, potassium nitrate), is the most important component of gunpowder by weight and by the physics of burning. As such, it was imperative for countries to have adequate supplies, and many nationalized its manufacture. At the time of the Civil War, saltpeter was almost entirely imported from India through British agents, a fact which would have important political and material considerations for both sides.

When considering powder supply in the Civil War, it is important to look beyond its obvious uses in firearms and artillery. Previously peacetime enterprises that relied on powder for blasting—the mining of gold and coal—became important military ventures. The successes of Confederate sea raiders prompted an increase in insurance rates and a tightening of permission to ship powder to California. A powder agent warned that if miners were not adequately supplied with powder, shipments of bullion to the East would be cut in half and that the effect of such a reduction to the country's currency would be "greater than would be experienced by the loss of a dozen battles."[12]

A similar warning came from an agent in Cincinnati anxious to keep his coal-mining customers in powder as well, "Coal cannot be mined without powder and the naval fleet on the Ohio and Mississippi will be powerless unless they can get coal for the boats . . . Cutting off the supply of coal from the fleet would be the very best kind of assistance to the rebels. Coal for the Furnaces is as important as Gunpowder for the Guns."[13]

Still, the *New York Times* felt so confident in the Union's supply of gunpowder that it proudly proclaimed in August 1861 that "We have more than enough already to drive a bullet to the heart of every traitor that breathes in our land." It had reason to be confident. When the war broke out, the North was home to more than fifty powder mills; the South, only two. However, most of the mills in the North were admittedly small: many were in the mining regions of Pennsylvania, producing crude blasting powder for use not far from the mills themselves.[14]

The chief producer of black powder, itself responsible for nearly forty percent of the country's production in 1860, was E. I. du Pont de Nemours and Company, located on the Brandywine River near Wilmington, Delaware. The role of the du Pont mills during the American Civil War is grand in its scope: keep powder out of enemy hands, protect itself from marauding enemies, supply the immense needs of the Union Army and Navy, and participate in secret missions. The company boasted authentic family heroes on sea and land and powdermen who gave the ultimate sacrifice by simply doing their job.[15]

When the *Scientific American* declared in a short notice in its July 20, 1850, issue that "the most extensive powder-mills in the world are those on the Brandywine, Delaware, and the best powder is made at these mills," the magazine was speaking of the du Pont gunpowder works. By the time the notice appeared, the du Ponts had already been manufacturing powder for nearly half a century.[16]

The du Pont powder mills were founded in 1802 by Eleuthere Irenee (E. I.) du Pont two years after he and his family fled France to escape the French Revolution and the guillotine. E. I.'s father, Pierre Samuel du Pont de Nemours, was a noted French intellectual; his writing on economics drew the attention of Voltaire and Adam Smith. As a diplomat, he was deeply involved in the talks that led to the Treaty of Paris that ended the American Revolution, for which he earned the friendship of Thomas Jefferson and Benjamin Franklin. An advocate of reform, Pierre was a welcome ally in the French Revolution and even led the National Assembly for a time.

During the subsequent "Reign of Terror," however, he was imprisoned and sentenced to death but escaped when his accuser, Robiespierre, met the guillotine instead.

Pierre, his sons E. I. and Victor, and their families sailed to America with the original purpose to invest in and develop real estate or manage international trade. Neither venture proved fruitful; instead, the du Ponts settled on E. I.'s plan: manufacturing gunpowder. His suggestion came from opportunity and estimable credentials: E. I. studied under the eminent French chemist Antoine Lavosier at the national arsenal in Paris and served an apprenticeship at the French government's powder works at Essonnes. French powder was recognized as first-rate and was the predominant powder used during the American Revolution.

In late 1800, E. I. visited a Philadelphia powder mill with Louis de Toussard, a French artilleryman who had lost an arm serving under Lafayette in the American Revolution and now supervised military gunpowder purchases. Recalling his experiences in France, E. I. found fault with almost every aspect of American powder-making. He concluded that if the process was poor, so must the powder be, and he declared that such competitors should not be formidable. He spent the next two years raising capital, buying land and equipment, and building the mills. "E. I. du Pont de Nemours & Company" shipped its first barrel of black powder in May 1804.

The du Pont's relationship with the United States government began with Pierre's friendship with Jefferson and remained unbroken up to and well after the Civil War. Indeed, the War Between the States marked only the latest instance in which the country relied on the du Pont powder mills in a national emergency. Still, despite Jefferson's friendship and the family optimism, government orders were small and slow in coming. E. I. blamed his fledgling firm's small share (less than $30,000 of nearly $250,000 of government business) on a burgeoning patronage system in Jefferson's administration, with Cabinet officers giving their orders to political friends, including a Philadelphia apothecary who du Pont thought did worthless work.

Granted, apart from suppressing the Barbary pirates—to which end du Pont had furnished more than 20,000 pounds of powder for American men-of-war sent to Algeria—there was not a great demand for powder for national security purposes. Within a few years, however, the prospect of another war with England became reality and in the War of 1812 the du Pont mills supplied more than 500,000 pounds of powder for the Army alone, with additional quantities sent to the Navy. E. I. acquired more property to expand the works and meet the wartime demand.

The next thirty years found the country at relative peace. Apart from the Seminole War and South Carolina's nullification crisis (in which du Pont refused the state's offer of $24,000 in cash for 125,000 pounds of powder) the government's need for powder was small. The du Pont mills used the intervening years—the "Era of Good Feeling"—to expand their peacetime base of business among sportsmen, traders, and miners, including John Jacob Astor's "American Fur Trading Company."

The du Pont mills provided more than a million pounds of powder during the Mexican War, in which the du Ponts saw at least two instances of a problem that they would face again during the Civil War: keeping their powder out of enemy hands. In the first, a firm in Havana ordered 200,000 pounds of powder weeks after war was declared. In the second, a Frenchman and a Spaniard—albeit with good references—submitted a similar order. Afraid that the powder was headed to Mexico, the du Ponts rejected both orders.

The drama of the du Pont powder mills and family during the American Civil War centers on two major players: Henry du Pont and Lammott du Pont. Henry, the youngest son of founder E. I. du Pont, entered the United States Military Academy at West Point at the age of seventeen and graduated in 1833. As a lieutenant in the Fourth Artillery he was posted first at Fort Monroe in Virginia and then served for a short time in the Creek country of Alabama. In June 1834 he resigned his commission and joined his father at the mills. In July 1850 he became head of the works, taking the reigns from his older brother, Alfred; a position he held until his death in 1889. Henry—known as "Boss Henry"—had little interest in the science of making powder but did have a keen business sense.

Lammot du Pont, son of former mill head Alfred, grandson of the founder, and nephew to "Boss Henry," was born on April 13, 1831, and raised at "Nemours," a home built for his parents by his grandfather. More than any of his family contemporaries, Lammot seemed to inherit the founder's interest in science (when as a boy his mother gave him a choice between a seaside vacation or a "box of instruments," Lammot chose the instruments). After attending school at a local academy, Lammot completed his studies at the University of Pennsylvania in 1849, where he excelled in science and mathematics.

Upon graduation, Lammot began working in the saltpeter refinery, and within months he was supervising refinery operations; his aptitude for science earned him the sobriquet "Our Chemist" from family members. In 1857, he secured his first patent for his "Improvement in Gunpowder"—a combination that included Peruvian niter and a graphite glaze to reduce moistening. Although not suitable for firearms, it proved ideal for blasting and industrial use and reduced the country's reliance on the British-controlled India niter. He also cooperated with the Ordnance Bureau to develop better large-grained powder—dubbed "Mammoth Powder"—for the large Parrott, Dahlgren, and Rodman guns that would come to play in the Civil War.

"We are not very warm politicians in our family, so we shall be glad when it is all over and quiet is restored. In about four weeks it will be decided," Lammot's Aunt Eleuthra wrote a relative in France in October 1860, weeks before Abraham Lincoln was elected. In fact, the du Pont family was *quite* political. Relatives, including her own uncle, Victor du Pont, had been elected to office in Delaware. Others had also served in the state legislature or as delegates to national conventions. The close association of the firm with the government since Jefferson's time required attention to political affairs at all levels.[17]

Opinion in the du Pont family as to the 1860 election was divided. Lammot, like his Uncle Henry, was a supporter of the Constitutional Union party and its presidential candidate, John Bell of Tennessee. When Bell polled poorly in the du Pont's home county, party loyalists threw their support to Lincoln. On the other hand, Henry's daughter, Ellen, had a decidedly different opinion of the President-elect. Writing of her misery at Lincoln's election, she commented that "it makes me feel like tasting green persimmons. . . . I wish the republicans and abolitionists were in the Atlantic, then we would be at rest."[18]

The du Ponts had close ties to the South, in terms of both family and business. Distant branches of the family had settled in Kentucky and South Carolina in the seventeenth century. Like most gunpowder firms, du Pont engaged agents throughout the country to sell their powder on a commission basis, including in the southern states. One of their first agents was Anthony Casenove, a Virginian, and the business relationship carried over into a close friendship; indeed, Lammot's own brother, Eleuthere, was married to a Virginia belle from the Casenove family. The du Pont mills had also developed a thriving business for its blasting and sporting powders in the South.

The sectional strife took an especially personal toll on Henry du Pont's son, Henry Algernon du Pont. Henry A. du Pont had followed in his father's footsteps to West Point, where he was set to graduate in May 1861 (first in his class). In a letter to his mother, Henry A. expressed regret that a number of his fellow cadets—including his own roommate, Llewellyn Griffith Hoxton, a Virginian—might soon be his sworn enemies, "The future certainly looks very dark and threatening and I cannot look forward to graduation with that pleasure that I did formerly, and if it is to be our lot

Figure 13. Lammot du Pont
Source: Hagley Museum and Library

to be employed in cutting our countrymen's throats and fighting our dearest friends and classmates, I am very sorry I ever came here."[19]

Even before South Carolina led other states in seceding from the Union, signs of the pending struggle could be found in correspondence between the du Pont mill headquarters and its Southern agents. An agent in Columbus, Georgia, informed du Pont in December 1860 that the state legislature had appropriated $1,000,000 for arms and ammunition and that he would try to get the concession for powder. Another, in New Orleans, ordered 30,000 pounds of powder—"as soon as it can be had and without delay" on behalf of the Louisiana government, with the stipulation "No Yankee Powder." Apparently he assumed Delaware, and by extension the du Pont mills, to be safely in the Rebel camp.[20]

In March 1861, P. E. Bowdre of Macon, Georgia, wrote Confederate Secretary of War LeRoy Pope Walker that "gentleman of this city" had "made up a purse . . . of nearly $3,000" and used the money to purchase more than 10,000 pounds of powder from the du Pont agent in Baltimore. Confederate and state officials seized powder from federal forts and arsenals throughout the South. In other cases they confiscated powder directly from du Pont agents. Anthony Casenove in Alexandria, Virginia, wrote the home office with regret that state authorities had "seized all your powder in our possession," but promised "to get an acknowledgment of their obligation to pay."[21]

When the du Pont balance sheet was tallied at the end of 1861, records showed that Confederate authorities had seized more than 300 tons of powder, valued at more than $100,000, from nearly twenty company agents throughout the South. Still, if they couldn't keep powder from being seized, the du Ponts could keep powder from being shipped. When their agent in Richmond, Virginia, insisted that more powder be sent (to replace stores seized by the state), the company refused, and answered in return two days after the beleaguered Fort Sumter fell:

> With regard to [your] order we would remark that that since the inauguration of war at Charleston, the posture of national affairs is critical, and a new state of affairs has risen. Presuming that Virginia will do her whole duty in this great emergency and will be loyal to the Union, we shall prepare the powder, but with the understanding that should general expectation be disappointed and Virginia, by any misfortune, assume an

attitude hostile to the United States we shall be absolved from any obligation to furnish the order.[22]

News of the bombardment of Fort Sumter galvanized the community surrounding the du Pont powder works. Flags were raised, bells were rung, and meetings were held—including at the mills, where Henry du Pont insisted that all the powdermen take the oath of loyalty to the Union. Henry's wife wrote of the excitement to their son at West Point, "Everyone, even the wavering ones, have now come warmly in favor of the government, and will sustain it if possible. Today there are three American flags floating in the different workshops on the place, put up by the men. Your father and cousins are going to raise the old flag which belongs to the Henry Clay pole."[23]

Family partisanship and Southern ties were set aside. The company had cast its lot with the Union.

In an urgent appeal to Virginia's Governor Henry Alexander Wise, Charles du Pont Bird—a purported du Pont relative (he wasn't) and ardent secessionist—gave a description of the political and military situation in Delaware in April 1861:

> A strong feeling in the two lower counties of Delaware is aroused in favor of Delaware joining the Southern Confederacy. . . . With a man or two from you to give directions and a hint that arms would come if necessary, the people of Sussex themselves would destroy the Delaware railroad terminating at Seaford. . . . The arms that Delaware own are in the hands of the secessionists. The powder mills on the Brandywine (owned by relations of mine) should be secured at all hazards. With a not very large force, if we cannot hold them, they should be destroyed. If it is possible to guard these works for a few weeks the stock of powder for the southern confederacy would be largely increased. . . . Come to our help.[24]

As a border state, Delaware—like the du Pont family—was home to divided loyalties. Sussex and Kent counties, in particular, had southern leanings, while New Castle County, home to the powder mills, was strong for the Union. Mississippi authorities led an effort to lure Delaware into the Confederacy, but Delaware's legislature, led by a Unionist (albeit antiabolitionist) governor, rejected secession. Still, Delaware had sufficient Southern sympathizers to give the du Ponts pause.

Not unexpectedly, the security of the du Pont mills was a constant concern throughout the Civil War, for, as Bird had declared in his appeal to Governor Wise, their capture or destruction would have been a great coup for the Confederacy. Within days of the firing on Fort Sumter, Henry du Pont wrote to Secretary of War Simon Cameron on the tenuous situation in his state:

> I will remark that the gunpowder mills in this neighborhood, of which I am the head, are of importance to the Government in these times, from their extent and immense facilities of production. They are wholly unprotected, and there is not a musket or rifle in the place; but we have over 300 good men, true, and loyal, and if we could get some 200 or 300 stands of arms from Franklin Arsenal and accoutrements, if there, we could take care of ourselves for the present, as far as mobs and disaffected persons are concerned.[25]

Similarly, New Jersey's Governor Charles S. Olden, wrote directly to President Lincoln on the "exposed and defenseless condition" of important points on the Delaware River and the port of Philadelphia. Among specific targets of concern, Olden wrote that a rebel expedition of sufficient force "would with ease destroy the machine-shops and Du Pont powder mills at the city of Wilmington."[26]

The fears were well-founded. Although it would be more than a year before serious Confederate military movements would threaten the mills, Henry du Pont had to wait only a day after his letter to Cameron for the specter of Rebel sabotage to rear its head. On April 20, he received a telegram warning that a large band of Maryland secessionists—as many as 150 men—were planning to seize a du Pont powder magazine on the Delaware River. Cameron had not yet had time to respond to du Pont's appeal (he wouldn't till weeks later, anyway), so Henry, his nephews, and a party of workmen armed themselves and retrieved the powder in the middle of the night.

Less than two weeks later, a sordid-looking interloper was spotted on the mill grounds. Workmen—yelling "A spy! A spy!"—chased the stranger and might have beat him had he not been rescued by Lammot. Some of the powdermen claimed that the intruder had asked about the whereabouts of the powder magazines, but Lammot, after an interview with the "spy," let him go with a word of warning. The du Ponts were also put on alert over rumors that two men, dressed as women, had been seen near the yards; another warning had a "known desperado" from Philadelphia on his way to blow up the works.[27]

All the incidents proved to be false alarms, but Henry du Pont—keen to prevent sabotage—organized the workmen into the "Brandywine Home Guards" (Delaware's Governor William Burton appointed him as major general of the state militia in May 1861; he insisted on being called "General Henry" from that point on). Lammot, who turned thirty the day after Sumter, was named captain of Company A. He supervised the drilling in the manual of arms (still without guns); Lammot's cousin, Ellen, thought that his company "looked mighty well in ranks" and drilled "infinitely better" than Company B. Lammot's men bested the rival company in a May 1861 competition, winning a sword for their captain.[28]

While the du Ponts and the Home Guard guarded against *perceived* threats to the mills, there was in fact a very *real* and constant danger: explosions. Accidents had happened at the powder works about every fourteen months on average since their inception. The first had occurred on August 18, 1807; it broke windows in founder Irenee du Pont's home, but caused no deaths. The first fatal accident, on June 8, 1815, claimed nine lives and caused $20,000 in damage. The du Pont family was not immune. The founder's son, Alexis, was killed in an 1857 explosion.

The incidents made a great impression on Lammot du Pont; as a teen, he wrote his brother, "This morning just as I got out of bed I saw a flash of light and then a loud explosion. I dressed as soon as I could and ran down to the refinery. . . . There were two men killed, entirely blown to pieces, there were 4200 lbs of powder in the mill, all finished ready to pack, so you may know it made a pretty good crack. . . . Every window or door that was shut was burst open in our house."[29]

More than ten explosions occurred at the du Pont mills during the Civil Wars—an average of one about every *five* months. The first explosion, in October 1861, caused no fatalities, but did level a number of buildings. An explosion a month later claimed the lives of three men. Others that followed killed nearly forty more workmen. Newspapers across the country carried bulletins of the wartime explosions; of one incident, Gettysburg's *Adams*

Sentinel reported that "large pieces of timber and barrels were thrown by the force of the explosion entirely across the Brandywine creek, and for a great distance evidences of the disaster were visible." Of another, an Iowa paper reported with just amazement that a correspondent "distinctly heard the explosion of the du Pont powder mills at his residence [in Clifford, Pennsylvania]; the distance . . . he says, is 135 miles."[30]

None of the explosions could be categorically attributed to saboteurs; certainly the accelerated pace of production and inexperience of newly-hired hands contributed to the accidents, and any clues would be lost in the destruction. Still, one wonders whether Rebel saboteurs may have indeed been successful in attempts to damage the mills.

"The extra demand for powder for war purposes will not equal the regular demand which would have existed had peace continued without extraneous troubles," Henry du Pont confidently declared in May 1861. Like so many others, he based his predictions on a short war; so confident was Henry du Pont in a short struggle that he had cancelled the company's orders for additional niter. He was wrong. By late summer, great battles such as Bull Run in the East, Wilson's Creek in the West, and a Union blockade around the coast, were all testament to the prospects of a gigantic and protracted struggle.[31]

The *New York Times*'s bold pronouncement that the Union already had enough powder to "drive a bullet to the heart of every traitor that breathes in our land" was equally hasty. Any crisis in Union gunpowder supply would not be one of production capacity but of raw materials, especially the crucial ingredient of saltpeter. In April, the niter supply was thought to be more than sufficient. Henry had informed his cousin, then-Captain Samuel Francis du Pont, that the company had a six-month supply on hand; the War Department reported a stock of nearly four million pounds (albeit old—most was left over from the Mexican War) in its stores.

Within weeks, du Pont reversed his decision and placed a standing order of more than 100 tons a month (the du Ponts routinely accounted for nearly a third of all the country's saltpeter imports). At least two challenges likely caused the reversal. Rising prices resulted when speculators began buying niter on the market and were loath to sell their stocks, gambling that prices would continue to rise. Furthermore, the line of supply was tenuous. India exported most of the world's nitre for two centuries; since the trade was under British jurisdiction, supplies could be cut off "as swiftly as word could pass from Whitehall to . . . Calcutta."[32]

As spring passed into summer, the confidence in the supply began to wane. Captain du Pont expressed his concern to officials in the Navy's Ordnance Bureau, but nothing came of it. In October he expressed the same to Secretary of the Navy Gustavus Fox. Fox then conferred with President Lincoln. Secretary of State Seward and Secretary of War Cameron in turn called Henry du Pont to Washington to consult with them on the pending crisis and to formulate a plan. A couple of weeks later, Henry wrote Captain du Pont to update him on the situation, "I was called to Washington on the 30th ulto. & had an interview with Mr. Seward & Mr. Cameron which resulted in our sending Lammot on the mission to London for the purchase—as confidential agent—nothing is known on the subject by *any one*, outside of the Secretaries and ourselves."[33]

Lammot's instructions were clear. He was, with all possible speed, to purchase a year's worth of saltpeter—about three million pounds. More important, although actually spending the government's money, he was to carry out all the negotiations for the purchase and shipping as a representative of E. I. du Pont de Nemours and Company. After two weeks at sea, Lammot arrived in London on November 19, 1861; within days he had arranged to buy all available niter on the English market as well as additional supplies already en route from India. A week later, as British stevedores were loading the *Moses Grinnell*, the dockmaster surprised Lammott by announcing that all shipments of niter to America were suspended.

A hint of the trouble at the docks can be found in the concluding sentences of Henry du Pont's letter to Captain du Pont, "I trust he will succeed in getting it shipped before any trouble may grow out of the seizure of Mason & Slidell, which some people appear to apprehend, altho' I do not."[34]

Henry had guessed wrong again. There *was* trouble, indeed. His reference to "the seizure of Mason & Slidell" concerned what would become known as the "Trent Affair," a diplomatic crisis that brought the United States and England to the brink of war and nearly cost the Union the saltpeter that its "confidential agent" had secured, such that the critical raw material might have become the proverbial nail for which a "kingdom was lost."

Keen to gain support from Europe, the Confederacy dispatched two diplomats, Virginian James M. Mason and Louisianan John Slidell, as ministers to England and France, respectively, on board the RMS *Trent*. The *Trent* departed from Havana, Cuba, but was stopped by Captain Charles Wilkes of the USS *San Jacinto* on November 8, 1861, when Lammot was just three days out to sea. The two diplomats and their party were removed despite the protests of the *Trent's* captain, who was allowed to resume his voyage.

The *San Jacinto* made port in Boston on November 23 to deliver the prisoners. Northern papers praised Wilkes's conduct and the House of Representatives passed a resolution honoring him. It took more than two weeks for news of the incident to reach Britain—a delay that allowed Lammot to do his important business—where the reaction was understandably different. Prime Minister Lord Palmerston considered the affair to be an insult to British honor and a flagrant violation of maritime law.

Opinion on the British streets and in the press was equally inflamed and anti-American. Lammot relayed his opinion of the situation to his Aunt Sophie, who in turn wrote her husband, "[Lammot] heard many persons say . . . 'We must have the northern part of Vermont and New Hampshire, & all Maine,'" and added that Lammot believed "we *will* have a war with England, because England is determined on it."[35]

Lammot's transactions did not escape notice. A "J. Mackenzie" alerted the Foreign Secretary, Lord John Russell, of the suspicious nature of the purchases and the apparent celerity of the shipment, "It is more than a year's supply for that Government even in a time of War, and the very rapid way it is being shipped off within three days of its purchase are altogether unusual, and look as if the federal government, having decided on a rupture with this country, was desirous of first laying in a supply of saltpeter."[36]

Others reported similar suspicions and details, such as names of the vessels on which du Pont's niter was being loaded. On November 30, Palmerston championed an order banning exports—to *any* country—of arms, powder, and saltpeter. With the shipments on hold (at least), Lammot headed back to America, arriving on Christmas Day. The next day, Lammot was in Washington to confer with Seward and report on his mission. It was an important day; England had set December 26 as the deadline for an apology and the release of Mason and Slidell. Absent a solution, Lincoln faced the loss of the saltpeter he needed for his present war, let alone a global conflict with England and her allies.

Lincoln concluded that one war was plenty and satisfied England's demands. With the diplomatic crisis apparently averted, Lammot sailed back to England on New Year's Day (on the same ship as Mason and Slidell!).

Arriving on January 13, 1862, he found the prohibition of exports of saltpeter still in place. Lammot shrewdly advised his agent in London that he would begin "dumping" his stores on the market at a loss. The threat alarmed other agents in the city, and they used their influence to have the embargo removed. In May 1862, General James W. Ripley could report—with just confidence—that sufficient saltpeter was on hand to carry on the war for at least three more years.

With the du Pont mills under careful watch of the Home Guards and a plentiful supply of saltpeter on hand, the du Pont principals and the powdermen went to work in earnest. Lammot in particular poured himself into work at the mills. Aunt Sophie wrote her husband that Lammot was "killing himself in the refinery, working day and night." His Cousin Sallie testified to the same, writing her brother, Henry A., "They have night work all the time in the refinery; and as it is all lighted up with kerosene-lamps, the illumination is quite splendid all night, from the back windows. Cousin Lammot and Gene work there, night bout; and are both there all day, so are never visible."[37]

Orders poured in from the Union Navy and Army ordnance bureaus on a regular basis for thousands of hundred-pound barrels of powder at a time, to be delivered within weeks to depots in Philadelphia, Boston, Portsmouth and elsewhere. Although government orders took first priority, du Pont did its best to keep up with its regular trade (including gold miners in California and coal miners in Ohio). The du Ponts sold more than $1,000,000 worth of powder every year of the war, with a peak of $1,625,305 in 1864—more than twice their best year ever before the war.

The war made the du Ponts quite wealthy—especially "Boss Henry," who held the greatest number of shares. Income tax returns for 1863 (Congress passed the Revenue Act of 1861, which included a tax on personal incomes, to help pay war expenses; it was repealed ten years later) show that Henry du Pont's income of $123,968 was the largest in Delaware that year. Though they didn't reach the scale of Henry du Pont's share, the workmen did benefit from the increased production and sales. Wages increased from $22–26 a month in 1861 to $32–35 in 1865. Actual take-home pay was even higher; with the mills operating 'round-the clock, many of the men put in several days of overtime each month.

In the summer of 1862, threats of sabotage were replaced by the dangers of concerted military movements as the Confederate Army moved through Virginia and into Maryland. In order to fill its quota of volunteers to meet the emergency, Delaware drafted nearly four-dozen men from the powder works into the ranks. Lammot was keen to volunteer himself, but was dissuaded by his mother, his Uncle Henry, and his Aunt Sophie, who wrote to Lammot's "Uncle Frank":

> Lammot, it seems, has been wanting to go for a good while, but the consciousness that he was absolutely needed here withheld him from volunteering. It is perfectly absurd, for he serves his country far more usefully here, not only in making powder, but in other ways. Any Irishman could be drilled to make as good a soldier in the ranks—but there is not one man in a thousand with Lammot's scientific genius and knowledge, and his acute mind.[38]

Henry's plea that his remaining workers be exempted from the draft was approved with dispatch. Nevertheless, Lammot got his wish to serve. The Brandywine Home Guards were incorporated into the Fifth Regiment of Delaware Volunteers, with Lammot receiving a commission as captain of Company A. For Lammot, the move required more attention to drills and an officer's uniform, which—according to his cousin Ellen—he declared "a humbug" (and officers, "nonsense").[39]

Despite a proviso that the companies were only to be used (and paid when doing so) to protect industry in and around Wilmington, the two companies were dispatched to the Union's Fort Delaware on Pea Patch Island to quell a riot of Rebel prisoners kept there. As a captain, Lammot pulled several 24-hour-long stints as officer-of-the-guard or officer-of-the-day, which, he wrote his mother, gave him "the fort to look after as well as 4,000 prisoners. So you see my hands are full." Lammot fell ill—a victim of the typhoid endemic to the POW camps. The disease, nearly fatal, left him "42 days delirious without intermission." Even when the danger had seemed to pass, he was plagued with inflamed eyes and a sore back.[40]

Though the specter of sabotage seemed to have passed with the first months of the war, the remaining years saw the mills guarding against seemingly annual crises as Rebel movements threatened the mills. The first came during the Antietam campaign in the fall of 1862. On reports that 3,000 Confederate cavalrymen were set to ride across Maryland to destroy the mills, Secretary of War Edwin Stanton wrote to General-in-Chief Henry Halleck of the "immediate necessity of a military force to protect the powder mills of Messrs. du Pont, on the Brandywine. You are aware that a large portion of the Government ammunition is made there, the works being the largest in the world. I have been informed that in the last war with Great Britain a guard of 4,000 men was kept there. It seems to me that at least an equal force is now necessary."[41]

Halleck could not spare anywhere close to 4,000 men; with the emergency at Sharpsburg, he wrote that "every man must be sent to General McClellan." He did, however, telegraph Brigadier General John Reynolds with the suggestion "that a guard of Pennsylvania militia be sent to guard these mills," with the promise they could be soon replaced by volunteers. Within a day, an advance guard of several hundred men from the Third Regiment Pennsylvania Reserve brigade arrived and camped within a half-mile of the works and remained there until month's-end.[42]

The powder works were threatened again during the Gettysburg campaign in the summer of 1863. Henry du Pont asked Union authorities to alert him when the enemy approached so that he could dump powder stores into the creek. Lammot's Aunt Sophie, sure their home would be burned in retaliation for her husband's signal victory at Port Royal, South Carolina, boxed the Admiral's papers and had them ready to secret away. Despite the temporary states of "alarm and anxiety" that beset the mills over the course of the war, Henry du Pont's wife wrote to her son that she was confident that "as a people and family we du Ponts are not easily frightened."[43]

"Such a night as we have had!" Lammot's Aunt Joanna wrote her daughter, Fanny, on April 10, 1865. A "commotion in Wilmington" had begun around 11 o'clock and by 3 o'clock it had picked up at the du Pont's powder yards with, as she wrote, "all the bells ringing, drums beating and guns firing!" Unable to sleep, she woke her son, Eugene, who, on asking what all the fuss was about, heard that Lee and his army had surrendered. "Everybody here is half crazy," she added. "The men have holiday, and all the bells, including the Church bell, have never ceased ringing! It is a great day! How thankful we should be!"[44]

Likewise, Louisa du Pont wrote her son, Henry A., that the people "were beside themselves with joy. The houses covered in flags, streets crowded with people—every bell in the town ringing—some people were running through the streets with dinner bells." At the mills, she added, they "had flags and a holiday for the men." Perhaps more relieved at her son's safety than joyful over the surrender, she confessed that she couldn't "get into the spirit of these celebrations" and, complaining about the celebrating workmen, wrote that "two of them have already come reeling down the road at this early hour."[45]

The celebrating came to an end a week later on news of the president's assassination. Henry du Pont—who had come to admire Lincoln—trusted the act was "intended by the Almighty for some special purpose and that all will be well," but considered it a "fearful blow at Republican institutions." His wife, again writing their son, expressed that they "all feel deeply his loss" and were "filled with horror at the wickedness" of the assassination "just when he [Lincoln] was showing such consideration and gentleness to those miserable men."[46]

The du Ponts no doubt took great pride in the role the family had played in the Civil War. Samuel Francis du Pont had become one of the country's early and great heroes for his naval exploits; Henry A. du Pont rose to Chief of Artillery in the Department of West Virginia and earned the Medal of Honor for bravery at the Battle of Cedar Creek in October 1864 (a local paper wrote of his heroics that the du Ponts "do not only know how to make the best powder in the world, but when made they know how to use it."); the mills had supplied nearly half the Union's gunpowder with more than forty men losing their lives in the process and dozens more serving in the ranks. The only official nod came in a short mid-war note from P.H. Watson, Assistant Secretary of War, sending his thanks "in the name of the Government, for the zealous efforts which now, as heretofore, you and your house have made to promote the interests of the public service whenever called upon."[47]

With the war over, Henry resolved to recapture du Pont's prewar business in the South. He sent a trusted employee, George Breck, on an extended trip to visit town and cities where it had agencies before the war with hopes of renewing agreements—or establishing new ones—to handle and sell du Pont powder. Although Breck complained at his reception in some Southern circles ("Northern men are insulted in every possible manner and an opportunity is never allowed to pass both from males and females," he wrote), he also reported success in reestablishing markets for du Pont powder. By December, Henry could write his son that all was "running with as great demand as we had during the war." Still, with powder prices depressed by a postwar glut of unused powder and saltpeter, it would be 1872 before the firm would surpass its peak war sales.[48]

Lammot gave new attention and energy to improvements that were laid aside when the war began. On January 2, 1865, he penned a list of more than forty tasks he had in mind for the New Year; from the mundane to the experimental. On October 24, 1865, the United States Patent Office granted Lammot Patent No. 50,568 ("Improvement in Presses for Pressing Gunpowder") for his horizontal press that could be loaded more efficiently—and safely—than the older vertical presses. The same day, the Patent Office granted Patent No. 50,617 to Swede Alfred Nobel for an "Improved Substitute for Gunpowder"—nitroglycerin.

Nobel's 1865 invention—and his more important invention of dynamite in 1867—heralded the era of high explosives. The naturally curious Lammot recognized the potential of dynamite and pressed his uncle to enter the field, but Henry du Pont thought nitroglycerin in all its forms "vastly more dangerous than gunpowder" and declared "no man's life is safe who uses them." Henry was eventually persuaded to enter the business, and in 1880 the du Ponts, with powder makers Hazard and Laflin & Rand, formed the Repauno Chemical Company, with Lammot at its head.[49]

The new plant was located on the New Jersey side of the Delaware River, in an isolated tract of Gloucester County. Production at Repauno began in mid-1880, and Lammot declared with characteristic optimism, "We have begun here what will some day be the biggest dynamite plant in America." Repauno quickly expanded, and Lammot ensured that the factory had the latest features in safety and technology. Still, making nitroglycerin was a dangerous business, and on March 28, 1884, Lammot du Pont—the man fondly called "our chemist" by his family and to whose inventive mind can be traced the institutionalized research that would mark the future of the company—was killed in an explosion.[50]

Figure 14. Surgeons at work at the rear during an engagement.
Source: *Harper's Weekly*

Figure 15. Closeup of label on wartime U. S. Army medicine chest prepared by E. R. Squibb, M.D.

Source: Bristol-Myers Squibb Corporate Archives (photography by F. Terry Hambrecht, M.D.)

CHAPTER SIX

Medicine Man

I firmly believe if the whole materia medica, *as now used*, could be sunk
to the bottom of the sea, it would be all the better for mankind and all
the worse for the fishes. —Dr. Oliver Wendell Holmes, Sr.

THE LAST TIME James Churchill's parents had heard from their son, an officer in the 11th Illinois Volunteer Infantry, was in his letter of February 10,
1862, just days before the Battle of Fort Donelson, Tennessee. All they had
received since was a letter from a "Mrs. Filley" letting them know their son
had been wounded in the said battle and assuring them that James would
write as soon as he was strong enough.

April came, and with it, thankfully, a letter from James in which he gave
his parents details on his two-month ordeal. He began with details of his
brigade's tactical disposition then turned to details of the fight in which
his unit suffered terribly (thirty-three of fifty-seven men killed or wounded
in his company and a similar proportion for the regiment). As his brigade
retreated they were surrounded by Rebel cavalry. His men—now on the
run—obeyed orders to change course, face to the rear, and charge the enemy
horsemen. "When I had gone, I suppose, about 100 feet," James wrote, "I felt
as though I was suddenly struck with a leaden whip across the thighs, and
was pitched headlong into a hole."[1]

Though hit in the left thigh, Churchill nevertheless managed to get up,
and he continued with his advance. Nearly successful in breaking through,
he saw an enemy cavalryman with his carbine pointed at him. Churchill
drew his revolver, but "Before I got a 'bead' on him, he fired and I fell on,
and among, a pile of dead and wounded," he wrote, adding "This time it was
a 'minnie' ball that had struck me in the center of the right hip-socket from
above, splitting off the outer half, and passing down by the thigh bone, frac-
tured it four inches below the head, and lodged above the knee."[2]

Churchill tried to get up, but could only raise his head ("my hips and lower
limbs were as of lead," he told his parents). Within minutes the enemy's
infantry had passed, and rebel shirkers were picking the pockets of the
Illinois dead ("the stragglers of an army are usually the worst men in it,"

Churchill added). As the air filled with the pitiful cries of the wounded, a handful of Confederate surgeons arrived and began to examine the fallen. Churchill asked about his prospects, to which the surgeons informed him his right hip and thigh were broken, he was bleeding heavily from his left leg, and he would likely "peg out" before the new day.[3]

The battle waxed and waned as Union infantry, then Confederate cavalry and infantry, and then again bluecoats crossed over the ground and fought as Churchill watched. "The 'Rebs' fired low and bullets 'sist' all around me," he wrote, "but as I was not in a condition to dodge, I had to take what came. Several struck the log near me, and the splinters flew in my face." As the firing grew fainter, night came, and with it bitterly cold temperatures ("I judged it must be 15 or 20 degrees below freezing," Churchill told his parents). His hair had frozen to the ground; after prying it loose with his fingers, Churchill raised his head and filled his mouth with snow to quench his thirst. Small icicles had formed on his uniform, and his wounds had frozen over, the effect of which almost certainly saved his life.[4]

Mid-morning on Sunday, nearly a full day since he fell wounded, Churchill raised his head and saw his regiment's assistant surgeon, O. G. Hunt, looking among the dead. Churchill hailed the doctor, who in turn shared the contents of his whiskey-filled canteen and promised to get help. A short time later a squad of men carried Churchill away on a camp cot. Arriving at the river, the men found all the hospital ships full, so they carried Churchill to General Grant's headquarters boat, *The New Uncle Sam*. Grant's chief surgeon examined Churchill but reported there was little he could do "as all the appliances, such as the case required, were in use."[5]

A week later, Churchill was transferred to the *City of Memphis*, a hospital ship headed for Cairo, Illinois. The four surgeons in charge there examined Churchill's wounds thoroughly and then stepped aside to consult. They returned to Churchill and reported that, although they did not all agree, a majority recommended his right leg be amputated at the hip and one of the four felt his left leg should be amputated as well. "I told them then I should decide with the minority," Churchill wrote, "and that under no circumstances would I consent to either . . . they told me if I would allow them to give me some chloroform they would not touch either."[6]

Churchill consented. The surgeons administered the chloroform and he was insensible shortly thereafter. He awoke, and looking at his watch, found that he had been under for several hours. His right leg was elevated and tightly bound in bandages holding together a patchwork appliance presumably designed to bring his broken bone back to its original position. Churchill considered the contraption a "weak affair" and was dubious of its benefit.[7]

Days later, Churchill was transferred yet again, this time to the *War Eagle*, a steamer bound for St. Louis, where he was transferred to a hospital at the southwest corner of Fifth and Chestnut Streets. Dr. John T. Hogden, the surgeon in charge, examined Churchill thoroughly (this was quite fortunate for Churchill, as Hogden was to become one of America's great surgeons, a founding member of the American Surgical Association, and later president of the American Medical Association).

Hogden immediately removed the contraption the Cairo surgeons had bound to Churchill's right leg, calling it the "the most murderous machine I ever saw on a man." He then placed Churchill in a novel block-and-tackle apparatus designed to realign his thigh (Hogden would later invent an effective splint that carried his name). He also had a nurse coat Churchill's throat, neck, and chest liberally with iodine as he feared his patient's sore throat might develop into diphtheria. Churchill called the attention he received upon arriving in St. Louis "the first proper treatment" that he had received in the two weeks since he had been wounded.[8]

Ten days later, Hogden told Churchill that his chances of recovery were very favorable. Churchill's ordeal was not over, though. He was still in a great deal of pain. "Proud flesh" invaded the wound on his left thigh, which required repeated treatments with caustic to burn it away. Nurses gave him glasses of whiskey or wine every two hours, from six in the morning to six in the evening, as a stimulant.

During the night, the various pains would orchestrate into what Churchill called a "nerve concert" at which point, he wrote his parents, "I would get my stick and tap on the floor for Tom, the nurse . . . I would take out a dollar and say, 'Another glass of morphine, Tom'; he would quietly slip out and bring it to me. It would deaden the sensitiveness of the nerves so much that I would lie quietly for some time."[9]

In April 1862, fully two months after his wounding, Churchill was still in the St. Louis hospital, the "oldest patient here, but one out of six hundred." He wrote that as soon as he could be safely moved on a cot, Dr. Hogden would have him transferred and promised his parents that he would write as soon as he arrived.[10]

Four years of fighting during the American Civil War left more than 600,000 soldiers dead, two-thirds of whom succumbed to diseases rather than shot, sword, or shell. More important from a medical standpoint, the war left millions of wounded and sick soldiers, such as James Churchill, in the hands of surgeons, hospital stewards, and nurses. Churchill's journey was truly an "everyman" experience: he received medical attention on the field, on hospital ships and transports, and finally in a general hospital; his attending surgeons ranged from the (sometimes) too-eager-to-amputate to innovative experts; he received a variety of medicines, some that were effective and others that did no good; and he received tender care from nurses, both male and female.

The Union Army's medical department was ill-equipped and overwhelmed at the war's start. The "old-school" leadership in place in 1861 was more concerned with politics and budgets than in considering changes to the existing system. The fruits of this lack of foresight were unmistakable after the war's first major battle at Bull Run in July 1861. Wounded soldiers were left unattended for hours, ambulance service was nonexistent, and regimental surgeons often refused to treat soldiers from other units. Any real improvement would require the medical department to face a number of challenges: advances in military technology, prevailing medical philosophy, and supply acquisition.

As for advances in military technology, the Civil War witnessed the advent and implementation of technologies that inflicted huge numbers of casualties. Most devastating was the soft, leaden conical "Minie" ball, (named for French Captain Claude E. Minie), which, when fired from a rifled musket, resulted in significant damage to soft tissues and bony structures of its victims.

Understanding medical care during the Civil War requires perspective. Medical knowledge, as we understand it now, was still emerging; basic medical theories and surgical techniques had remained relatively unchanged for hundreds of years. Significant advances in understanding the link between infectious organisms and wound contamination—including the important work of Pasteur and Lister—were not reported and published until after the war's end. Doctors of the day still talked of "miasmas"—foul odors and vapors in the air that spread infection. The misunderstandings were compounded by a lack of basic hygiene in camps and hospitals.

It was also an era of "heroic medicine"—physicians believed in the healing power of a complex array of drugs administered in massive doses and in older treatment methods such as bleeding and purging. Indeed, the Army's own drug supply table included more than a hundred distinct pharmaceutical preparations, including the infamous mercurial purgative known as "blue mass." Still, Oliver Wendell Holmes's famous quote notwithstanding, some of the medicine applied during the Civil War actually had a therapeutic benefit, and Churchill refers to a number of medicines that were demonstrated to provide relief.

Contrary to popular belief (and decades of misinformed Hollywood dramatizations of soldiers "biting the bullet"), anesthetics *did* exist and were used frequently. Opium and morphine were employed to relieve pain and make patients comfortable following surgery. Alcohol, which James Churchill received on the battlefield and in the hospital, was the most commonly prescribed medicine during the Civil War. Unfortunately it was prescribed contrary to its actual mode of action. Alcohol was thought to be a stimulant and was given in small doses to combat shock and other depressive conditions. Used properly, it could have been of great use as a sedative, analgesic, amnesic, or topical antiseptic. Perhaps the most effective and popular drug was quinine, which was routinely given to soldiers to prevent and treat malaria.

Although some raw materials used in these medicines were gathered in the United States, most crude drugs were imported. The imported materials were then sold through brokers to large companies or wholesalers—mostly in the North—who inspected the material and converted them to finished medicines (extracts, tinctures, and the like). These in turn were sold to physicians, retail pharmacists, or even directly to patients.

Before the war, the United States military purchased medicines on the open market and thus had to contend with the vagaries of free enterprise: erratic prices, fluctuating exchange rates, and unpredictable supplies. Speculators—some savvy and some naïve—bought up large quantities of popular items in hopes of garnering quick profits on rising prices, all in competition with the Army's desperate needs. To complicate the business further, European exporters and merchants tried to increase their profits by shipping worm-eaten substances or adulterating their offerings with sand, chalk, twigs, and other foreign objects.

Once the medicines were available in the large quantities required, there was still the challenge in getting them to various supply points and then again to where they were most needed and could be dispensed: on the march, on the battlefields, and in the hospitals. Prior to the Civil War, the Army's medical and hospital supplies were shipped through the medical purveying depot in New York to a few smaller depots in the South and West for distribution. The war required an expansion in this system. Philadelphia became another major depot, and as many as thirty purveying depots in cities such as Memphis, Cincinnati, and St. Louis, completed a network that by war's end evolved into a highly efficient distribution system.

How and where did the Union Army acquire a reliable supply of the large amount of medicines to distribute? At times, state governments and civil relief agencies, such as the United States Sanitary Commission, provided the military with medicines. Many soldiers treated themselves with home remedies, nostrums, and "patent medicine" available from camp sutlers. In the main, though, the Union's military medical department supplied the great bulk of medicines to the troops.

The army's medical purchasing agents tried to avoid the widely fluctuating prices and unreliable quality by bypassing the drug brokers; instead they purchased medicines from wholesalers and drug companies whose prices, inventories, and quality could be trusted. However, there were few firms that had the capacity to meet the army's needs in either scale or immediacy. To state that America's antebellum pharmaceutical industry was nascent is an exaggeration; it was nearly nonexistent. The total value of the country's annual chemical industry output, of which drugs were included, was less than $4 million. Still, the Army found a few firms to meet the need.

Chief among those few was the drug house of Edward R. Squibb, M.D., founder of the pharmaceutical company that still carries his name. A number of factors in Squibb's early years had an impact on his experiences during the Civil War: his service in the Navy, friends and customers in the South, a dedication to quality, and a talent for innovation and invention.

Squibb was born on Independence Day in 1819, in Wilmington, Delaware, to Quaker parents. He demonstrated an early interest in a medical career, but his family's financial situation did not allow for it. At the age of eighteen, Squibb began apprenticeships with two Philadelphia apothecaries, and after five years he saved sufficient funds to attend Jefferson Medical College in the same city. He received his M.D. degree in 1845 and set up a private practice while simultaneously holding a number of positions at Jefferson, including assistant instructor in anatomy, curator of the museum, and clerk of the school's hospital clinic.

In 1847, upon the outbreak of the Mexican War, Squibb joined the U.S. Navy as an assistant surgeon, a decision that did not sit well with his Quaker family or local Meeting, which disowned him on the grounds that he had violated his pledge of pacifism. Squibb saw no contradiction in his service, arguing that as a doctor he would be assuaging suffering and participating in the Navy's mission to eradicate the overseas slave trade.

Squibb served more than four years at sea, first for more than two years as Medical Officer on a brig in the Caribbean, then for a few months on a store ship, and finally on a cruise of nearly two years on a frigate in the Mediterranean. Squibb was an energetic diarist, filling more than a thousand journal pages in tidy script and great detail. From his first entry—"Land ho at daylight this morning!"—the pages teem with wonderful descriptions of voyages and ports of call that have enchanted sailors for centuries, including Gibraltar, Naples, and Pompeii.[11]

The pages also abound with disgust with his captains and with living conditions at sea, including discipline, diet, and hygiene, all of which left the sailors in his care vulnerable to disease. The situation was made worse by the primitive medicine and pharmacy practiced on the ships. Squibb was especially dismayed at the poor quality of the drugs available on board. The Navy purchased its medical supplies the same way it purchased rope and oakum—from the lowest bidder with few specifications for quality. The experience set Squibb on a lifelong advocacy of regulatory standards for drug purity.

In January 1852, Squibb was ordered to the Naval Hospital in Brooklyn where the Navy, supported by limited funds from Congress, established a drug manufacturing and research laboratory. As assistant director, Squibb was responsible for outfitting and operation of the laboratory, a duty in addition to his other obligations that included serving as staff surgeon, supervising employees, and even preparing menus.

Eager to see that the Navy would benefit from medicine manufactured to an exacting standard, Squibb went straight to work making drugs for the hospital, ships calling at the Brooklyn yard, and other stations. He didn't limit his experiments to the laboratory's intended mission of improving the quality, quantity, and ready availability of medicines for the fleet. He also examined adulterations in provisions, clothing, soap, tobacco, lighthouse oils, sheathing copper, and other supplies provided by contractors. Squibb also performed a good deal of original and applied research; indeed, the first dozen of his more than one hundred published scientific papers were based on work conducted at the Navy laboratory.

The economic pressures of raising a growing family—Squibb had married in 1852 and his first son was born the next fall—prompted him to write the Secretary of the Navy (through channels) for an increase in pay, arguing that his salary was not commensurate with his duties and success at the laboratory. Despite the endorsements from several influential people at the hospital and in Washington, the Secretary rejected Squibb's request.

Squibb's work at the Naval Laboratory had attracted attention, and he had a number of prospects, including a long-standing proposition from his long-time friend and roommate at Jefferson—Dr. Sam White—to join a profitable private medical practice in Georgia. He resigned his commission in late 1857 to supervise the laboratory of the Louisville Chemical Works in Kentucky. A year later, with promises of contracts from Dr. Richard Satterlee, then the Army's chief medical purveyor, Squibb borrowed $1300 from White and opened his own firm in a small brick building in Brooklyn.

Squibb spent the fall of 1858 buying and installing apparatus for his laboratory as carpenters, mechanics, masons, and painters put on finishing touches. He printed circulars detailing his credentials and a list of drugs he intended to manufacture and sell. Squibb filled his first order in early December, and with samples in the hands of the army and influential druggists and physicians, the future of his enterprise seemed bright indeed. But less than three weeks later, on the night of December 29, 1858, disaster struck, as detailed in an account carried in the following day's *Brooklyn Eagle*, "About 6 o'clock last night a fire broke out in the chemical factory of Dr. Edward K. [sic] Squibb, No. 149 Furman Street. The firemen were promptly on the ground, and obtaining a good supply of Ridgewood water, soon suppressed the flames. About 9 o'clock it again burst out and the contents were totally destroyed."[12]

As Squibb later explained it, a boy—new to the lab—had accidentally broken a small bottle of ether, and the fluid spilled near a flame the young man had been using to wax stoppers. He cried for Squibb, who upon arriving found "the whole table and a portion of the floor in a voluminous blaze." Squibb tried to extinguish the flames, nearly succeeding, but soon found himself trapped behind the fire without a safe exit. He quickly grabbed some journals and research notebooks, and "took the longest possible run, closed [his] mouth and eyes and jumped through it." By the time he reached safety most of his clothing had been seared away and his face and hands were burned horribly.[13]

Insurance covered all but nearly a thousand dollars of the losses, so that while Squibb recuperated, the landlord rebuilt the damaged floors, and mechanics refitted the laboratory with apparatus and fixtures. At the same time, a group of distinguished men—physicians, pharmacists, and others—subscribed more than $2,000 to help fund the resurrection of the laboratory. The men, appreciative of Squibb's efforts to relieve them from "the manifold evils of adulterated and noxious drugs imposed upon [us] by the dishonesty and criminal cupidity of unprincipled manufacturers," offered the money as a gift, insisting, "we look upon your cause as our cause, your enterprise as the inauguration of a new era, and yourself as the exponent of the great principles of Truth and Humanity."[14]

By the next spring, workers had cleaned out debris and demolished the burned-out floors of the laboratory. Soon after, craftsmen were hard at work painting and building the new structure. By summer, Squibb was accepting special orders and re-employing assistants, including the boy whose accident had caused the fire, who was hired at $2.50 a week, an increase of fifty cents over his previous salary. All his hands received two weeks of holiday with pay, which was a progressive benefit for the time.

By the close of 1859, a year after the fire, Squibb's laboratory was again in full operation and in a position to meet many of the medical needs of the Army. However, Satterlee's promised orders—the premise on which Squibb started his business—were minimal; Army purchases in 1859 accounted for less than $600 of Squibb's total receipts of just over $5000. The lack of orders was in accord with supplying the needs of the pre-war's small standing army and not for want of confidence in Squibb, for, as Satterlee wrote, the quality of Squibb's products was directly tied to the health of the army:

> Many of the chemicals and preparations which I supply habitually, namely those prepared by Dr. Squibb, cannot be had elsewhere except through uncertain channels and . . . I believe them to be better and more nearly officinal than similar preparations from other sources, and . . . uniform sources of supply for the most important articles such as these, is desirable

if not necessary to any good degree of uniformity in practice and results upon the sanitary condition of the Army.[15]

The situation changed when war broke out. Satterlee doubled his orders in early 1861 after the first Southern states seceded and doubled them again in April when President Lincoln called for volunteers to put down the rebellion.

Soon Satterlee was pleading with Squibb to enlarge his operations to meet the demands of a rapidly expanding force. At first Squibb hesitated, perhaps thinking—as many Americans did—that the rebellion would be no more than a three-month's war. Squibb's principal biographer, Lawrence Blochman, suggested that the motivation for his eventual decision to increase capacity was "mixed feelings about the McClellan family."[16]

Squibb had great respect for brothers Dr. George McClellan (founder of Jefferson Medical College) and Dr. Samuel McClellan (professor of anatomy at Jefferson) and Squibb's neighbor and close friend Dr. C. M. McClellan, the brothers' cousin. It was C. M. McClellan who had chaired the committee whose donations helped rebuild the laboratory.

Squibb, though, was apparently less enthusiastic about Dr. George McClellan's two sons: Dr. John N. McClellan (for his "know-it-all attitude . . . need to talk loudly during lectures . . . and his more than slight tendency to circumnavigate the truth") and General George B. McClellan, who, Blochman wrote, "had always struck [Squibb] as too ambitious and too successful a promoter . . . with McClellan running things it was bound to be a long war."[17]

Whatever the reason, in early 1862 Squibb chose property not far from his present works on which to erect a new building. The cornerstone was laid in late May and Squibb moved in just before Thanksgiving. With the December 1858 fire burned into his mind (and literally on his hands and face), Squibb gave careful thought to the design of the new laboratory. He insisted that the contractors use heavy posts and beams, thick flooring, and fireproof brickwork, all to ensure slow burning in the event of another disaster.

In February 1863, Squibb circulated a price list for more than two hundred products and announced the new location:

The large amount of medical supplies required for the army during the past two years so increased the demand for that part of them furnished from this laboratory, that it has been difficult, with a small building to keep up the supply and attend promptly to other demands. Hence, as it became possible and proper to do so, a large and moderately complete laboratory has been built, furnished, and organized wherein it is supposed all the business with which the undersigned may be entrusted can be done with more care, accuracy, and promptitude, than has been hitherto attained.[18]

By early 1863, Squibb was turning out all but a handful of the hundreds of medicines listed on the Army's official supply table. Frank Hastings Hamilton, an influential wartime military surgeon wrote:

Most of the medicines used in the United States Army are manufactured and supplied by E. R. Squibb, M.D. . . . The name of Dr. Squibb is a complete guarantee of their excellence to all who have a personal acquaintance with the man, or who have used his drugs. Of one thing we may be certain, therefore, however poorly our soldiers may be clothed or fed, they are in no danger from impure or adulterated drugs.[19]

The endorsement of Squibb was certainly welcome, but Hamilton's claim that Squibb supplied "most of the medicines" was exaggerated. By his own account, Squibb estimated that he supplied about one-twelfth of all the medicines consumed by the Army (this fraction of wartime supplies may not seem like much, but a "market share" of that magnitude can be claimed by only the top two or three global pharmaceutical companies today), with total sales of nearly $300,000 in the first few years of the war.

Many of Squibb's drugs found their way into a useful wartime innovation, his "medicine pannier," which helped to standardize the distribution of medicines to individual units and to make their use more convenient (less than a century later, in time for World War II, the "House of Squibb" introduced another important wartime invention—the morphine syrette). In addition to medicine wagons, the Union Army used large, heavy boxes to carry drugs and supplies while on campaign. These containers had to be transported in supply train wagons, and were thus generally unavailable to surgeons during an engagement.

Squibb's pannier—and similar containers supplied by other contractors—was constructed of iron-reinforced wood and equipped with robust iron handles, which rendered it sturdy enough to withstand the rigors of march, yet compact enough to be carried in an ambulance or by a horse or mule and aid the medical staff closer to the front lines. The pannier was divided into two tiers; bandages, instruments, and other supplies were stored in a removable upper tier, while the lower tier contained medicines. Each pannier contained nearly ninety items—from "A to Z" (*argenti nitras* to *zinci sulphas*)—but a diagram on the inside of the chest lid showing the location of each item made locating a specific medicine very convenient. Squibb also distributed a "medicine chest," which was smaller than the pannier but offered many of its advantages.

Squibb also supplied Rebel surgeons with medicine, at least indirectly. While the Confederacy maintained at least one naval medical laboratory and no less than eight more for its armies, the success of the Union blockade forced the Confederates to rely on blockade running, smuggling, and capture of Union supplies to fully meet its medical supply needs. Years after the war, Squibb's son Charles recalled, "our chief distributor [in the South] was General [Nathaniel] Banks. The Johnnies always managed to capture his well-equipped trains. Our goods went all through the Confederacy and were appreciated" (the hapless general earned the moniker "Commissary Banks" for his penchant for leaving supplies behind).[20]

As further evidence that the Squibb enterprise was busy supplying two armies, in a letter that accompanied his $182 check to Squibb, Thomas Smith, a pharmacist in St. Joseph, Missouri, speculated that his missing shipment of medicine could be explained by the fact that "the rebels seem to be having their way in Missouri."[21]

The combination of overwhelming casualties and disease—and the occasional loss of supplies to the Rebels—prompted Satterlee to persuade Squibb to expand his operations even more. Squibb was uncertain that he could give a larger plant, or expanded operations at his existing laboratory, the close personal attention required to maintain the purity and reliability of his products. He also doubted that orders from a presumably smaller standing army after postwar demobilization would justify the expense and risk of another expansion.

When Charles Darwin was asked his opinion on the most important discovery of the nineteenth century, he answered, "painless surgery." Although physicians and dentists had privately used ether with patients in the early 1840s, it was October 1846 before its value in surgery was made public in a well-attended demonstration hosted by Dr. William T. G. Morton at Massachusetts General Hospital. Still, surgeons hesitated to use ether (as well as chloroform, introduced at about the same time) because the preparations then available varied so much in quality, and their action was so uncertain that they proved more of a risk than a benefit. In addition, ether's manufacture was very dangerous as the volatile and highly inflammable liquid was prepared in crude stills over an open fire.[22]

Edward R. Squibb did not invent anesthesia, but he is justly remembered for his production of safe, standard, and effective anesthetics by equally safe and effective manufacture. Ether was the foundation of Squibb's business and he established a standard for quality that stood well after his passing. It is largely to Squibb's credit that the Union Army had a ready *and* reliable supply of ether and chloroform for its surgeons to use (and perhaps Confederate surgeons, also; one historian claimed that "Abraham Lincoln himself chose to overlook the smuggling of Squibb ether to the South").[23]

Squibb was certainly aware of the Jefferson Medical College faculty's first uses of ether in 1846 and 1847. In 1851—on leave from the Navy—he took three months of refresher courses at Jefferson ("rubbing up," it was called) with an eye towards promotion and a raise. While there, he filled his journal with careful notes about the chemistry and preparation of ether and his impressions of its use, including an operation on a fifty-year old man whose swollen leg required amputation, "The patient was not easily etherized, but was finally brought under the full effect and kept so during the entire operation. . . . The double-flap operation was performed just above the knee, the bone being sawed through at about its middle. . . . At the end, just before the dressing, the patient was asked if he felt the operation and replied that he did not know it was done . . . The operation was very well and prettily and quickly done. . . . A large audience and one case of fainting."[24]

Squibb's experiences during the "rubbing up" at Jefferson had also shown him that the effect of ether was quite variable, even on patients of similar age and stature. Now at his laboratory at the Brooklyn Naval Hospital, he had an opportunity to discover why this was so. Squibb bought six samples of ether on the market and after putting them to careful tests of purity, color, density, and clarity, found them to be widely variable. He published his results and conclusion—that the doubtful reliability of ether in surgery was due to its careless manufacture from ingredients of dubious quality—and worried that the poor ether being used brought to surgery "an uncertainty which does not belong to it"; rather, the discredit "justly belong[ed] to the preparation which [the surgeon] employs."[25]

Squibb then set his mind to discovering a method of manufacturing ether of standard strength and purity in a safe manner. After well over a year of experiments, and nearly two dozen attempts at labyrinths of pipes, flasks, and boilers, he developed a process using steam (rather than an open fire) as a heat source that resulted in very pure ether and a much less dangerous procedure. Unwilling to capitalize on his discovery personally (Morton, who had received a patent in 1846, claimed a ten percent royalty on each use of ether for anesthesia), Squibb published in 1856 a full account of his process with drawings, directions, formulas, and costs.

After his success with ether, Squibb then turned to perfecting the manufacture of chloroform, and published his results of equal success a year later. His ether and chloroform were put to good use in the Navy; Squibb wrote that of the nearly 200 pounds he had manufactured for the Navy, most of it had been used and "as yet without a single reported case of bad results." Others thought as highly when Squibb made the anesthetics for profit. Dr. Valentine Mott, a well-respected surgeon of the era, wrote that in his practice, "I have been in the habit of using the Scotch Chloroform of Duncan, Flockhart, & Co., of Edinburgh, but have also employed that of Dr. Squibb, of Brooklyn, and with pleasure commend the latter for its purity and reliability."[26]

Ether and chloroform were used to great effect in the Civil War and Union authorities purchased many tons of each. Official records from the war suggest that anesthesia was employed in no fewer than 80,000 cases. As impressive as the widespread use of ether and chloroform during the war is their safety record; fewer than fifty deaths were attributed to anesthesia in the tens of thousands of cases in which it was used.

Morton—whose demonstration in 1846 was the genesis of the widespread use of anesthesia—did not make a fortune from royalties. Squibb—who never sought royalties—prospered nonetheless by selling reliable and safe products. There is no evidence that Squibb ever begrudged Morton his legal right to a fortune; he carried on a correspondence with Morton when he was still at the Navy laboratory. There is no doubt that both men's inventions did great good during the Civil War. In 1862, Morton joined the Union Army as a volunteer surgeon and performed valuable service as an anesthesiologist (almost certainly using Squibb's products). Of his experience at the Battle of the Wilderness in May 1864, which produced more than 30,000 casualties on the Union side alone, Morton gave witness to Darwin's declaration that "painless surgery" was the great discovery of the nineteenth century, "How little did I think . . . when originally experimenting with the properties of sulfuric ether on my own person, that I should ever successfully administer it to hundreds in one day, and thus prevent an amount of agony fearful to contemplate."[27]

At the same time he was pressing Squibb to expand, Satterlee was getting pressure from his own boss—Surgeon General William A. Hammond—to agree to a plan to establish pharmaceutical manufacturing laboratories in New York (specifically, Astoria, Long Island) and Philadelphia, in competition with the firms that had been supplying him to that point. Hammond saw a number of advantages in this plan, including ensuring the purity of purchased raw materials and finished drugs, protection from rising prices, uniformity and centralization of distribution, and savings to the government of at least part of the profits being made by the private firms. He also had a worthy model to follow—the Navy's medical laboratory that had been so ably administered by Squibb.

To be sure, by mid-war, Hammond was facing some problems in terms of drug supply. Despite Hamilton's assurance that Union soldiers had the benefit of a pure and unadulterated drug supply, there had been some complaints. John Wyeth & Brother in Philadelphia—one of Hammond's favorite contractors—was accused of furnishing supplies to the medical purveyor there that were "inferior in quality, deficient in quantity, and excessive in price." Even Squibb had received complaints about his morphine and opium.[28]

Prices of medicines and raw materials had certainly risen early in the war, but mostly due to speculation, higher exchange rates, and tariffs. In 1863, as chairman of the American Pharmaceutical Association's "Committee on the Drug Market," Squibb penned an extensive and economically sophisticated report on that year's market (of the timeless greed of speculators, Squibb wrote derisively, "They commonly overstand a rising market and miss the highest point, but will rarely pass through a depression without selling near the lowest point."). Regarding Hammond's concern, Squibb admitted that an early and unsettled drug market had driven up prices, but also noted that in the months leading up to his report there had been a "downward tendency . . . with a strong probability that prices have not yet 'touched bottom.'"[29]

Hammond plowed ahead with establishing the Philadelphia laboratory, but he met resistance from Satterlee and Squibb in starting at Long Island. Satterlee—an "Old Army" man—clashed early and often with the Surgeon General, in no small part due to his friendship with Squibb. Conservative in nature and jealous because Hammond held a post that he coveted himself, Satterlee did not share the progressive Surgeon General's optimism in the virtues of the Army labs, and wrote his superior in certain terms, "Taking into account the expense of the laboratory, viz. building, apparatus, operations, etc., I doubt if we can manufacture anything to advantage. That is, and has been . . . my opinion."[30]

Hammond, equally adamant, replied that he doubted "that manufacturing chemists and druggists generally are so superior in skill and business qualifications . . . that our efforts alone should be prosecuted to disadvantage while theirs are attended with success" and concluded with the expectation of Satterlee's "cordial cooperation."[31]

Certainly Squibb was disappointed in the potential loss of Army business; when he caught wind of the planned government rivalry, Squibb wrote a friend, "Othello's occupation is (nearly) gone." Squibb, like Satterlee, also had very personal reasons to oppose the lab, and expressed them to the same friend with more poison than poetry:

> The Surgeon General has decided to have laboratories of his own. Dr. McCormick is to have one near here and Dr. A.K. Smith one in Philadelphia. Dr. McCormick is just starting his at great expense and under such circumstances that I predict for it a disastrous and disagreeable failure. From all I can learn, Dr. McC is, as the author and vendor of a 'Magic Waverly Pill,' but little more than a great quack and I think him an unreliable man, but Dr. Wood knows more of him than I do. It is, however, a great pity that the best interests of the Medical Corps of the Army should fall into such keeping.[32]

Squibb had a running feud with McCormick—it was the "great quack" who had reported through official channels that "intelligent physicians" in the Army of the Potomac complained about the inferior strength of Squibb's opium. At the beginning of the war, Squibb had disproved complaints about his morphine. Claims about the unworthiness of Squibb's opium were disproved in the surgeon general's own laboratory (it was found to be superior in strength to a competitor's rather than inferior), but McCormick continued to repeat the charge through his subordinates. Squibb finally demanded that Hammond require McCormick to cease and desist.

Hammond visited Squibb in Brooklyn but was still not persuaded by Squibb's argument that "the establishment of Army Laboratories might at . . . [that] time prove otherwise than economical or advantageous to the Government." When Squibb could not force a change in policy through force of his personality or logic, he concluded he would do so by transparency, and wrote Hammond, "I would suggest that one or more sound men and judicious medical officers be ordered for a month or more, to inspect closely the entire operations of my laboratory. . . . I will expose to inspection all my bills, accounts and transactions freely. . . . To obtain the best practical result they should be in the laboratory every day during the working hours, and keep notes which may be summed up . . . and embraced in a concise report."[33]

Hammond—progressive but tactless—had the temerity to suggest McCormick as the observer. Squibb rejected the suggestion. Hammond instead assigned a young medical officer, Joseph H. Bill, to spend time in Squibb's laboratory. Bill spent most of March and April 1863 in Brooklyn, as he wrote Hammond, he had "availed [himself] of all the opportunities afforded me for obtaining information on the manufacture of chemicals" and penned his report on the "Arrangements and Operations and Operations of Doctor E. R. Squibb's Laboratory."[34]

The document is unique in its insight into the operation and design of a large-scale manufacturing laboratory of the day. Bill began with a detailed description of the four-story physical plant then proceeded to explain the organization of the various departments, including his estimates of the costs involved to duplicate the apparatus and labor at the government laboratories (which Squibb surely hoped would prove that Hammond's plan was too expensive). Among the interesting details is Bill's description of women employed in Squibb's wartime operation:

> On the fourth floor is a room devoted to compounding of medicines, etc. . . . The pill masses when thoroughly mixed are taken to the second story and placed in the hands of females. Six girls at present are so

employed. They make about five thousand pills apiece per day. In the same room are four large tables. On these [another] six girls and one man label and wrap bottles after they have been filled and corked. There are in all twelve women employed at an average wage of three dollars and fifty cents apiece.[35]

In the conclusion to his report, Bill noted that with an increase in his staff, Squibb "had sufficient capacity to furnish supplies for a million men," with the presumed implication that Hammond's pet proposal might not be necessary. Nevertheless, Hammond proceeded with his plans. Still, Squibb's fingerprints can be found on the Army labs. When McCormick was sacked for his clumsy direction at Astoria, Bill succeeded him, and his experience in Brooklyn almost certainly contributed to his success there. Likewise, John M. Maisch—an erstwhile Squibb employee and exceptionally talented chemist—was the Philadelphia lab's chief scientist.

The Civil War also had a profound personal impact on Squibb apart from his professional activities. The first involved an important link to his service in the Navy. Squibb's home for two years on the Mediterranean had been the USS *Cumberland*. Squibb's tour on the *Cumberland* resulted in his first published contributions to public policy and science. The first was a 2,500-word letter published in Philadelphia's *North American and United States Gazette* titled simply "Punishments in the Navy," in which he rebuked the service for the lack of discipline on its ships, placing part of the blame on Congress for recently banning the practice of flogging. It was certainly an audacious step for a junior officer.

The second, and more important, was an article summarizing the medical care aboard the *Cumberland* during his two year tour. Published in the *American Journal of the Medical Sciences*, it is a great work of scientific, statistical, and clinical observation, even by modern standards; not to mention an exceptional contemporary and first-hand look at life aboard a man-'o-war in the antebellum Navy. In his paper, Squibb detailed a record of more than 1,600 cases of disease among a ship's company numbering less than 500 men. He supposed that no community like in number and in any other condition would exhibit as much disease in two years. Why then the *Cumberland*? Squibb pointed his finger at the Navy's stubborn attachment to outdated routine and tradition. Squibb did not just grumble; he made specific suggestions as to how changes in diet and ship construction could improve the health of the men on board.

After Squibb left the ship to work at the Navy Laboratory in Brooklyn, the *Cumberland* was converted to a sloop of war. The vessel was anchored off Newport News, Virginia, on March 8, 1862, when the ironclad CSS *Virginia* came out to attack Union warships in Hampton Roads. In a battle that signaled the age of the armored steam-powered warship and the demise of the wooden ship-of-the-line, *Cumberland* was rammed and sunk. One can only wonder what Squibb thought when he read that the ship from which he had seen the world, filled hundreds of pages of in his diary, and about which he wrote his first important medical paper, now lay at the bottom of the ocean.

The Civil War also cut Squibb off from old and dear friends in the South, especially his old roommate and patron, Dr. Sam White, White's extended family in Georgia, and physicians and pharmacists in Southern towns who were his customers. Fleming Grieve, owner of the "Grieve & Clark" pharmacy in Milledgeville, Georgia, was one of Squibb's first customers. White wrote Squibb throughout the war, especially about family and friends who had been captured but whose whereabouts among the many Union prison camps were unknown.

Squibb's biographer characterized White's letters as "terse, impersonal, and very short." Kate Davidson—an old acquaintance of Squibb and White—was a Georgian expatriate (and ardent Confederate) who lived in Connecticut during the war. She explained the terseness to Squibb, writing "I suppose Dr. White does not quite understand how much he might say to you in his notes without compromising you. Neither does he understand your feelings toward him. This accounts for his very brief notes."[36]

White needn't have worried; more often than not during the war, Squibb did what he could to help his old friend. When, in November 1863, White inquired into the whereabouts of a relative of Squibb's old customer Fleming Grieve, Squibb wrote a note to the commanding officer at Fort Delaware:

Dear Sir:

If not improper, nor against the regulations of your command, I beg you will allow the enclosed note to be given to a prisoner of war taken at Gettysburg and now believed to be in your charge, named John Grieve. He is a Georgian, and I believe was serving in the 2nd Georgia Battalion.

Should he have been transferred from Fort Delaware, will you have the kindness to tell me where he may be found?

Should he still be in the Fort, and reply to my note (which you will please read), be so kind as to guard me against sending him anything that will interfere with your regulations or compromise him.

Very Respectfully

Your obed. Servt.

E. R. Squibb"[37]

The commander replied that Grieve had been transferred to Point Lookout, Maryland, adding that Squibb was free to send money or clothing (except in blue or gray, of course!), which Squibb did.

In early 1864, White wrote again with the salutation "Friend Squibb," and asked that he inquire into the condition of his kinsman Batt Jones, a prisoner at Johnson's Island. Squibb contacted Jones, and when the prisoner asked that Squibb send him money, clothing, food, and blankets, Squibb obliged (drawing on an account he had set aside for White's interests). Squibb also inserted a notice in the *New York Herald* stating that "Lt. Col. Batt Jones, prisoner of war at Johnson's Island, is well. Richmond papers please copy."[38]

Later that year, facing the harsh winter that would certainly plague the prison set on Lake Erie, Jones wrote Squibb asking him to participate in a "pious fraud . . . for the preservation of my health." He requested that Squibb send him a hundred pounds each of bacon and flour and a bushel each of corn meal and dried peaches. Since packages to Johnson's Island could only be sent from outside of federal lines, Jones asked that Squibb address the package so it appeared to have come from Atlanta. Squibb's generosity—tempered by his Quaker scruples—had its limits. If the provisions could not be sent legitimately, they would not be sent at all, for as Squibb wrote, "Col. Jones should be as ready to offer his health and his life to his cause, as a prisoner, as he did in going into the war as an officer."[39]

Nevertheless, when the unreconstructed Kate Davidson sent to Brooklyn the very provisions Jones had asked for (via Jones's brother in Augusta, Georgia), Squibb happily forwarded them to Johnson's Island.

"The United States Army laboratory, located at Astoria, L.I., was consumed by fire on Monday morning last," the *New York Times* declared on Wednesday,

Figure 16. Edward Robinson Squibb
Source: Bristol-Myers Squibb Corporate Archives

February 15, 1865. Prompted by warnings from Washington that arsonists might attempt to sabotage the laboratory, Bill had ensured that a "guard of five additional men . . . from among the male employees and armed with muskets" were kept on alert and rotated daily (an added expense to the government labs that Squibb did not face; watchmen were not described in Bill's 1863 report, in any event). But it wasn't arson that destroyed Hammond's experiment in Astoria, it was—as it had been for Squibb—an accident.[40]

"The fire commenced about 9 a.m., in the ceiling over the drying-room," the *Times*'s report continued, "and so rapidly did the flames spread, that all efforts to stay their progress were of no avail." The article noted that "the employees worked faithfully to save the various articles, and by their efforts much that was explosive was removed." The paper put the government's loss at $50,000, including Bill's office. Satterlee visited Squibb in person within days of the fire with a proposal that Squibb take the work of the Astoria laboratory, sell the Squibb works to the government, or at least take up a portion of the slack.[41]

Squibb traveled to Washington for an audience with the Surgeon General, Joseph K. Barnes, who had replaced Hammond. Squibb discussed the merits of Satterlee's various proposals; he even offered to sell his laboratory, but Barnes politely declined. When he returned home, Squibb reorganized his staff to absorb the Army's orders and bought two adjoining lots for $4500 for an expansion.

On April 25, 1865, Squibb marched with the King's County Medical Association in a daylong procession for the fallen President Lincoln, whose funeral train had reached New York that morning. A month later, Squibb hosted the now-released Lt. Col. Batt Jones at his home. "He is supplying himself with a few necessaries," Squibb wrote, "and will go home when he can." A few days later Captain Tom White—a cousin to Sam White and newly-freed from Fort Delaware—appeared at Squibb's door and shared the guestroom with Jones. After dinner, Squibb took White to shop for clothing, and the following day found all three men reunited with Kate Davidson.[42]

Just after the New Year 1866, Squibb joined his friend Dr. C. M. McClellan in trying to revive a mutual neighbor and friend, banker George Sampson, but to no avail. The sudden passing of Sampson depressed Squibb greatly. He had depended on his banker friend for financial advice and for a safety note in those rare times he was overextended. Now was one of those times. Squibb had invested a substantial amount of capital in land, equipment, and new staff when the Astoria lab burned to the ground, but the expansion was completed just in time for the surrender at Appomattox. Unable to secure a $25,000 mortgage on the laboratory, Squibb advertised his factory for sale in the papers but had only a few inquiries; happily, his note was approved a few weeks later.

Just as the Civil War had accelerated the pace of invention in the "arts of death," it also advanced many of the "arts of life." James Churchill, the badly hurt soldier first abandoned on the battlefield of Fort Donelson and then hauled through the Civil War's nascent but improving health care system, survived his wounds. By war's end, he was a quartermaster and Brevet Lieutenant Colonel. Thirty years later, speaking to a group of veterans gathered in St. Louis, he read the February 1862 letter he had written to his parents.

The war also hastened the development of a burgeoning drug industry. Such were the scales involved that in early 1865, the editor of the *American Journal of Pharmacy* justly declared "It is altogether certain, that no gigantic pharmaceutical operations have ever been carried on in Europe, as the past three years have witnessed in the supply of the armies of the United States." Squibb, like many others, had to endure a postwar depression, but the drug business eventually recovered, such that in 1870 the number of firms engaged in making medicines had nearly doubled; the number of people employed in the trade more than quadrupled; and capital investment in the pharmaceutical industry had increased from two million dollars in 1860 to more than twelve million.[43]

Firms that would become household names in the twentieth century—Pfizer, Wyeth, Lilly, Merck, Warner, Parke-Davis—can all trace their roots to the Civil War itself or the boom that followed, in no small part due to the training that talented chemists received either at the government laboratories or in industry. Squibb, having passed control of the company to his sons, died in 1900 and was eulogized with great acclaim by the members of his profession: "Pharmacy has lost a Nestor, medicine a leader, and the world the noblest work of God—an honest man."[44]

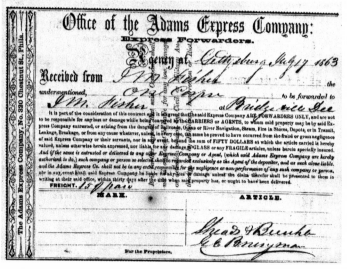

Figure 17. The express office at City Point, Virginia, on payday.
Source: *Harper's Weekly*

Figure 18. Adams Express receipt to ship William Fisher's corpse.
Source: Gettysburg National Military Park

CHAPTER SEVEN

Special Deliveries

Get posts and letters, and make friends with speed;
Never so few, and never yet more need.
—*Henry IV*, Part II, Act 1

IN AUGUST 1861 Isaac and Sarah Fisher saw their son William off to war. Only seventeen, he had nevertheless received a commission as a second lieutenant in the Tenth United States Infantry, and the following months found him writing home regularly of his experiences in camp, on the march, and in Washington, where he had occasion to meet and shake hands with President Lincoln.

In short time William gained the respect of his fellow soldiers as a "really excellent officer" and was admired by others for his "fine soldierly qualities, his gentlemanly deportment and his extreme kindness and unassuming manners." Another soldier wrote of Fisher that "there was not a man in the regiment but what thought a great deal of him and when on duty with him he wasn't cross like some of them he was kind and genteel to all of us." [1]

William saw a lot of action. In two years of service his regiment fought in the Seven Days campaign, and the battles of Antietam, Fredericksburg, and Chancellorsville. In those engagements a fellow soldier in the Tenth, First Sergeant Terrance McCabe, thought that William "behaved with a coolness, intrepidity—and personal bravery almost unequalled" during McCabe's time of service. John Buchan, another soldier in Fisher's company, added that William was "as cool in the battle [at Fredericksburg] as he was out of it and as brave a man as there is in the regiment." [2]

In late June 1863, the Tenth Infantry—reduced to a complement of three under-strength companies—made forced marches for several days, and arrived at Gettysburg, Pennsylvania, mid-day on July 1. The next afternoon, Fisher—lately promoted to first lieutenant—talked and laughed with his comrades, wondering when they would enter the fight. At about three o'clock in the afternoon, the Tenth moved forward at the double quick and into the midst of some of the heaviest fighting that day. The unit took heavy fire and suffered greatly.

As reports from the battle filtered into homes across the country, the Fishers joined thousands of families in the anxious routine of scanning newspapers for any information on the fate of their sons, husbands, and brothers. On July 9th, the following line appeared in a long ledger of dead and wounded in *The New York Times,* "1st Lieut. W. J. Fisher—10th Infantry—killed."[3]

The Fishers knew that casualty lists were famously inaccurate. Military authorities could do little to identify the remains, and the "fog of battle" led soldiers to innocently spread erroneous information concerning the whereabouts of missing comrades. Leading newspapers even incorrectly reported important officers of both armies as being killed or wounded. Families submitted notices to local newspapers begging for information concerning loved ones.

Unable to bear the suspense, Isaac decided to go to Gettysburg, one hundred and forty miles away from his Delaware home to search for his son. En route, Isaac found Lt. James H. Bradford at his home in Wilmington, recovering from his own wounds suffered in the battle. A friend of William's and an officer in a regiment that fought alongside the Tenth, Bradford was able to shed some light on William's fate.

Late that night, Isaac Fisher began penning a letter to his wife, as he sat in his hotel room in Wilmington:

> My dear, it is 10 o'clock and I have retired to my room to grieve in private. Our worst fears are realized and I know that William is no more . . . I have seen Lt. Bradford who is at home slightly wounded in the foot and he told me that he saw the dead body of our dear boy. He was killed on Thursday the 2nd of July as we supposed, by a musket or rifle ball in or through the body and was buried with the other officer named in the list . . . he thinks they were put in coffins and that I shall be able to obtain his body and if I do I will have it with me when I get home.[4]

With Bradford's information in hand, Isaac traveled by coach to Gettysburg. After reaching the battlefield two days later, he made his way to the farm of Jacob Weikert, where he had been told his son could be found. A little less than two hundred yards northwest of the Weikert home, Isaac found a temporary grave marker made from a wooden cigar box with the hastily carved inscription: "L. T. Fisher 10th US INFT."[5]

Survivors of the battle left a trail of temporary cemeteries in their wake as they left Gettysburg, and gravediggers were doing a brisk business removing bodies interred only days before. Embalmers, engaging in a relatively new trade perfected during the war, charged $50 for officers and $15 for enlisted men. Undertakers did their best to keep up with the demand for coffins and cases. In all probability, Isaac engaged such services in this grim chain of commerce.

His last stop was at the Adams Express office in town. The agent, now probably all too familiar with the process, wrote William's name and regiment on a crudely cut piece of wood and tied it to the boy's toe. He wrote the same in tidy script on a piece of glossy paper and placed it inside the coffin. As the agent completed the waybill, Isaac handed over the thirty dollars it took to ship William's body back to Delaware. In the space where the description of the freight was to be written, the agent summarized in two words a looming lifetime of sorrow for the Fishers: "one corpse."[6]

The express industry was an inestimable force in industry, transportation, communication, and westward expansion in the nineteenth century. First tested as an enterprise in the late 1830s by a handful of pioneering entrepreneurs, within a decade a growing number of companies were moving eastern goods westward, precious ores from western mines eastward, and money, mail, and other documents in all directions. One historian wrote enthusiastically of the breadth of services the express companies offered and concluded there is no modern equivalent, "Imagine a business that combines the communication aspects of letter mail, e-mail, faxes, and the telephone; the transportation of heavier goods by parcel post and express mail, such private carriers as United Parcel Service and Federal Express, and an armored car service; and the plethora of financial arrangements supplied by modern . . . full-service banks."[7]

One period express executive defined the business as "carrying parcels and packages as fast as possible, with special care to their safety in transportation and their sure delivery." An early motto of another company succinctly expressed the industry's principle: "Safety and Dispatch." However it was put, the express system stood as a superior alternative to the costly and risky choices of the day; the postal service and complete strangers.[8]

"I view [the post road] as a source of boundless patronage to the executive, jobbing to members of Congress and their friends and a bottomless abyss of public money," Thomas Jefferson wrote James Madison in 1796. "You will begin by only appropriating the surplus of the post-office revenues; but other revenues will soon be called in to their aid and it will be a source of eternal scramble among the members, who can get the most money wasted in their states; and they will always get most who are meanest."[9]

Jefferson's prediction proved true. In the early and mid-1800s, the United States Post Office was the largest commercial enterprise in the country. It employed nearly three-fourths of all the nation's civil servants, mostly as deputy postmasters or clerks. While Great Britain's postal service yielded profits of greater than two hundred percent, America's turned over no revenue to the Treasury; instead, it most often reported losses. It was not for a lack of return—large profits *were* earned, but they were distributed to favored groups, especially newspaper editors, southerners, and westerners. In turn, the politicians—eager to keep the money and their constituency of thousands of employees—protected the postal service from privatization.

Whether the hidden profits caused high prices or vice versa, one thing was for certain—in the early 1800s, the high rates were compounded by poor service. Before the first price reform in 1845 (forced largely by the express industry), an average one-page letter cost nearly fifteen cents to send (charges were added for each additional sheet). Newspapers noted with dismay that a person could ship a 200-pound barrel of flour down the Hudson from Troy to New York City for less than a letter over the same route. If money or other valuables were included, they might be stolen.[10]

A common and inexpensive but equally risky practice was to entrust mail, packages, and valuables to an acquaintance or even an unknown (albeit respectable-looking) gentleman who happened to be going the same way by ship, stage, or rail. The proliferation of stagecoach lines—Boston had more than a hundred lines running in 1832—found the drivers carrying letters, parcels, and large amounts of money. When the railroads were built, bankers and brokers in the big cities employed their own messengers, entrusted with important papers and valuables, to make the journey to neighboring cities.

The concept of the "express" was born when enterprising men saw an opportunity to charge a nominal fee for delivering packages. A number of expresses were formed, but they were limited in both the distances they covered and in their ambitions. It was left to William F. Harnden to expand the idea to a larger and more profitable scale. An erstwhile train conductor and ticket agent, Harnden quit his job and in early 1839 began advertising daily trips from Boston to New York as a messenger and carrier. He soon earned an estimable reputation as witnessed in an editorial in a Boston newspaper, which noted that his business "is found highly convenient to those who wish to send small packages or parcels from one city to the other. Mr. Harnden may be confided in for honesty and fidelity in the discharge of his engagements, and it affords us much pleasure to recommend his 'Express' to the notice of our readers."[11]

Before long, Harnden had more clients than he could handle alone. His business expanded in scale and in scope. He began carrying parcels in a bag, then a trunk, then in large freight boxes; first from New York to New England, then to other cities, and then overseas. As the advantages of the express industry became widely recognized, others started their own concerns so that gazetteers and business directories of large cities listed dozens of firms—large and small—offering express services.

Harnden died in early 1845 at the age of thirty-three, just six years after he started his business. Some attributed his passing to the effects of hard work and worry—which attended his life as an express pioneer—on an already delicate frame. So appreciative were the others who had capitalized on and profited from Harnden's lead that they erected a monument to the "Founder of the Express Business in America" over his grave. Carved into the sixteen-foot tall shaft is the iconography of the express business—a bulldog, dove, and hourglass—and an inscription from the Old Testament: "Because the king's business required haste"[12]

Sending the bodies of slain soldiers like William Fisher back to their homes was only one of the important services that express companies performed during the Civil War. In doing the "king's business," they also shipped arms, munitions, and other supplies; delivered packages from the home front to soldiers in camps and hospitals; and forwarded soldiers' pay and messages back to their homes. The principal companies of the Civil War all remain in business today: American Express, now a global leader in travel and financial services; Adams Express, a successful investment trust; and Wells Fargo, one of the country's best known banking interests. Though the companies' missions have changed over the years, their names have not, and each points with pride to its Civil War heritage.

On March 18, 1850, seven men—the principals being Henry Wells, William Fargo, and John Butterfield—merged their modest but successful businesses to form the American Express Company. Wells, born in Vermont, attended school until he was sixteen, at which time he was apprenticed as a tanner. In his mid-thirties, he became the Albany agent for Harnden. His vision for the express was even more ambitious than Harnden's, and when he was unable to convince his boss to expand westward, he left to become proprietor of the "Wells & Co." express, which operated between Buffalo and Detroit.

William Fargo, born in New York, was the oldest of twelve children in an old Connecticut family. At thirteen, he rode a mail route of thirty miles twice a week. Over the next decade, he helped in a village inn, worked in a grocery store, failed as a grocery owner himself, and was then the first freight agent on the newly completed railroad that connected Auburn to Syracuse. In 1844, he became a messenger for Wells & Co., then partner, and then owner of the "Livingston and Fargo" express, which operated at points farther west than Wells.

John Butterfield was the scion of old New England stock, his family having settled in the Bay Colony on 1638. Born near Albany, New York, Butterfield had minimal formal schooling but became very rich. He began his professional career as a stage driver, then owner of several smaller stage lines and a steamboat line, a promoter of railroads and the telegraph, and finally owner of the "Butterfield, Wasson, & Co." express.

Cutthroat business tactics marked the express industry as the various companies fought bitterly for the valuable and exclusive contracts granted by the railroads. The companies slashed shipping rates, hoping to woo each other's customers. Contests among the messengers provided good sport, but also added prestige—and presumably new customers—to the winner. Smaller expresses, some of them one-man operations, began to disappear as the larger and stronger firms purchased them or put them out of business.

Indeed, it was this atmosphere that led to the founding of American Express. Wells dropped his rates in a bid to capture Butterfield's customers. Both Wells and Butterfield were losing money, but Butterfield had deep pockets and could afford several months of losses. In time, one or the other—no one is entirely sure—suggested a merger, and thus the March 1850 meeting of Wells, Fargo, Butterfield, and others. Eight days into their meeting, the principals agreed to form the "American Express Company" with Wells as president and Fargo as secretary; Butterfield, meanwhile, maintained significant power of the board. By capitalizing on advances in transportation, the mass emigration west, and a commitment to its customers, American Express became an extremely successful enterprise.

Behind the scenes, however, American Express was marked by factionalism among the men who founded it, especially between Butterfield and Fargo. In 1852, Fargo offered a resolution to extend American's operations to California. The gold rush was in full swing, tens of millions of dollars of the precious metal were being mined each year, and the lucrative express business was going to the company's rivals. Despite the fact that the proposal made good business sense, it was defeated—largely through the machinations of the powerful Butterfield—with only Wells and Fargo voting in the affirmative. Days later, on March 18, 1852 (two years to the date from the founding of American Express), Wells and Fargo met with a group of investors, and founded "Wells, Fargo & Co."

Alvin Adams—who, with Harnden, is considered one of the two great pioneers of the express industry—provided the stiffest competition to American Express. Adams was orphaned at an early age and raised by his older brothers. He set out on his own at the age of sixteen and worked for several years assisting a stage and hotel operator in Vermont. Adams then failed twice in the produce business.

In 1840, impressed by the prospects of the express service, he established "Adams & Company" by purchasing two season tickets for the train from New York to Boston and back. On one day, Adams would start from Boston to New York and his partner, Ephraim Farnsworth, rode from New York to Boston; they reversed directions the following day. Within a few years Adams had purchased many of Harnden's routes and expanded his service to other cities in the East and Midwest. He incorporated the "Adams Express Company" in 1854 with $10 million capital and was soon competing on equal terms with American.

Given the Yankee roots of the major express concerns, there was little doubt which side they would take when the war began. Even before hostilities commenced, American Express signaled its allegiance to the Union by aiding beleaguered abolitionists in "Bloody Kansas." In the minutes of a February 12, 1861, board meeting, Fargo noted the receipt of a congratulatory letter from Seth B. Hunt, Chairman *pro tem* of the "New York Relief Committee." There, Hunt wrote, the committee had unanimously agreed to a resolution that "the thanks of the public are due to the American Express and United States Express Companies for their generous aid to the suffering people in Kansas by conveying to them clothing and medicine free of expense."[3]

Adams Express also made a splash in pre-war abolitionist circles when a slave named Henry Brown used the firm to make an inventive escape. Brown was separated from his family as a teenager and brought to Richmond to work in a tobacco factory. An exceptional worker, Brown used the extra money he earned exceeding his daily quotas to pay his wife's master for the time she spent caring for her family. In 1848, the master sold Brown's wife and their children to another slave owner, who in turn sent them to North Carolina.

Enraged and devastated, Brown was determined to escape. He found a willing accomplice in a Richmond shoemaker, who agreed to ship Brown as "dry goods." Brown—at five-foot-eight and two hundred pounds—squeezed into a small wooden crate with a few provisions and three small holes for air. The shoemaker wrote "This Side Up" on the box and addressed it to abolitionist friends in Philadelphia. Adams Express then carried Brown in an adventure that lasted twenty-six hours. He arrived safely in Philadelphia, where abolitionists "unpacked" him. News of his novel escape spread, and the now-styled Henry "Box" Brown became a *cause celebre* among abolitionist circles in New England and overseas.[14]

In California, Wells Fargo was on the periphery of the war; still it showed its Union stripes in a number of ways. Louis McLane, the firm's general agent, conferred regularly with officers in the Union Army's Department of the Pacific as to the best disposition of troops to protect the Overland Mail route. Several times in 1862, in cooperation with General George Wright's authorized suppression of "treasonable publications" in California and Oregon—such as the *Stockton Argus, San Jose Tribune, Albany Enquirer,* and Visalia's colorfully-named *Equal Rights Expositor*—McLane instructed his agents to "comply with the above orders [not to express the named papers] STRICTLY (his emphasis)." Despite the state's distance from the battlefields, Californians contributed a full quarter of the millions of dollars raised in Sanitary Commission fairs, and Wells Fargo expressed, without charge, donations from the interior to San Francisco.[15]

Both the Union and Confederacy exempted certain occupations from military service, including newspapers editors, ministers, physicians, shoemakers, and druggists—as well as others of conveniently presumed importance, such as Congressmen. Though not explicitly listed, both sides excused expressmen from service due to their association with critical railroad, telegraph, and riverboat operations. Nevertheless, in answer to a railroad executive seeking exemptions for his workers, U. S. Secretary of War

Edwin M. Stanton noted that the "Adams Express Company encouraged their employees to enlist in the service."[16]

Daniel Butterfield, son of American Express co-founder John Butterfield and in 1861 superintendent of the company's eastern division, was one of the first at American Express to volunteer. He had been active in the local militia before the war and, despite having little military experience, rose through its ranks to colonel. Butterfield joined the Union Army as a sergeant in Washington, D.C., in April 1861, and within weeks he obtained a commission as a colonel in the 12th New York Militia (later the Twelfth New York Infantry). By summer he commanded a brigade, and by fall he was a brigadier general.

While at the front, Butterfield received a copy of a resolution passed at an August 15, 1861, board meeting in which the directors of American Express expressed their appreciation of his "patriotic and prompt services . . . in behalf of their country" and added, "That his position in this company is open for him, and that should he feel disposed to devote his services 'to the war for the preservation of the Union,' the company will, in consideration of the high appreciation entertained of him by the National Government and the flattering honor confirmed on him, continue his salary during the war, while he is doing service for his country."[17]

Figure 19. Daniel Butterfield
Source: Library of Congress

The company later extended this generous policy to all its employees by keeping them at no less than half their salary if they volunteered for military service; American suspended the policy for conscripts later raised through the draft, but faithfully kept its promise to the employees who volunteered. In a unanimous resolution, American's directors challenged other corporate leaders to match their patriotism, "It behooves all men who are true and loyal to come forward in their individual and corporate capacity to arouse by every effort the dormant energies of the people, awaken them to a sense of the danger that overhangs us and our liberties, and send men at once to the support of the authorities. The influence of the company we represent is wide and extended over the whole country; its example will stimulate others to like patriotism. Our country's necessity will justify us, our large increased earnings will sustain us."[18]

Gestures of patriotism and declarations of fidelity notwithstanding, some citizens accused the express companies of the very opposite, especially Adams Express, which historically had stronger commercial ties to the South. The problems began when Postmaster General Montgomery Blair ordered the cessation of U.S. mail service throughout the South on May 31, 1861. In doing so, he created a heavy business for the express companies, and a ready (and for awhile, legal) means for Confederate sympathizers in northern states to transmit to the South intelligence such as information about troop movements, and materiel, such as tactical and drilling manuals, firearms, and medicine.

Wartime arrest records of "Suspected and Disloyal Persons" include cases of attempted smuggling via express. In October 1861, U.S. marshals in New York arrested John F. Parr on suspicion that he purchased items in New York to transmit to his native Tennessee. Evidence against the man included a trunk seized in Buffalo—sent there by American Express—containing a large amount of quinine intended for Confederate surgeons. During an intense deposition in a separate case, a member of the "Order of American Knights"—a secret association whose members were suspected of disloyal and treasonable actions—admitted that the Order had members purposely placed in express offices.[19]

In a single week in late August 1861, Secretary of State William H. Seward received several complaints from prominent citizens in the North, including a New Yorker who wrote, "It is well known here that Adams Express daily conveys information in every shape to all quarters of the Southern Confederacy." In another letter, a self-described "Union man to the backbone" complained "considering the facility the enemy has for letter transportation [via Adams] it is not to be wondered at that they know our movements so well," and demanded that "something be done to suppress such a dangerous conveyance."[20]

Northern newspapers printed caustic accusations that the express companies carried mail and packages to and from the South. After a Philadelphia paper reported that the Adams Express would be brought to trial for the purported traffic, Adams's General Superintendent in the city wrote a strongly worded rebuttal to the War Department with a demand that it "make someone responsible for statements of this character."[21]

On the authority of E. D. Gazzam, chairman of the "Committee on the Transportation of Contraband Goods," other papers published allegations that American Express had "gone around to various houses which had been shipping this kind of goods by the Adams Express Company . . . and informing those houses that if they would ship their goods by the American Express Company such goods would pass safely by other and more northern routes."[22]

In response, Henry Wells, President, and Alex Holland, Managing Director, of American Express, issued a rebuttal:

> This company has, on the contrary, through its officers and agents, issued orders to all their collectors and receivers of freight to take nothing like arms or munitions of war, or any kind of contraband articles for any point in the seceding States . . . besides which they have stopped on the way and refused to forward many articles which they had only a doubt in their nature . . . The officers of the federal, State, and city governments are fully aware of the course we have pursued from the beginning, and approve of the same, and are constantly employing us in transporting for them."[23]

Critics might have tempered their accusations had they known the risks that expressmen took in performing their services on behalf of the Union. Confederate sympathizers surrounded express offices in Union-held territory in states such as Mississippi and Kentucky, and Rebel cavalry and guerillas fired on trains, made off with packages and money, and took expressmen as prisoners. In April 1862, at the Battle of Shiloh, a cannonball passed through and nearly destroyed the log house the Adams agent used as an office. Charles Woodward, a wartime superintendent for Adams, was captured several times, once by the Rebel cavalryman Nathan Bedford Forrest; in another episode he was pressed into service as an ersatz artillery-man in an emergency defense of the Union-held fort at Helena, Arkansas.

If American and Adams were closer to the "sword," then Wells Fargo was closer to the "purse," and distance from the battlefields did nothing to protect its expressmen or the treasure in its charge. The daily shipments of California gold and Nevada silver—by land and sea—made an inviting target for Rebel sympathizers and guerillas. Capture of the valuable metals put badly needed cash into Confederate hands while damaging the Union's purchasing power and weakening its credit.

Recognizing the threat, Wells Fargo joined more than thirty other banks and merchants and petitioned Secretary of the Navy Gideon Welles for protection in April 1862. The businessmen, acting on information that there were "citizens of Spain and other foreign countries who are . . . in possession of letters of marque, granted by the Confederate states, who are likely to seize upon the California steamers, on the Pacific and Atlantic, having on board large amounts of treasure," petitioned Welles to "detail a Government steamer on the Pacific to act as a convoy."[24]

Their fears were well founded—on December 7, 1862, the *Ariel*, a packet steamer owned by shipping magnate Cornelius Vanderbilt, was rounding Cape Maysi, Cuba, when the Confederate raider CSS *Alabama*, commanded by the intrepid Raphael Semmes, came upon her rapidly. The *Alabama* fired twice, striking the *Ariel's* foremast. Facing a faster ship with superior fire-power, the *Ariel's* captain had no choice but to ransom the ship to Semmes. In doing so, he surrendered more than $15,000 belonging to Wells, Fargo & Co.

Wells Fargo treasure was also at the center of what one historian called "without question the most daring and desperate undertaking by any of California's Secessionist movement." The instigators were the so-called "Captain Ingram's Partisan Rangers," named for Rufus Ingram, an erstwhile member of William Quantrill's band of guerillas. Ingram's band had spent weeks observing the comings-and-goings of Wells Fargo shipments. The targets were two stagecoaches that had left the Virginia City, Nevada, mines with nearly $30,000 in bullion.[25]

On the night of June 30, 1864, the coaches reached a bend in the road at Placerville, California where the "Rangers," masked and armed with pistols and shotguns, were lurking. Ingram jumped in front of the lead coach and demanded the silver bars and gold dust. The driver retorted "Come and get it," at which point two of Ingram's men threw the bags to the ground. Ingram sent the lead coach on its way when he saw the trailing coach come around the bend. Ingram declared, "Gentleman, I will tell you who we are. We are not robbers, but a company of Confederate soldiers . . . All we want is Wells, Fargo and Company's treasures to assist us to recruit the Confederate Army."[26]

As the band of Rebels removed treasure from the second coach, Ingram handed the driver a receipt stating, "This is to certify that I have received from Wells, Fargo, & Co. the sum of $_____ cash [in his haste, Ingram failed to enter his take], for the purpose of outfitting recruits in California for the Confederate States Army."[27]

Lawmen, aided by citizen posses, pursued the robbers and surprised them at a boardinghouse not far from the crime scene where a firefight ensued. A deputy sheriff was killed, another was wounded, and one of the robbers was captured. The pursuit continued, and by early September all of the Rangers had been killed or captured, except for Ingram and another who made it to Missouri. At trial, one of the guerillas testified to the band's motive, "They were robbing our people back home and it was nothing but right to rob the Federal Government, or rob Wells, Fargo, & Co.'s Express. We had a right to retaliate."[28]

"Oh! It makes my mouth water every time I think of what I am likely to get in my box," Sgt. John Hartwell wrote his wife. In doing so, he expressed the sentiment of every Union soldier who missed many of the special things he took for granted while at home. Soldiers eagerly anticipated receiving boxes from home containing warm clothing, shoes, prayer books, quilts, and, especially, good things to eat. Small luxuries they were; still, they eased the monotony of life in camp and gave a much needed boost to morale. Winslow Homer drew overjoyed soldiers reveling in the contents of Adams Express boxes from home for the first *Harper's Weekly* Christmas cover of the war.[29]

Alexander Stimson, himself a wartime expressman, described the scene of excitement when packages were delivered to camp:

[The express agent] would have a proper tent assigned to him by the general in command, with a soldier or two to guard it, and, in this canvas office, deal out his promiscuous stack of boxes, parcels, letters, &c., to the eager-eyed blue-coats. . . . A crowd of them would gather around the door of the tent, across which a board, supported by two barrels, served as a counter, and the scene was not without interest, even to the casual spectator. . . . See one of them asking the agent . . . if he has anything for him; and he gives his name, regiment, and company. Yes, there is something; and his sallow face flushes, his eyes moisten, and with tremulous hand, he signs the receipt-book and essays to lift the little box of goodies and comforts which his dear old mother has sent to her soldier boy.[30]

Both American Express and Adams Express advertised they would ship packages to soldiers at half their regular rates and shipped some items, including Bibles and blankets, free. Still, the rates for a large package sent across the country could be expensive, and some families saved on charges by combining their gifts in boxes intended for other men. This practice annoyed Andrew Chestnut of the 126th New York Infantry, who instructed his loved ones, "When you send my box I don't want you to put in anything that Baker's folks wants to send let them send a box to Eugene they are as able to pay Express as I am they had the impudence to stick in a lot of things in Henry's Barrell."[31]

In addition to forwarding packages from home to the camps, the express companies did a healthy amount of return business by carrying huge sums of money. The more responsible soldiers sent some or all of their monthly pay home, almost always by express. Indeed, regiments took great pride in reporting the amount of money sent home. The chaplain of the Second Iowa Cavalry wrote the *Davenport Daily Gazette* that he "took from New Madrid to Cairo, to express to the families of soldiers, fourteen thousand and six hundred dollars, nearly all from our regiment." Likewise, a New York paper reported that the members of "Jenny's Battery"—then on Morris Island, South Carolina, before Charleston—had "sent home a considerable amount of money, which has been received at the office of the American Express Company, where it may be obtained. . . . One day the past week the packages received by Express here, for distribution in Oswego, Cayuga and Wayne counties, contained over $15,000."[32]

A *Harper's Weekly* artist marveled at the "vast amount of business transacted on board" the "floating" express office moored at a wharf near the Union Army's supply depot at City Point, Virginia on a typical day:

Having to do . . . the banking business of the thousands comprising an army, one may suppose is no ordinary labor; but very few who have not witnessed the *modus operandi* can realize how immensely that labor is increased by the necessary lack of all those technical facilities by which banking establishments are carried on, and which it is impossible to find at the temporary base of an army constantly in motion. It is an average thing, irrespective of the large amount of freight constantly going to and from the office at City Point, for from 50,000 to 75,000 dollars in money to be daily transmitted, in individual packages, from the soldiers to their friends at home; and there are days when the aggregate can not fall short of 150,000 dollars.

He continued, describing the protocol and diligence by which money was sent home, "These packages, after having their contents duly counted and receipted, have to be sealed up with five large impressions of sealing-wax, stamped by the Company's seal, and then read over and tallied—a tedious mechanical labor often reaching far into the night."[33]

On at least one occasion, Adams Express actually provided funds to the United States government to make its payroll. Due to a mistake on the part of paymasters in early July 1862, not enough money was delivered to New Orleans to pay troops stationed there, many of whom had already gone without for six months. General Benjamin F. Butler, military commander in New Orleans, ordered Asa S. Blake, agent of the city's Adams Express office to lend him $25,000 on a personal note. In a letter to William Dinsmore, President of Adams Express, Butler remarked that Blake "strongly resisted me in this matter, not wishing to deviate from . . . the rules of your company," but Butler appealed to the dictum that "necessity knows no laws" to explain his actions.[34]

Added to care packages, pay, battlefield souvenirs, and government treasure, the express companies also handled (probably unwittingly) a number of banned items, especially liquor. A wartime American Express circular warned that in addition to other items prohibited by the Treasury Department and military authorities, agents were "specially enjoined not to receive . . . any package or article of freight which they have reason to believe contains spirituous liquor." Generals and provost marshals ordered express agents to subject every box to strict inspection and confiscate such items, but ingenious subterfuges still worked—peaches in glass jars were awash in liquor instead of syrup; bottles of patent medicines, emptied of their contents, were filled with something more intoxicating; and trunks with false bottoms concealed bottles of wine.[35]

Even authorized shipments of liquor were not always safe. Adams's superintendent Woodward recalled an incident when one of his messengers was to deliver a barrel of whisky to the Union Army military hospital in Jackson, Tennessee. The expressman delivered the barrel at the train station platform and took the railroad agent's receipt. A freight car loaded with soldiers was on the rear of the train that carried the whisky. Woodward remembered, "As the car slowly passed the platform when the train had started, four of the soldiers jumped upon the platform, and, though the train was still in motion, succeeded in pitching the barrel of whisky into the car in the presence of the agent who could not stop them." The agent informed the commanding general, who telegraphed ahead to authorities in Corinth, Mississippi, to arrest every man in the car on arrival. After their capture and arrest the men were sentenced to forfeit two months' pay and reimburse Adams Express for the value of the whisky.[36]

Seemingly innocent clothing sent from home to the camp also proved a bane to maintaining discipline in the Union army. In February 1863, from his camp near Falmouth, Virginia, an adjutant sent a letter to officials of Adams Express stating that packages containing certain attire would not be allowed for soldiers' use. He made exceptions for underclothing, mittens, and "other little items that may be desired," but strictly forbade outer garments, adding that the policy was necessary due to the "pernicious practice of treasonable persons sending citizens' clothing to soldiers here to encourage and facilitate desertion."[37]

Commenting on the flip side of this problem, another wartime expressman wrote of his bemusement at the "habits of rigid economy" of soldiers from Maine who were "exceedingly careful" with their worn clothes, "After a new fit-out was furnished a regiment, the ragged, filthy, and worthless duds were packed in boxes and sent home to their friends from sadly mistaken motives of economy—thousands of these boxes constantly arriving per express to their destination . . . a large proportion of them freight unpaid, at burdensome charges to the almost destitute families . . . from five to twenty-five dollars and upwards, the contents of which were utterly worthless unless as paper stock."[38]

The White House was also the source and destination of express traffic during the war. Important papers, including the orders informing Ulysses S. Grant he had been elevated to the revived rank of lieutenant general, were sent out; others, including a copy of Edward Everett's remarks at the dedication of the cemetery at Gettysburg, were received. Over the course of his presidency, Abraham Lincoln received by express: gifts, such as a boomerang, ebony cane, and carved busts of Generals Winfield Scott and George McClellan; food, including a saddle of English mutton, a barrel of flour, and Mackinaw salmon; and clothing, including hats, suits, and a coat of chain mail. All that most asked for in return was a short note from the president acknowledging the gift. When Mary Frazier did not hear back from Lincoln about the "pr of slippers with the Stars & Stripes & the American Eagle" that she had sent, she concluded that the box had never been sent and blamed the Adams Express agent, whom she deemed "a regular Copperhead."[39]

Certainly in the running for most unusual express items were the live animals sent to Lincoln, including a turkey and several bald eagles, all from admirers and patriotic citizens. After apologizing in a note that his gift had lost a foot when caught in a trap, D. M. Jenks of Johnsburgh, New York, added "But he is yet an Eagle & perhaps no more cripled [sic] than the Nation whose banner he represents. . . . Please accept it as a present from a true Republican friend."[40]

Undoubtedly, the saddest traffic was carrying the bodies of soldiers slain by disease or battle back to their homes, as thousands of families shared Isaac Fisher's saga with variations unique to their own sorrow. While most of the war's dead were buried without ceremony—and often anonymously—on the field where they fell, families who could afford the cost of shipment stood a chance to have their loved ones returned if they could locate the body. A decade after the war's end, an article in *Harper's Monthly* told of this heartbreaking commerce, "One of the most melancholy duties these brave fellows had to execute was the transmission of the bodies of the slaughtered to their relatives and friends. The delivery at the home office often occasioned heart-breaking scenes, as 'somebody's darling,' wrapped in a coarse shroud was presented to the woman who had kissed his handsome face good-bye scarcely six months before."[41]

Still, the grim duty had its moments of gallows humor. Woodward remembered an instance of a young Union officer killed in Tennessee whose wealthy father sent a very fine burial case in which his son's remains were to be returned home. Woodward wrote, "The corpse was placed in the casket, and as the weather was warm and the train did not leave until the next morning, the case was placed on the platform at the depot . . . What was our surprise the next morning to find the corpse lying on the platform and the casket gone!" The casket was never found, and Adams Express had to pay for another.[42]

In 1864, the express companies played a part in securing Abraham Lincoln's re-election. The contest demanded attention to every possible constituency, including the vast Union Army. New York itself had between three and four hundred thousand soldiers scattered all over the South, and the state legislature set up the legal machinery to allow them to vote in the field. The law made it the duty of New York's secretary of state, Chauncey Depew, to provide ballots to every unit, gather the votes, and transmit them to the hometown of each soldier.

First, Depew needed to find where the New York troops were, so he traveled to Washington to ask Secretary of War Edwin M. Stanton to give him the information. Depew later wrote that he "took [his] weary way every day to the War Department, but could get no results. The interviews were brief and disagreeable and the secretary of war very brusque."[43]

Time was getting short, and Depew insisted that he must have the information at once, but Stanton angrily refused. Depew told Illinois Congressman Elihu Washburne, a good friend of Lincoln, of his difficulties, and Washburne acted on the beleaguered Depew's behalf to get the information ("You don't know [Lincoln]," Washburne told Depew, "While he is a great statesman, he is also the keenest of politicians alive. If it could be done in no other way, the president would take a carpetbag and go around and collect those votes himself.").[44]

"I left Washington that night with a list and location of every organization of New York troops," Depew remembered. "When I reached New York I summoned the officers of the express companies of that day to know if they could get the packages containing the blanks for the soldiers' vote to the various regiments and companies and batteries . . . Without consultation, they said it could not be done."[45]

Depew then sent for American Express co-founder John Butterfield, now retired. Butterfield "was intensely patriotic and ashamed of the lack of enterprise shown by the express companies," Depew recalled. "He said to me, 'If they cannot do this work they ought to retire.'" Butterfield "then undertook to arrange through the various express companies, by his own direct superintendence, to secure the safe delivery in time to every company."[46]

In the end, Lincoln won with 212 electoral votes to McClellan's twenty-one. Lincoln carried the Empire State, and while New York Democrats pointed fingers at voting irregularities to explain their loss at the polls, Depew attributed the victory to Butterfield's express efforts, concluding it was "a gigantic task . . . successfully executed by [a] patriotic old gentleman."[47]

The American Express directors' prediction of increased earnings during the war was fulfilled as the express industry reaped huge profits. In 1862, American maintained nearly 900 offices and ran freight over nearly 10,000 miles of railway. The American directors voted themselves a $5,000 bonus each in consideration of their extra load of wartime duties, raised their salaries, and paid out millions of dollars in dividends to shareholders.

Wells Fargo paid out dividends at rates of twelve to more than twenty percent, and Adams Express stock rose as high as five hundred dollars per share, from a par value of one hundred dollars. Many principal shareholders of the express companies also owned shares in other expresses and in railroads and shared in their huge wartime returns as well.

To be sure, the express companies made money, and they—and the railroads on whose rails the freight traveled— were roundly criticized during and after the war for profiteering. But if the Civil War proved a boon to the express business, World War I spelled its doom; in 1918, the express companies were nationalized into the Railway Express Agency to meet the national emergency. Indeed, even before the "Great War," the profitability of the companies was dealt a serious blow when Congress enacted the "Parcel Post Law" in 1913, enabling the postal service to carry packages up to eleven pounds (and then more) as ordinary mail.

In 1914, H. F. Millard, an American Express travel agent in Springfield, Massachusetts, wrote a poignant letter to the manager of American's Boston office, expressing his disappointment in the government's action. After recounting the contributions American Express had made during the Civil War (he had been reading Depew's memoir that very afternoon), Millard lamented, "And now the same country that the express companies served so well is trying to drive them out of business."[48]

Despite the charges of profiteering, the express companies did sow a healthy amount of public goodwill by providing an efficient and secure means of communication between the soldier and the home front. Thousands of families, including the Fishers, must have especially appreciated the ability to return the remains of their loved ones home. Still, the comfort of having their son's body back could not assuage all their sorrow, as witnessed by the closing lines in Isaac Fisher's letter to his wife:

> My heart sinks as I contemplate this sad information. We have made the most costly sacrifice that we could possibly offer on the altar of our country, and if it is not sufficient we must perish. How my heart bleeds as I call up past reminisces of our poor boy. I well remember the first sound I ever heard issue from his mouth, poor little innocent babe. If I have ever done wrong by him in any thing I trust I may be forgiven.[49]

Notes

Introduction

1. *Cincinnati Gazette*, September 17, 1861, p.1.
2. Ibid.
3. "The Civil War: Its Impact on a Border Community," n.p.
4. Wilson, pp. 127-28.
5. "Border Community," n.p.
6. Ibid.
7. Ibid.
8. "men of fair repute" in Wilson, p. 149; "been given out at . . . " in "Border Community," n.p.
9. Schisgall, p. 18.
10. "all business must be . . . " in *Cincinnati Gazette*, September 2, 1862, p. 1; "was the only factory allowed . . . " in "Border Community," n.p; Terry notes (p. 107) that while P & G certainly received an exemption, it could not have been the only business allowed to remain open.
11. "Border Community," n.p.

Chapter One

1. Ware, p. 5.
2. Ibid, p.64.
3. Ibid, p.66.
4. Ibid, pp. 70-71.
5. Ibid, p.79.
6. Ibid, p. 80.
7. "Regarding the First Iowa . . . " in Ware, p. 155-56; "[They] were a mixture . . . " in Lindberg, p. 12.
8. *Dubuque Herald*, June 26, 1861, p. 2.
9. "resembled a rabble more than . . . " in Lindberg, p. 17; "tinfoil shoulder straps . . . ." and "Jackson's white plug at . . . " in Lindberg, p. 15.
10. Piston and Hatcher, p. 255.
11. Ware, p. 340.
12. "No troops hereafter furnished . . . " in *Official Records of the Union and*

Confederate Armies in the War of the Rebellion (hereafter, OR) Series 3, Vol. I, p. 531; "still in the gray uniform . . . " in OR, Series 1, Vol. X, Part I, p. 84.

13. "could never find . . . " in Wiley, pp. 59-60; "uniformed in dark roundabout . . . " in Wilkie, p. 34.

14. "He looked like a . . . " in *Arms and Equipment*, p. 99; "I have been promoted . . . " in letter, G.K. Warren to Richardson, Spence, & Thomson, 10 August 1863, Dennis Buttacavoli Collection.

15. "I enclose herewith a draft . . . " in letter, Jno. Pope to Richardson, Spence, & Thomson, 30 June 1863, Dennis Buttacavoli Collection.

16. Cooke, p. 20.

17. Ibid, p. 16.

18. "Commencing in a moderate way . . . " in Ibid, p. 23; see entries for the Brookses in Beach, p. 14.

19. Ware, pp. 26-27.

20. Joselit, p. 9.

21. Cooke, pp. 23, 26.

22. "60 French Imported . . . " in Coates, p. 50; "That we telegraph to . . . " in entry, 19 April 1861, Orderly Book, Company C, Second Regiment, Connecticut Militia, Connecticut Historical Society.

23. *New York Times*, September 5, 1861, pp. 2-3.

24. "stripes of gray ran . . . " in McAfee, "The New York State Jacket, 1861," *Military Images*, March/April 2000, http://findarticles.com/p/articles/mi_qa3905/is_200003/ai_n887166; "coarse, fluffy, flimsy . . . " in *Arms & Equipment*, p. 89.

25. *New York Times*, September 5, 1861, p. 2.

26. *Janesville Daily Gazette*, September 7, 1861, p. 3.

27. "any knowledge of any . . . " in *New York Times*, September 5, 1861, p. 2.

28. Ibid

29. Ibid.

30. *Scientific American*, 22 September 1860, p. 195.

31. "and patronize those that . . . " in Ibid; "no less impressed by . . . " in Zakim, pp. 101-102.

32. Dubuque *Democratic Herald*, 7 March 1865, p.1.

33. "make or buy": for an excellent discussion of the evolution of the "mixed military economy" in the Civil War, see Wilson, pp. 73-106.

34. Ibid, p. 72.

35. Ibid, pp. 93-94.

36. *New York Times*, 11 November 1861, p. 2.

37. Ibid.
38. "From the first of the . . . " in *Harper's Weekly*, August 1, 1863, p. 494; "Brook's clothing store was . . . " in *Brooks Brothers Centenary*, p. 24.
39. Barnes, p. 33.
40. Ibid., p. 33.
41. "Hailed with terror by most . . . " in Ibid, pp. 33-34; "Upwards of a hundred shots . . . " in Ibid, p. 37; "had he been but . . . " in Ibid, p. 34; "was fired at by a man . . . " in Ibid, p. 40.
42. *Brooks Brothers Centenary*, p. 25.
43. Cooke, p. 25.
44. McFeely, p. 233.
45. *New York Times*, June 8, 1865, p.1.
46. McFeely, p. 233.
47. Shanks, p. 646.
48. Kennett, p. 99.
49. "He may have been honest . . . " in Roberts, p. 21; "awkward and ungainly . . . " in Richards, p. 82.
50. Guelzo, p. 165.
51. Tarbell, p. 169.
52. For details on Lincoln's coat, see "Fact Sheet: Lincoln's Great Coat Tale," Brooks Brothers, n.d.
53. Brandes, pp. 71-72.
54. Ackerman, p. 107.
55. For brief notes on the historiography of the exaggerated claims against the Brooks Brothers uniforms, especially that they disintegrated in the rain, see Brandes, p. 307, n. 18; for a listing of the leading clothing suppliers to the Union armies, see Wilson, p. 235; for the uniform challenges faced by quartermasters in the years between the World Wars, see Kirsner, H., "Uniformity for Uniforms," *The Quartermaster Review*, July-August 1931, http://www.qmfound.com/uniformity.htm.
56. McMurtry, p. 3.
57. *New York Times*, January 3, 1968, p. 42.
58. Ware, p. 345.
59. Ibid, p. 346.
60. Ibid, p. 347.
61. Ibid, p. 353.

Chapter Two

1. Letter, Charles Ramsay to his wife, Kate, October 3, 1861, http://www.soldier-studies.org/index.php?action=view_letter&Letter=321.

2. Letter, Kate Ramsay to Charles, October 19, 1861, Author's collection.

3. Letter, Charles Ramsay to Kate, October 19, 1861, http://www.soldierstudies.org/index.php?action=view_letter&Letter=325.

4. Letter, Kate Ramsay to Charles, October 20, 1861, Author's collection.

5. Letter, Charles Ramsay to Kate, October 24, 1861, Nate D. Sanders Collection.

6. Letter, Kate Ramsay to Charles, November 9, 1861, Author's collection.

7. Letter, Charles Ramsay to Kate, November 11, 1861, Author's collection.

8. Letter, Kate Ramsay to Charles, Kate, November 16, 1861, http://www.soldier-studies.org/index.php?action=view_letter&Letter=421.

9. Letter, Charles Ramsay to Kate, November 19, 1861, http://www.soldierstudies.org/index.php?action=view_letter&Letter=423.

10. Davis, p. 10.

11. "I will not move my army . . ." in Nonnecke, p. 294; "I have been up to see . . ." in Yates, vol. 1, p. 325; Freeman, p. 538; "An army is a big . . . " in Fiske, p. 289.

12. "No government ever . . . " in Davis, p. ix; for a detailed comparison of the Union ration versus the other standing armies of the era, see Horsford, p. 6; "Some days we live . . . " in Wiley, p. 225.

13. "Have been making money . . . " in *Scientific American*, November 9, 1861, p. 297; "the process of cooking . . . " in Davis, p. 1; "culinary hints for the . . . " in Davis, p.9; "I am thinking seriously . . . " in Davis, p. 29.

14. Davis, p. 26.

15. "good and wholesome provisions . . . " in Callan, p. 67; "unmitigated curse" in Lord, p. 41.

16. See Wooster, p. 236; Wooster also declared meatpacker Philip Danforth Armour among his Top 100" (p. 238).

17. Frantz, p. 221.

18. *Scientific American*, March 23, 1850, p. 213.

19. "I am greatly encouraged . . . " in Frantz, p. 217; "so full of the milk . . . " in Burleson, p. 729.

20. Hassall, p. 440.

21. Ibid, pp. 440-41.

22. Ibid, p. 441.

23. Frantz, p. 211.

24. "unpalatable" in Ibid, p. 211; "It may answer . . . " in Olmsted, p. 81.

25. "Villainous" and "a plot" in Frantz, p. 212; "how much I would . . . " in Frantz, p. 217.

26. "We do not meet half . . . " in Frantz, p. 260; "all manner of patent compounds . . . " in Sherman, Vol. 2, p. 391.

27. *Scientific American*, October 29, 1864, pp. 281-82; for another wartime exposition on Borden's factory, see also *Scientific American*, January 21, 1865, p. 53.

28. "Borden's condensed milk . . . " in Tyler, p. 132; "Only a recruit with . . . " in Billings, p. 118; "pass through the casemates . . . " in Palmer, pp. 42-43.

29. "in extensive use . . . " in Hammond, p. 508; "I took a can of . . . " in Holland, p. 397; "Oh! That precious . . . " in Wormeley, p. 107.

30. "Peaches and cream in . . . " in Douglas, p. 23; "I well remember . . . " in Howard, p. 307; "[We] shared our food . . . " in Flood, p. 18.

31. Frantz, p. 258.

32. Ibid, pp. 256-57.

33. Ibid, p. 257.

34. Ibid, p. 258.

35. Homans, p. 129.

36. Frantz, p. 262.

37. "I have known the skirmish line . . . " in Sherman, Vol. 2, p. 392; "Dress appropriately and devote . . . " in Homans, p. 128.

38. "Borden's meat biscuit may . . . " in *Report of Committee*, p. 17; "Mr. Borden's long-continued labors . . . " in Horsford, p.26; "was going to make . . . " in Janesville *Weekly Gazette*, September 9, 1864, p. 7.

39. Frantz, pp. 274-75.

40. Ibid, p. 276.

41. Letter, Kate Ramsay to Charles, December 5, 1861, http://www.soldierstudies.org/index.php?action=view_letter&Letter=451.

42. Letter, Charles Ramsay to Kate, December 14, http://www.soldierstudies.org/index.php?action=view_letter&Letter=457.

Chapter Three

1. From a list of the various state companies called to Madison to form the Second, Third, and Fourth Regiments of "Wisconsin Active Militia," by proclamation of Governor Randall, in *Wisconsin Daily State Journal* (Madison), May 16, 1861, p. 2.

2. Descriptions of company presentation flags in Madaus and Zetlin, pp. 7-8.
3. Nolan, p. 5.
4. Ibid, p 6.
5. Description of regimental color in Madaus and Zeitlin, p. 12.
6. Ibid, p. 3.
7. Quiner, p. 454.
8. "shorthand of history . . . " in Fox-Davies, p. ix; "desire to be bedecked . . . " in Du Bois, A., "Heraldry, Flag and Insignia Work of the Office of The Quartermaster General," *The Quartermaster Review*, May-June 1928, http://www.qmfound. com/heraldry1928.htm; Today, the United States Army's Institute of Heraldry is responsible for the design, development, standardization, quality control, and other services relating to official symbolic items: seals, decorations, medals, insignia, badges, flags, and other items authorized for official wear or display by government personnel and agencies, see http://www.tioh.hqda. pentagon.mil.
9. August 17, 1782, General Orders, George Washington Papers, Library of Congress
10. Callan, p. 540.
11. Heydt, p. 13.
12. Purtell, p. 24.
13. *Harper's Weekly*, December 14, 1861, p. 799.
14. For a detailed description of "Rockwell's Combination Union Army Camp Chest," see "Campaign Luxuries," *Scientific American*, November 2, 1861, p. 280; "Business in the diamond department . . . " in Purtell, p. 36.
15. Purtell, p. 38.
16. "Officers studying the . . . " in *Army and Navy Journal*; December 24, 1864, p. 288; "[we] have in store . . . " in *Harper's Weekly*, December 28, 1861, p. 831.
17. *Scientific American*, October 3, 1863, p. 210-211.
18. Ibid, pp. 210-211.
19. For a list of Tiffany-crafted wartime testimonials, see Heydt, pp. 36-37; "Books were opened . . . " in *Scientific American*, May 7, 1864, p. 296.
20. Purtell, p. 40.
21. *Scientific American*, May 7, 1864, p. 296.
22. *Harper's Weekly*, July 4, 1863, p. 430.
23. *Harper's Weekly*, November 28, 1863, p. 764.
24. Purtell, p. 37.
25. *Harper's Weekly*, October 24, 1863, p. 674.

26. OR, Series 1, Vol. 27, Part I, p. 281.

27. Curtis, p. 40.

28. OR, Series 1, Vol. 27, Part I, p. 268.

29. Dawes, pp. 194-195.

30. *History of the North-Western Soldiers' Fair*, p. 29.

31. Curtis, pp. 203-204.

32. Dawes, pp. 205-206.

33. Sherman, Vol. 2, p. 363.

34. OR, Series I. Vol. 33, p. 837.

35. Beckendorf, p. 26.

36. Lyman, p. 320.

37. "Ohio Veteran Volunteer Medals," http://www.48ovvi.org/oh48medals.html; for a list of other Tiffany-crafted medals, see Heydt, pp. 36-37.

38. Beckendorf, p. 23.

39. Wittenberg, p. 125.

40. Purtell, p. 40.

41. *Morning Oregonian*, April 2, 1873, p. 4; for an announcement of the exhibition at Tiffany's, see *New York Times*, April 1, 1873, p. 8.

42. Purtell, p. 207.

43. Madaus and Zeitlin, pp. 62-63.

44. Ibid, p. 78.

45. Ibid, p. 107.

Chapter Four

1. "Buoying Vessels Over Shoals," Letters Patent #6469, issued to Abraham Lincoln, Springfield, Illinois, May 22, 1849, United States Patent and Trademark Office.

2. Sandburg, p.108.

3. Herndon, p. 239.

4. "Continual thinking . . . " in Ibid; "I am never . . . " in Sandburg, p.472.

5. Herndon, p.240.

6. Foster, p.1.

7. Ibid, p. 1.

8. "It affords me . . . " in Letter, Zenas C. Robbins to Abraham Lincoln, April 13, 1849, Abraham Lincoln Papers, Library of Congress (hereafter Lincoln Papers); "to A. Lincoln . . . " in *Scientific American*, June 2, 1849, p. 294.

9. "a streak . . . " in Bruce, p.10; "an inventive faculty . . . " in Biographical Notes, James Q. Howard, May 1860, Lincoln Papers.

10. *Scientific American*, August 3, 1861, p. 75.

11. Lipman, p. 8.

12. *Scientific American*, August 28, 1845, p. 2.

13. Forsyth, p. 153.

14. *Scientific American*, August 28, 1845, p. 2.

15. *Scientific American*, April 3, 1861, p.223.

16. "Our Secession Troubles" in Ibid; "it would interest . . . " and "The merits of . . . " in *Scientific American*, December 1, 1860, p. 356.

17. *Scientific American*, April 3, 1861, p.233.

18. Ibid.

19. Ibid; The editors (and the angry Northern correspondent) were almost certainly referring to an engraving in the May 8, 1858 issue of the *Scientific American* (p. 280), which featured an engraving and description of "Hosford & Avery's Cotton Picker." In commenting on the magazine's "Secession Troubles," a senior researcher at *Scientific American* wrote me "You'll be glad to know that that some of our readers are as irate today as they were then." (e-mail, Daniel C. Schlenoff to James Schmidt, February 22, 2006).

20. *Scientific American*, August 17, 1861, p. 105.

21. Ibid.

22. Ibid.

23. F. L. Mott, p. 6.

24. "We lost . . . ." in *Biblical Repertory and Princeton Review*, October 1865, p. 657, as quoted in F. L. Mott, p. 6; circulation numbers from entries in unpublished diary of O.D. Munn, September 24, 1862 and February 26, 1863, as quoted in Borut, p. 216.

25. *Scientific American*, November 22, 1862, p.329.

26. *Scientific American*, May 11, 1861, p.297.

27. Borut, p. 72.

28. *Scientific American*, June 1, 1861, p. 338.

29. "Learning to Shoot" in *Scientific American*, May 11, 1861, p. 298; "Careful Loading . . . " in Ibid; "Purifying Water . . . " in Ibid, p. 297; "The *Scientific American's* Advice . . . " in *Scientific American*, July 20, 1861, p. 42.

30. *Scientific American*, May 25, 1861, p. 327.

31. *Scientific American*, June 15, 1861, p. 371.

32. "Spectacles which would . . . " in *Scientific American*, July 6, 1861, p. 14; "Your

shell filled . . . " in *Scientific American*, May 24, 1862, p. 334; "An arrangement of . . . " in *Scientific American*, September 21, 1861, p. 190; "The attachment to . . . " in *Scientific American*, September 7, 1861, p. 158; "Your submarine-gun port . . . " in *Scientific American*, June 14, 1862, p. 382; "The attachment of . . . " in *Scientific American*, June 15, 1861, p. 382.

33. *Official Records of the Union and Confederate Navies in the War of the Rebellion* (hereafter ORN) Series I, Vol. 7, p. 754; Mallory was almost certainly referring to the March 22, 1862 issue of *Scientific American*, pp. 177-178, which featured a handsome engraving of the USS Monitor as well as a long article. The editors noted: "we . . . intended to give sectional views which would fully illustrate the peculiarities of her construction, but the government does not deem it advisable to have such views published at present, and it is hardly necessary for us to say that we comply with the suggestion with the most hearty acquiescence."

34. ORN, Series I, Vol. 21, p. 331.

35. OR, Series I, Vol. 28, Part II, p. 501.

36. Ibid.

37. *Scientific American*, July 19, 1863, p. 41.

38. Bruce, p. 27.

39. OR, Series III, Vol. 1, p. 264.

40. *Scientific American*, September 19, 1863, p. 178.

41. "fog of mutual . . . " in Bruce, p. 71; "our inventors have . . . " in *Scientific American*, February 28, 1863, pp. 137-138; "We do not think . . . " in *Scientific American*, January 17, 1863, p.42.

42. *Scientific American*, September 19, 1863, p. 178.

43. *Scientific American*, May 6, 1865, p. 287.

44. "a method that . . . " in *Scientific American*, November 19, 1864, pp. 330-331; "the present state of . . . " in *Scientific American*, May 6, 1865, p. 287.

45. *Scientific American*, May 6, 1865, p. 287.

46. *Scientific American*, January 28, 1865, p. 68.

47. *Scientific American*, April 15, 1865, p. 247.

48. "Our Calamity" in *Scientific American*, April 22, 1865, p. 263; "a model of . . . " in *Scientific American*, May 27, 1865, p. 340.

Chapter Five

1. Hunt, pp. 452-53.

2. Ibid, p. 453.

3. Alexander, p. 245.

4. Sears, p. 394.
5. "Let the batteries . . . " in OR, Series 1, Vol. 51, Pt. II, p. 733; "We were not . . . " in Hess, p. 127; "indescribably grand" in Hunt, p. 453.
6. "Simply to make . . . " in Alexander, p. 245; "as if the heavens . . . " in Trudeau, p. 464; "producing such a . . . " in Sears, p. 396.
7. "made the ground . . . " in Trudeau, p. 464; "like gusts of wind," Trudeau, p. 466.
8. "The atmosphere was . . . " in Trudeau, p. 464-65; "Turn your eyes . . . " in Sears, p. 396; "lazy air was . . . " in Hess, p. 128.
9. Kelly, p. 212.
10. Ibid, p. ix.
11. Brown, p. 4.
12. Hancock and Wilkinson, "Manufacturer in Wartime," p. 219
13. "Coal cannot be mined . . . " in J.W. Donohue & Co., Cincinnati, to Messrs. E. I. du Pont & Co. (hereafter du Pont), March 18, 1863, Hagley Museum and Library (hereafter HML), Accession 500, Series 1, Box 52.
14. *New York Times*, August 10, 1861, p. 3.
15. The convention for spelling the family name is "du Pont" when quoting an individual's full name but "Du Pont" when speaking of the family as a whole (and for some individuals, most notably Civil War naval hero Samuel Francis Du Pont). The name of the chemical company founded by the family is properly spelled DuPont. For simplicity, the author has chosen to use "du Pont" throughout.
16. *Scientific American*, July 20, 1850, p. 347.
17. Wilkinson, *Lammot*, p. 70.
18. Ibid, p. 72.
19. McNinch, p. 6.
20. "as soon as it . . . " and "No Yankee Powder" in Philip Rotchford, New Orleans, to du Pont, February 12, 1861, HML, Accession 500, Series 1, Box 314.
21. "gentleman of this city . . . " in OR, Series 4, Vol. I, pp. 188-189; "seized all your powder . . . " in Anthony Casenove, Alexandria, VA, to Du Pont, April 20, 1861, HML, Accession 500, Series 1, Box 58.
22. du Pont, pp. 86-87.
23. Wilkinson, "Operation Sabotage," p. 6.
24. OR, Series 1, Vol. LI, Part II, p. 46.
25. OR, Series 1, Vol. LI, Part I, pp. 328-329.
26. OR, Ser 3, Vol. I, pp. 765-766.

27. Wilkinson, *Lammot*, p75.

28. Ibid, p. 75.

29. Parker, p. 29.

30. "Large pieces of timber . . . " in the *Adams Sentinel*, August 2, 1864, p. 4; "distinctly heard the . . . " in Burlington *Weekly Hawk Eye*, March 14, 1863, p. 4; an exceptionally detailed report of a wartime powder works explosion at the Hazard Powder Company (a chief competitor to du Pont) can be found in the *Berkshire County Eagle*, July 31, 1862, p.3.

31. Hancock and Wilkinson, "Manufacturer in Wartime," p. 223.

32. Hancock and Wilkinson, "Devil to Pay," p. 20.

33. Ibid, p. 22.

34. Ibid, p. 22.

35. Ibid, p. 26.

36. Ibid, p. 24.

37. "Lammot is killing himself . . . " in Wilkinson, *Lammot*, p. 87; "They have night work . . . " in Sallie du Pont to Henry A. du Pont, April 20, 1862, HML, Group 8, Series B, Box 11.

38. "Lammot, it seems, has been . . . " in Mrs. S. F. du Pont to S. F. du Pont, August 16, 1862, HML, Winterthur Manuscripts, 9/D/106.

39. Parker, p. 17.

40. "the fort to look after . . . " in Wilkinson, *Lammot*, p. 97; "42 days delirious with . . . " in Wilkinson, *Lammot*, p. 104.

41. OR, Series 1, Vol. XIX, Part 2, p. 307.

42. Ibid, p. 307.

43. Wilkinson, *Lammot*, p. 91.

44. "Such a night . . . " and all others in Joanna (Smith) du Pont to daughter Fanny Coleman, April 10, 1865, HML, Accession 178, Box 1.

45. "were besides themselves . . . " and "had flags and . . . " in Louisa du Pont to Henry A. du Pont, April 16, 1865, HML, Winterthur Manuscripts, 7/B/Box 15; "get into the . . . " and "two of them have . . . " in Wilkinson, *Lammot*, p. 123.

46. "intended by the . . . " and fearful blow at . . . " in Ibid, p. 123; "all feel deeply . . . " and remaining in Louisa du Pont to Henry A. du Pont, April 16, 1865, HML, Winterthur Manuscripts, 7/B/Box 15.

47. "do not only know . . . " in Wilkinson, *Lammot*, p. 118; "in the name of the . . . " in OR, Series 3, Vol. III, pp. 1074-1075.

48. Hancock and Wilkinson, "Manufacturer in Wartime," pp. 235-36.

49. Parker, p. 35.

50. Parker, p. 36.

Chapter Six

1. Churchill, p. 150.
2. Ibid, p. 150.
3. Ibid, pp. 150-151.
4. Ibid, p. 154-155.
5. Ibid, p. 159.
6. Ibid, p. 160.
7. Ibid, p. 160.
8. Ibid, pp. 161- 162.
9. Ibid, p. 164.
10. Ibid, p. 168.
11. Squibb, *Journal*, p. 1.
12. *Brooklyn Eagle*, December 30, 1858, p.3.
13. Squibb, *Papers*, pp. 173-174.
14. Blochman, p. 126.
15. Smith, *Medicines*, p. 38.
16. Blochman, p. 132.
17. Ibid, p. 133.
18. "Circular," February 1, 1863, Bristol-Myers Squibb Corporate Archives.
19. Hamilton, p. 109.
20. Blochman, p. 136.
21. Ibid, p. 136.
22. Stearns, p. 309.
23. Wickware, p. 12.
24. Blochman, p. 43.
25. Squibb, *Papers*, p. 304.
26. "as yet without . . . " in Squibb, *Papers*, p. 110; "I have been in . . . " in V. Mott, p. 15.
27. Albin, p. 112.
28. Stevens and Murphy, p. 560.
29. "they commonly overstand . . . " in Squibb, *Papers*, p. 308; "downward tendency . . ." in Squibb, *Papers*, p. 302.
30. Smith, *Medicines*, p. 37.
31. Ibid, p. 37.

32. "Othello's occupation is . . . " in Smith, *Medicines*, p. 34; "The Surgeon General has . . . " in Blochman, pp. 136-37.
33. Smith, *Medicines*, pp. 41-42.
34. Smith, "Squibb Laboratory," p. 383.
35. Ibid., p. 391.
36. "terse, impersonal, and . . . " in Blochman, p. 137; "I suppose Dr. White . . . " in Blochman, p. 142.
37. Ibid, p. 138.
38. Ibid, pp. 138-39.
39. Ibid, p. 139-40.
40. "The United States Army Laboratory . . . " in *New York Times*, February 15, 1865, p. 8; "guard of five additional . . . " in Smith, *Medicines*, p. 60.
41. *New York Times*, February 15, 1862, p.8.
42. Blochman, p. 173.
43. Procter, p. 75.
44. Ibid, p. 351.

Chapter Seven

1. A remarkable collection relating to William J. Fisher, including correspondence and artifacts, was purchased by the Friends of the National Parks at Gettysburg (FNPG) in 2001 and donated to the Gettysburg National Military Park (GNMP); "really excellent" in Shoaf, p. 56; "fine soldierly qualities . . . " in letter, Terrance McCabe to Isaac Fisher, September 25, 1863, GNMP; "there was not one man . . . " in letter, John H. Buchan to Isaac Fisher, September 8, 1863, GNMP.
2. "behaved with a coolness . . . " in letter, Terrance McCabe to Isaac Fisher, September 25, 1863, GNMP; "as cool in the battle . . . " in letter, John H. Buchan to Isaac Fisher, September 8, 1863, GNMP.
3. *New York Times*, July 9, 1863.
4. Letter, Isaac Fisher to Sarah Fisher, July 13, 1863, GNMP.
5. Among the pieces of memorabilia in the Fisher collection is the original headboard that Isaac Fisher found on the battlefield; "L. T. Fisher . . . " as seen on photograph of headboard provided by GNMP.
6. Also among the pieces in the Fisher collection is the original Adams Express receipt for shipping William's body back to Delaware and the "toe tag" that was placed in his coffin; "one corpse" as seen on photograph of express receipt provided by GNMP.

7. Fradkin, p. 1.

8. Ibid, p. 4.

9. Randolph, p. 321. To be fair, Jefferson's critique—while oft-quoted—was specific to his skepticism of public works projects. While he also complained of his letters being opened, the post office did continue to expand in his administrations.

10. For criticism of operations of the United States Postal Service in the early and mid-nineteenth century see Olds, K. B., "The Challenge to the U.S. Postal Monopoly," The *Cato Journal Magazine*, Spring/Summer 1995, Vol. 15, No. 1, pp. 1-24. Still, Olds's essay has been criticized by some historians for lacking depth in research, or for being highly polemical. See the "Essay on Sources" for other works on the history of the postal system.

11. Harlow, p. 17. As to a "nominal fee," some historians arrgue that it depends on one's definition of "nominal." To be sure, the expresses underbid the Post Office in delivering letters, but charged higher rates for large parcels.

12. Ibid, p. 31.

13. Board of Director Meeting Minutes, February 14, 1861, American Express Corporate Archives (hereafter AECA).

14. For details on Brown's escape via Adams Express see Stearns, C., *Narrative of Henry Box Brown* (Boston: Brown and Stearns, 1849).

15. For examples of McLane's correspondence with the Union's Department of the Pacific, see OR, Series 1, Volume L, Part I, pp. 620, 730-31, 766, and 954; "Comply with the orders . . . " in circulars to agents, from Louis McClane, Wells, Fargo, & Co., September 16 and October 4, 1862, Wells Fargo Historical Services (WFHS).

16. OR, Series 3, Vol. 2, p. 310.

17. Butterfield, p. 46.

18. Massengill, p. 26.

19. For the case of John H. Parr, see OR, Series 2, Vol. II, p. 1023; also see mention of express companies in the deposition of Green B. Smith of the "Order of American Knights," in OR, Ser. 2, Vol. VII, p.648.

20. "It is well known here . . . " in OR Ser. 2, Vol. II, p. 579; "Considering the facility . . . " in OR, Ser. 2, Vol. II, p. 44.

21. OR Ser. 2, Vol. II, p. 87.

22. Stimson, p. 115.

23. Ibid, pp. 115-16.

24. ORN, Series 1, Vol. I, pp. 10-11.

25. Boessenecker, p. 133; Robert Chandler, Senior Research Historian, Wells Fargo Historical Services, San Francisco, CA, has concluded that the raid's daring was matched in its foolhardiness because the gang robbed the "down" coach—carrying heavy silver bars—rather than the "up" stage to Virginia City carrying cash in gold coin (letter from Chandler to author, 24 April 2007).

26. Ibid, p. 142.

27. Ibid, p. 144.

28. Fradkin, p. 74.

29. Britton and Reed, p. 177.

30. Stimson, p. 149.

31. Tobey, p. 3.

32. "Took from New Madrid to Cairo . . . "in Jennings, Norma, "Articles from the Davenport *Daily Gazette*, May 1-6, 1862," http://iagenweb.org/civilwar/other/gazette/gazette-1862-5a.htm (accessed by author on 23 April 2007); "had sent home a considerable . . . " in New York State Division of Military and Naval Affairs: Military History, "New York's 1st Artillery Regiment (Light) Civil War Newspaper Clippings," http://www.dmna.state.ny.us/historic/reghist/civil/arti llery/1stArtLt/1stArtLtAllCWN.htm (accessed by author on 23 April 2007)

33. *Harper's Weekly*, November 5, 1864, pp. 709-710.

34. "strongly resisted me . . . " in OR, Ser. 1, Vol. XV, p. 514; see also Butler's letter to Scott in OR, Ser. 1, Vol. LI, Part I, pp. 446-47.

35. Circular to Agents, February 6, 1863, AECA.

36. Woodward, p. 139.

37. OR, Ser. 1, Vol. 25, Part II, p. 73.

38. Tucker, p. 69.

39. Mary A. Frazier to Abraham Lincoln, March 4, 1864, Abraham Lincoln Papers.

40. D. M. Jenks to Abraham Lincoln, June 10, 1862, Abraham Lincoln Papers.

41. Rideing, p. 319.

42. "The corpse was placed . . . " in Woodward, p. 138.

43. Depew, p. 54.

44. Ibid, p. 55.

45. Rice, p. 431.

46. Ibid, p. 431.

47. Depew, p. 53.

48. Letter, H.F. Millard to C. W. Robie, December 13, 1914, AECA.

49. Letter, Isaac Fisher to Sarah Fisher, July 13, 1863, GNMP.

Sources

FOR MANY READERS, this book will be the first word on the role of well-known companies and brands in the Civil War; this author sincerely hopes it will not be the last. To that end, I have provided the following essay on sources used for this book, which I hope will inspire new lines of inquiry and scholarship.

Introduction

Procter & Gamble is the subject of a number of histories, each of which gives some attention to the firm's role in the Civil War. They include Alfred Lief's *It Floats: The Story of Procter & Gamble* (New York: Reinhart, 1958) and Oscar Schisgall's *Eyes on Tomorrow: The Evolution of Procter & Gamble* (Chicago: J.B. Ferguson, 1981). The most recent study is Davis Dyer, et al, *Rising Tide: Lessons from 165 Years of Brand Building at Procter & Gamble* (Boston: Harvard Business School Press, 2004) which stands as the only well-annotated history of P & G.

Another volume, *Into a Second Century with Procter & Gamble* (Cincinnati: privately printed, 1944) is short, but gives a glimpse into the company's operations during World War II. Equally short, but very informative, is the pamphlet, "The Civil War: Its Impact on a Border Community" (Cincinnati: Procter & Gamble Educational Services, 1984), which focuses specifically on the role of P & G during the Civil War and includes excerpts from a number of sources, most important the reminiscences of wartime employee John Donnelly.

The saga of P & G during the Civil War is closely tied to the wartime experience of Cincinnati. The best scholarly study on the Queen City during the war, and an estimable model for any equivalent study of a city in wartime, is Clinton W. Terry's unpublished Ph.D. dissertation, "The Most Commercial of People: Cincinnati, the Civil War, and the Rise of Industrial Capitalism,

1861-1865" (University of Cincinnati, 2002). Terry gives attention to many of the city's businesses, including P & G, and comments on some of the firm's "corporate mythology."

Chapter One

Only two official histories of Brooks Brothers have been published, both by the company. The first, *Brooks Brothers Centenary,* was published in 1918 on the occasion of the firm's one hundredth anniversary. The most recent is John Cooke's *Brooks Brothers: Generations of Style* (2003). Cooke's volume is lavishly illustrated but contains only a few paragraphs on the company's role in the Civil War. The *Centenary* is more a pamphlet than book; it does contain some excerpts from period accounts of the draft riots, but no mention is made of its role in supplying uniforms to the Union Army.

Of general histories of the nineteenth-century clothing industry, the best is Michael Zakim's *Ready-Made Democracy: A History of Men's Dress in the American Republic, 1760-1860* (Chicago: University of Chicago Press, 2003). Zakim drew somewhat on the Brooks Brothers archives and makes excellent points on how the firm has shaped (then reshaped) its own history over time. Stuart Brandes' *Warhogs: A History of War Profits in America* (Lexington: University Press of Kentucky, 1997) includes an account—and rethinking—of the importance of the early uniform scandals. Mark Wilson's *The Business of Civil War: Military Mobilization and the State, 1861-1865* (Baltimore, MD: Johns Hopkins University Press, 2006) includes an excellent discussions of army seamstress activism and the evolution of a "mixed military economy"—balancing private and public interests—in the Civil War era.

For general information on Civil War uniforms, the following were particularly useful: *Arms and Equipment of the Union* (Alexandria, VA: Time-Life Books, 1998), *Don Troiani's Regiments & Uniforms of the Civil War* (Mechanicsburg, PA: Stackpole Books, 2002), and Michael McAfee's numerous monographs on Civil War uniforms, especially in the publication *Military Images.*

Chapter Two

Though dated, Joe B. Frantz's *Dairyman to a Nation* (Norman: University of Oklahoma Press, 1951) remains the best full-length and scholarly biography of Gail Borden. Harold W. Comfort's address to the Newcomen Society of America, "Gail Borden and his Heritage Since 1857," was later (1953) published by the Society, and contains some interesting details on Borden's life and the subsequent success of the company, all informed by Comfort's position then as executive vice president of the firm. More than any of the other principals of this book—almost certainly owing to his place in Texas history and as an inventor—Borden has also found a place in the juvenile literature, most recently in Mary Dodson Wade's *Milk, Meat Biscuits, and the Terraqueous Machine: The Story of Gail Borden* (Austin, TX: Eakin Press, 1987).

For background on soldier's provisions in the Civil War, the author relied heavily on William C. Davis's *A Taste for War: The Culinary History of the Blue and Gray* (Mechanicsburg, PA: Stackpole Books, 2003) and the chapter, "Hardtack, Salt Horse and Coffee," in Bell I. Wiley's classic, *The Life of Billy Yank* (Baton Rouge: Louisiana State University Press, 1978). In his *Civil War Sutlers and their Wares* (New York: T. Yoseloff, 1969), Francis A. Lord describes the importance of canned goods—including Borden's milk—in supplementing the soldiers' diet. Readers will also find other familiar brand names of food—Durkee, Lea and Perrins, Guldens, Tetley, and others—in his several appendices of sutler wares.

As stated by Davis in *Taste of War*, "every soldier's letters and diary commented more on the awfulness of his diet than on anything else." Published memoirs, diaries, or collections of letters—such as John Billings's oft-quoted *Hardtack and Coffee: Or the Unwritten Story of Army Life* (Boston: George M. Smith, 1887) and Samuel W. Fiske's *Mr. Dunn Browne's Experiences in the Army* (Boston: Nichols and Noyes, 1866)—are rich primary sources of firsthand comments on food and cooking in the Civil War armies.

Chapter Three

The earliest of the Tiffany histories is George F. Heydt's *Charles L. Tiffany and the House of Tiffany and Co.* (Tiffany and Co.: Union Square, NY, 1893). Like many "corporate histories" of the late nineteenth century, it is self-published, short, and unashamedly hagiographic. Still, it is well-illustrated and relatively rich in information on the firm's role in the Civil War. Of special note is the appendix of "War Testimonials," which includes a list of Tiffany's most notable presentation pieces. Period newspapers are rich sources of information on presentation ceremonies—especially for swords and flags—especially as they became increasingly public affairs.

The next comprehensive company history did not appear until Joseph Purtell's *The Tiffany Touch* (New York: Random House, 1971). Though un-annotated, Purtell's is an estimable history that gives good attention to the firm's early history, including the Civil War years. The most recent accounts include John Loring's sesquicentennial history, *Tiffany's 150 Years* (Garden City, N.Y.: Doubleday, 1987). Loring is a longtime director of design at the firm and has also published more than a dozen other works on Tiffany's influence in American taste and jewelry. *Tiffany's 150 Years* and others of his books are richly illustrated and include full color plates of items from the Civil War era. There is less emphasis on history, but, given his important experience and place in the company, his monographs are well-informed.

The story of Tiffany & Co. in the Civil War is less about the firm itself, or its principals, than the lasting legacy of the things it created, including swords, flags, and other materiel. In general, the author recommends *Arms and Equipment of the Union* (Alexandria, VA: Time-Life Books) for photographs of Civil War artifacts, including Tiffany swords and flags. In regards to swords specifically, the author depended on Richard H. Bezdek's *American Swords and Sword Makers*, 2 vols. (Boulder, Col.: Paladin Press, 1994, 1999).

Howard Michael Madaus and Richard H. Zeitlin's *The Flags of the Iron Brigade* (Madison: Wisconsin Veterans Museum, 1997) combines the authors' articles on flags, especially those created by Tiffany, that originally appeared in the *Wisconsin Magazine of History*. Interested readers should consult the unmatched scholarship of the late Madaus—the acclaimed "godfather" of Civil War vexillology—who published widely on flags in American history.

After the Iron Brigade, the most fully documented and cited Tiffany-crafted flags are those of the Army of the Potomac's Irish Brigade. The banners are mentioned without fail in brigade histories and memoirs. Peter J. Lysy, in his *Blue for the Union and Green for Ireland: The Civil War Flags of the 63rd New York Volunteers, Irish Brigade* (Notre Dame, Ind.: Archives of the University of Notre Dame, 2001), documents the succession of flags that the regiment carried—including its famous Tiffany colors—and, as Madaus and Zeitlin do in *Flags of the Iron Brigade*, places the flags in the larger context of wartime politics (although ethnic, rather than regional).

The Tiffany & Co. archive department is responsible for the collection and preservation of records and artifacts that document the history of the firm from its founding to the present day. The archives are not open to the public, but interested persons can contact archivists for information on individual pieces. The archives are open to scholars after approval of a written research plan.

Chapter Four

There are four "official" histories of the *Scientific American*, all published in the pages of the magazine: "Fifty Years of the *Scientific American*," July 25, 1896; "Seventy Years of the *Scientific American*," June 5, 1915; "The Diamond Jubilee of the *Scientific American*," October 2, 1920; and Albert G. Ingalls, "A Century of *Scientific American*," December, 1945.

A "coffee table-style" book, *Free Enterprise Forever! Scientific American in the 19th Century* (James Shenton, ed., New York: Images Graphiques, 1977), includes a historical sketch of the magazine but in the main consists of reproductions of selected covers and pages from the inaugural issue through the end of the nineteenth century, including some from the Civil War years.

The best scholarly history of the magazine is Michael Borut's unpublished Ph.D. dissertation, "The *Scientific American* in Nineteenth Century America" (New York University, 1977). The study charts the history of the periodical from its inception through Beach's death in 1896. In writing the dissertation, Borut drew extensively on the unpublished diaries of Orson D. Munn, which remain privately held by the Munn family.

Biographical sketches of the magazine's principals—Porter, Munn, and Beach—can be found in *Dictionary of American Biography, American National Biography*, and in obituaries printed in the *Scientific American*. Only Porter, in Jean Lipman's *Rufus Porter: Yankee Pioneer* (New York: C. N. Potter, 1968), has received a full-length biographical treatment.

On a more general level, Frank Luther Mott's *History of American Magazines, 1850-1865* (Cambridge: Harvard University Press, 1938) and David Forsyth's *The Business Press in America: 1750-1875* (Philadelphia: Clinton Book Company, 1964), in addition to their historical sketches of the *Scientific American*, were helpful in presenting an overview of journalistic practices of the era.

Likewise, Kenneth W. Dobyns's *The Patent Office Pony: A History of the Early Patent Office* (Fredericksburg, VA: Sgt. Kirkland's, 1994) is a highly readable account of the state of patent law and the Patent Office in nine-teenth-century America. Robert V. Bruce's *Lincoln and the Tools of War* (Indianapolis: Bobbs-Merrill, 1956) draws heavily on the *Scientific American* in describing Lincoln's role in arming the Union forces, and his Pulitzer Prize-winning social history, *The Launching of Modern American Science, 1846-1876* (New York: Knopf, 1987), encompasses the Civil War years in describing the maturation of American science and technology.

The economic and social impacts of invention and the public policy of intellectual property in American history, including the nineteenth century, continue to receive scholarly attention. Among the most recent and best of these studies is Zorina Khan's *The Democratization of Invention: Patents and Copyrights in American Economic Development, 1790-1920* (New York: Cambridge University Press, 2005). Even more relevant is Khan's unpublished white paper, "Creative Desctruction: Technological Change and Resource Reallocation during the American Civil War," in which she analyzes patents filed between 1855 and 1870 to closely examine the relationship between war and technology. She pays particular attention to socioeconomic factors of the inventors themselves, including their education, wealth, occupation, and location. In her article, "'Not for Ornament': Patenting Activity by Women Inventors" (*Journal of Interdisplinary History*, Fall 2000), Khan demonstrates that women also exhibited their "inventive faculty" with a significant increase in patent activity.

The real story of the *Scientific American* during the American Civil War is to be found in the wartime pages of the magazine itself. The index, published at the end of each twenty-six-issue volume during the war years, organizes the material by illustration, "miscellany," and patent claims. Researchers should not ignore antebellum issues as many technologies used effectively for the first time during the Civil War were actually prewar innovations.

Many large libraries have period issues on microfilm. In addition, Cornell University Library's "Making of America" collection, a digital library of primary sources in American social history from the antebellum period through reconstruction, includes electronic access to digitized pages of the *Scientific American* from 1846-1869. Optical Character Recognition (OCR) has been performed on the images to enhance searching the texts by keyword (http://cdl.library.cornell.edu/moa/browse.journals/scia.html).

Reading wartime issues of the *Scientific American* will naturally lead researchers to interest in the specifics of Civil War-era patents. Patents issued by the United States Patent Office (USPTO) during the war years are very accessible. Printed copies of almost all of the patents issued since 1836 (and some issued before 1836), are available in the USPTO Public Search Room in Arlington, Virginia, in chronological order on microfilm, and in Patent Depository Libraries throughout the country. If one knows the patent number, the USPTO will supply a copy by mail for a nominal fee ($3.00 at this writing). The USPTO has also made digital full-page images of all patents issued since 1790 available on its website (http://www.uspto.gov).

In 1948, Munn & Co., owners of the *Scientific American* for a century, sold the magazine to Gerard Piel, Dennis Flanagan, and Donald Miller for $40,000. A German-based publishing group, Verlagsgruppe Georg von Holtzbrinck, bought *Scientific American*, Inc., in 1986. Unfortunately, all of the archival material was disposed of when Munn & Co. transferred ownership of the magazine to Piel, except for some of the more interesting material relating to Thomas Edison, which was transferred to the Smithsonian Institution.

Chapter Five

The body of literature on the du Pont family and the du Pont powder mills in the American Civil War is immense and can be divided into several categories: official company histories, histories of the family as a whole, biographies of the principals, special studies of the explosives industry in America, relevant monographs in the periodical literature, and the company archives.

The years following the 1902 centennial of the du Pont mills witnessed the publishing of several histories, including Atwood and Rideal's *The History of E. I. du Pont de Nemours Powder Company: A Century of Success* (New York: Business America, 1912), B. G. du Pont's *E. I. du Pont de Nemours and Company: A History, 1802-1902* (Boston: Houghlin Mifflin, 1920), and *A History of du Pont Company's Relations with the United States Government, 1802-1927* (Wilmington: du Pont, 1928). More recent publications marked other anniversaries, including the sesquicentennial history *Autobiography of an American Enterprise* (Wilmington: du Pont, 1952) and Adrian Kinnane's bicentennial history *From the Banks of the Brandywine to Miracles of Science* (Wilmington: du Pont, 2002).

The epic story of the du Pont family has been the subject of a number of works, all of which include sketches of the company's involvement in the

Civil War. They include William Carr's *The du Pont's of Delaware* (New York: Dodd, Meade, 1964), Marc Duke's *The du Ponts: Portrait of a Dynasty* (New York: Saturday Review Press, 1976), and Leonard Mosley's *Blood Relations: The Rise and Fall of the du Ponts of Delaware* (New York: Atheneum, 1980). The best, in terms of scope, writing, and scholarship is Joseph Wall's *Alfred I. du Pont: The Man and His Family* (New York: Oxford University Press, 1990).

Capsule biographies of the du Pont principals can be found in the *Dictionary of American Biography* and *American National Biography*. The best work on Lammot is Norman B. Wilkinson's *Lammot du Pont and the American Explosives Industry* (University of Virginia, 1999). An unpublished monograph, Nancy Parker's "Biographical Essay on Lammot du Pont" (Hagley Museum and Library, April 2005), draws heavily on Wilkinson, but also includes interesting original research.

Unfortunately, especially given his contributions as a soldier, statesman, and businessman, Henry du Pont has not received a full-length biographical treatment. The Hagley Museum and Library holds the manuscript of the late Harold B. Hancock's unfinished biography of him. He also appears in compilations of notable West Pointers, including W. H. Baumer's *Not All Warriors: Portraits of 19th Century West Pointers who Gained Fame in Other than Military Fields* (New York: Smith & Durrell, 1941).

For studies of the history of gunpowder and the development of the explosives industry in America, the following proved especially helpful: G.I. Brown's *The Big Bang: A History of Explosives* (Stroud, Gloucestire, UK: Sutton, 1998), Jack Kelly's *Gunpowder: Alchemy, Bombards, and Pyrotechnics* (New York: Basic Books, 2005), and Hugo Schlatter and Arthur van Gelder's *History of the Explosives Industry in America* (1927; reprint New York: Arno Press, 1972).

The saga of du Pont in the Civil War has also been the subject of several excellent monographs in the periodic literature, especially by Harold B. Hancock and Norman B. Wilkinson. They include "A Manufacturer in Wartime: Du Pont, 1860-1865" (*Business History Review*, Summer 1966) and "The Devil to Pay! Saltpeter and the Trent Affair" (*Civil War History*, 1964). Both articles are well-annotated and draw heavily on primary research, especially correspondence and business records in the du Pont archives. Wilkinson's "Operation Sabotage" (*Civil War Times Illustrated*, June 1960), while unannotated, is a lively and well-informed account of the challenges that the du Pont powder works faced from saboteurs and concerted military movements during the war. The most recent work includes Mark Wilson's "Gentlemanly Price-Fixing and Its Limits: Collusion and Competition in the U.S. Explosives Industry during the Civil War Era" (*Business History Review*, Summer 2003). Wilson examines both the general social foundations of industrial cooperation as well as the specific problems that the leading powder producers— including du Pont—faced in maintaining price agreements during the Civil War. He concludes that such price-fixing arrangements were not a guarantee of high profits as the ordnance bureaus could be demanding customers.

Few companies have maintained their historical record in original documents as well as du Pont. The collected business and personal papers of the company and the family form the core of the Hagley Museum and Library, which sits on the original powder works property on the Brandywine. Though dated, John Beverly Riggs's *A Guide to the Manuscripts in the Eleutherian Mills Historical Library* (Greenville, Del.: Library, 1970; supplement published in 1978) remains an essential starting point for the huge amount of material. Inventories and finding aids are available online through the library's website: http://www.hagley.lib.de.us/

Chapter Six

There is a fine body of literature on E. R. Squibb, M.D., himself, if somewhat less on the history of the company he founded. The only full-length biography is Lawrence Blochman's *Doctor Squibb: The Life and Times of a Rugged Idealist* (New York: Simon and Schuster, 1958); it is a lively account but is marred by its lack of annotation. Some of Squibb's personal journals were privately published in *The Journal of Edward Robinson Squibb, M.D.*, 2 vol., (Boston: George E. Crosby, Co., 1930); they cover the period from his first entries in the Navy and up to the fire in 1858. Happily, his many contributions to the medical and scientific literature were compiled and reprinted in Klaus Florey, ed., *The Collected Papers of Edward Robinson Squibb, M.D., 1819-1900*, 2 vols. (Princeton, N.J.: Squibb Corp., 1988).

The only official history of the company, Francis Wickware's *The House of Squibb* (New York: E. R. Squibb & Sons, 1945), has a capsule history of Squibb's role during the Civil War but in the main is about the important role that E. R. Squibb & Sons played in World War II. The Bristol-Myers Squibb corporate archive (New Brunswick, N.J.), maintains some material from the Civil War era, including artifacts such as panniers and period medicine containers. The collection includes period documents such as price lists but less in the way of manufacturing records or contracts. The archive still holds eleven of Squibb's journals; after the fire, it was 1862 before he resumed making journal entries. The wartime journal includes references to manufacturing and family matters, but there is little mention of business with the military. The archive also maintains a file of Blochman's notes; much of his material to support his narrative came from Squibb's journals.

The general body of literature on Civil War medicine is immense, but a number of special studies on drug supply in the era proved very helpful. The best of these is George W. Smith's *Medicines for the Union Army: The United States Army Laboratories During the Civil War* (Madison WI: American Institute of the History of Pharmacy, 1962; reprinted New York: Pharmaceutical Products Press, 2001), a major contribution to our understanding of the evolution of the government laboratories in Astoria and Philadelphia. The study is exceptionally annotated; Smith relied heavily on letters in the Surgeon General's Office and identified records from Hammond's court martial as an excellent source of material on dealings and contracts (including sales figures) with the various private drug firms.

Guy Hasegawa's "Pharmacy in the American Civil War," *American Journal of Health-System Pharmacy* (Vol. 57, 2000, pp. 475-89), is a well-annotated and amply illustrated introduction to Union and Confederate drug supply, with capsule histories of the various laboratories that were established by both sides. He also gives attention to the role of pharmacists and the actual distribution of drugs on the march, near the battlefield, and in hospitals. "The Supplies: Drug Distribution and Manufacturing," a chapter in Michael Flannery's *Civil War Pharmacy: A History of Drugs, Drug Supply and Provision, and Therapeutics for the Union and Confederacy* (New York: Pharmaceutical Products Press, 2004), is a good introduction to the role that civilian drug suppliers, including Squibb, played in the war.

Chapter Seven

Despite its importance in the history of American commerce, there are few modern general studies of the express industry; fortunately, there are a number of monographs written in the nineteenth century. Other sources include published company histories, corporate archives, and trade journals. None of the principals—Butterfield, Wells, Fargo, or Adams—is the subject of a full-length biography, but they are featured in standard biographical dictionaries. Period ephemera is a very rich source of information on the role of the express companies in the Civil War; indeed, few of the subject firms of this book are mentioned as often *by name* in soldier letters as are the express companies, especially American and Adams.

Of general histories, the following were particularly useful: Alvin F. Harlow's *Old Waybills: The Romance of the Express Companies* (New York; Appleton-Century, 1934; reprint New York: Arno Press, 1976), and David Nevin's *The Expressmen* (New York: Time-Life Books, 1974); both A.L. Stimson's *History of the Express Business* (New York: Baker & Goldwin, 1881) and T.W. Tucker's *Waifs from the Waybills of an Old Expressman* (Boston: Lee and Shepard, 1872) were written by former expressmen, and Stimson's, in particular, is marked by excellent first-hand accounts of his duties "at the front" during the Civil War. Both Harlow and Stimson provide excellent information on the "Southern Express Company" which operated Adams's territory in the Confederate States during the war.

American Express is the subject of a number of published histories, each of which includes a discussion of the company's role in the Civil War; they include Peter Grossman's *American Express: The Unofficial History of the People Who Built the Great Financial Empire* (New York: Crown, 1987) and Alden Hatch's *American Express: A Century of Service* (Garden City, N.Y.: Doubleday, 1950). Official histories include *Promises to Pay: The Story of American Express Company* (New York: American Express Co., 1977) and Reed Massengill's award-winning sesquicentennial history *Becoming American Express: 150 Years of Reinvention and Customer Service* (New York: American Express Co., 1999).

The American Express Corporate Archives (New York, NY) consists of more than 1,000 linear feet of holdings, including the papers of founding partners and executives, articles of association, board meeting minutes, financial records, company newsletters and publications, express business periodicals, annual reports, product samples, advertising material, and thousands of photographs.

Wells Fargo is the subject of a number of published histories including Edward Hungerford's *Wells Fargo: Advancing the American Frontier* (New York: Random House, 1949), Lucius Beebe and Charles Clegg, *U.S. West: The Saga of Wells Fargo* (New York: Bonanza Books, 1949), and Neill Loomis's *Wells Fargo* (New York: Clarkson N. Potter, 1968), all of which—justifiably—concentrate on the firm's part in advancing the frontier, but at the expense of its role in the Civil War.

The best sources are two recent works, Philip L. Fradkin's *Stagecoach: Wells Fargo and the American West* (New York: Simon & Schuster, 2002) and Robert Chandler's short, but richly illustrated *Wells Fargo* (Charleston, SC: Arcadia, 2006), which is part of the publisher's "Images of America" series; both give estimable attention to the role of Wells Fargo in the Civil War.

The Historical Services department of Wells Fargo & Co. (San Francisco, CA) is the steward of more than 8,000 linear feet of sources that document the origins, development, operations, and impact of Wells Fargo from 1852 to the present.

Unfortunately, apart from a company-published brochure celebrating the firm's sesquicentennial (The *Adams Express Company: 150 Years*, 2004), Adams Express is not the subject of any works specifically dedicated to its history, nor does the company maintain a historical archive; for now, Harlow's *Old Waybills* remains the best source on Adams Express

A number of nineteenth-century express trade journals, including the *Express Gazette* (1882-1926), *Expressman's Monthly* (1876-1881), and the short-lived *Our Expressman* (1874-1875), all contain published reminiscences of wartime expressmen. A good index for these journals would be a welcome contribution to the scholarship of the express industry and the American West.

To stress the importance of the express industry during the Civil War is *not* to discount the importance of the traditional postal system. Richard John's prize-winning *Spreading the News: The American Postal System from Franklin to Morse* (Boston: Harvard University Press, 1998) provides a thoroughly-researched history of the genesis of the country's postal system and its maturation into the mid-nineteenth century, with an emphasis on the important connection between public policy and social change. David M. Henkins's *The Postal Age* (Chicago: University of Chicago Press, 2007) picks up where Richard John leaves off; he emphasizes the importance of the postal system in the war with an estimate that nearly 200,000 pieces of mail were exchanged *daily* between the soldiers and the home front. The *U.S. Mail and Post Office Assistant* (1860-1872)—a monthly newspaper for postmasters—while in the main devoted to rates, schedules, and postal regulations is an important work for those serious about studying the wartime postal department.

Archives

Gettysburg, Pennsylvania
> Gettysburg National Military Park

Hartford, Connecticut
> Connecticut Historical Society
>> Civil War Manuscripts

Los Angeles, California
> Nate D. Sanders Collection

New Brunswick, New Jersey
> Bristol-Myers Squibb Corporate Archives

New York, New York
> American Express Corporate Archives
> Brooks Brothers
> Dennis Buttacavoli Collection

Republic, Missouri
> Wilson's Creek National Battlefield

San Francisco, California
> Wells Fargo Historical Services

Spring, Texas
> Author's collection

Washington, District of Columbia
> Library of Congress
>> Abraham Lincoln Papers
>> George Washington Papers, 1741-1799
> United States Patent and Trademark Office

Wilmington, Delaware
> Hagley Museum and Library (HML)

Newspapers

Adams Sentinel (Gettysburg, PA)
Army and Navy Journal
Brooklyn Eagle
Burlington (Iowa) *Weekly Hawk Eye*

Cincinnati Gazette

Dubuque (Iowa) *Herald*

Dubuque (Iowa) *Democratic Herald*

Harper's Weekly

Janesville (Wisconsin) *Daily Gazette*

Janesville (Wisconsin) *Weekly Gazette*

Morning Oregonian (Portland)

New York Times

Scientific American

Wisconsin Daily State Journal (Madison)

Books

Ackerman, K. D. *Boss Tweed: The Rise and Fall of the Corrupt Pol Who Conceived the Soul of Modern New York.* New York: Carroll & Graf, 2005.

Arms and Equipment of the Union. Alexandria, VA: Time-Life Books, 1998.

Barnes, D. M. *The Draft Riots in New York, July 1863, The Metropolitan Police: their Services During Riot Week, Their Honorable Record.* New York: Baker and Godwin, 1863.

Beach, M. Y. *The Wealth and Biography of the Wealthy Citizens of the City of New York.* New York: Sun, 1855.

Billings, J. B. *Hardtack and Coffee: Or the Unwritten Story of Army Life.* Boston: George M. Smith, 1887.

Blochman, L. G. *Doctor Squibb: The Life and Times of a Rugged Idealist.* New York: Simon and Schuster, 1958.

Boessenecker, J. *Badge and Buckshot: Lawlessness in Old California.* Norman: University of Oklahoma Press, 1988.

Britton, A.H. and Reed, T.J. eds. *To My Beloved Wife and Boy at Home: The Letters and Diaries of Orderly Sergeant John F. L. Hartwell.* Madison, NJ: Fairleigh Dickinson University Press, 1997.

Brandes, S. D. *Warhogs: A History of War Profits in America.* Lexington: University Press of Kentucky, 1997.

Brooks Brothers Centenary: 1818-1918. New York: Cheltenham Press, 1918.

Brown, G. I. *The Big Bang: A History of Explosives.* Stroud, Gloucestershire: Sutton, 1998.

Bruce, R. V., *Lincoln and the Tools of War.* Indianapolis: Bobbs-Merrill, 1956.

Burleson, G. J. *The Life and Writings of Rufus C. Burleson.* n.p., 1901.

Butterfield, J. L. ed. *A Biographical Memorial of General Daniel Butterfield, Including Many Addresses and Military Writings.* New York: The Grafton Press, 1904.

Callan, J. F. *The Military Laws of the United State.s* Philadelphia: G.W. Childs, 1863.

Cooke, J. W. *Brooks Brothers: Generations of Style.* New York: Brooks Brothers, 2003.

Coates, E. J., M. J. McAfee, and D. Troiani. *Don Troiani's Regiments & Uniforms of the Civil War.* Mechanicsburg, PA: Stackpole Books, 2002.

Curtis, O. B. *History of the Twenty-Fourth Michigan of the Iron Brigade.* Detroit: Winn & Hammond, 1891.

Davis, W. C. *A Taste for War: The Culinary History of the Blue and the Gray.* Mechanicsburg, PA: Stackpole Books, 2003.

Dawes, R. R. *Service with the Sixth Wisconsin Volunteers.* Marietta, OH: E. R. Alderman & Sons, 1890.

Depew, C. M. *My Memories of Eighty Years.* New York: C. Scribner's Sons, 1922.

du Pont, B. G. *E.I du Pont de Nemours and Company: A History, 1802-1902.* Cambridge, MA: The Riverside Press, 1920.

Douglas, H. K. and Green, F. M. ed. *I Rode with Stonewall.* Chapel Hill: University of North Carolina Press, 1940.

Fiske, S. W. *Mr. Dunn Browne's Experiences in the Army.* Boston: Nichols and Noyes, 1866.

Flood, C. B. *Lee: The Last Years.* Boston: Houghton Mifflin, 1981.

Forsyth, D. P. *The Business Press in America: 1750-1875.* Philadelphia: Clinton Book Company, 1964.

Foster, B. G. *Abraham Lincoln, Inventor.* Privately Printed, 1928.

Fox-Davies, A. *A Complete Guide to Heraldry.* New York, Grammercy Books, 1993.

Fradkin, Philip L. *Stagecoach: Wells Fargo and the American West.* New York: Simon & Schuster, 2002.

Frantz, J. B. *Gail Borden: Dairyman to a Nation.* Norman: University of Oklahoma Press, 1951.

Gallagher, G., ed. *Fighting for the Confederacy: The Personal Recollections of General Edward Porter Alexander.* Chapel Hill, NC: 1989.

Guelzo, A. C. *Abraham Lincoln: Redeemer-President.* Grand Rapids, MI: Wm B. Eerdmans, 1999.

Hamilton, F. H. *A Practical Treatise on Military Surgery.* New York: Bailliere Brothers, 1861.

Hammond, W. A. *A Treatise on Hygiene: With Special Reference to the Military Service.* Philadelphia: J. B. Lippincott & Co., 1863.

Hassall, H. A. *Food and Its Adulterations: Comprising the Reports of the Analytical*

Sanitary Commission of "The Lancet". London: Brown, Green, and Longman's, 1855.

Herndon, W. H. *Herndon's Life of Lincoln: The History and Personal Recollections of Abraham Lincoln*. Cleveland: World Publishing Co., 1949.

Hess, E. J. *Pickett's Charge: The Last Attack at Gettysburg*. Chapel Hill: University of North Carolina Press, 2001.

Heydt, G. F. *Charles L. Tiffany and the House of Tiffany and Co.* Tiffany and Co.: Union Square, NY, 1893.

History of the North-Western Soldiers' Fair. Chicago: Dunlap, Sewell, & Spalding, 1864.

Holland, M. G. *Our Army Nurses*. Boston: B. Wilkins & Co., 1895.

Homans, J. E. ed., *The Cyclopædia of American Biography, Vol. VIII*. New York: The Press Association Compilers, 1918.

Horsford, E. N. *The Army Ration*. New York: D. Van Nostrand, 1864.

Howard, M. *Recollections of a Maryland Confederate Soldier and Staff Officer Under Johnston, Jackson and Lee*. Baltimore: Williams & Wilkins, 1914.

Joselit, J. W. *A Perfect Fit: Clothes, Character, and the Promise of America*. New York: Metropolitan Books, 2001.

Kelly, J. *Gunpowder: Alchemy, Bombards, and Pyrotechnics: The History of the Explosive that Changed the World*. New York: Basic Books, 2004.

Kennett, L. B. *Sherman: A Soldier's Life*. New York: HarperCollins, 2001.

Lipman, J. *Rufus Porter: Yankee Pioneer*. C. N. Potter: New York, 1968.

Lord, F. A. *Civil War Sutlers and their Wares*. New York: T. Yoseloff, 1969.

Lyman, T. *Meade's Headquarters, 1863-1865: Letters of Colonel Theodore Lyman from the Wilderness to Appomattox*. Boston: Atlantic Monthly Press, 1922.

Madaus, H. M. and R. H. Zeitlin. *The Flags of the Iron Brigade*. Madison: Wisconsin Veterans Museum, 1997.

Massengill, R. *Becoming American Express*. New York: American Express Company, 1999.

McFeely, W. S. *Grant: A Biography*. Boston: W. W. Norton, 1982.

Mott, F. L. *A History of American Magazines, Vol. 2, 1850-1865*. Harvard University Press: Cambridge, 1938.

Mott, V. *Pain and Anæsthetics: An Essay Introductory to a Series of Surgical and Medical Monographs*. Washington: Government Printing Office, 1862.

Nolan, A. T. *The Iron Brigade: A Military History*. Bloomington: Indiana University Press, 1994.

Nonnecke, I. L. *Vegetable Production*, New York: Van Nostrand Reinhold, 1989.

Official Records of the Union and Confederate Armies in the War of the Rebellion, 130 vols. Government Printing Office: Washington, DC, 1880-1901 (cited as *OR*).

Official Records of the Union and Confederate Navies in the War of the Rebellion, 30 vols. Government Printing Office: Washington, DC, 1894-1927 (cited as *ORN*).

Olmsted, F. L. *A Journey Through Texas*. New York: Dix, Edwards, & Co., 1857.

Palmer, A. J. *The History of the Forty-Eighth Regiment New York State Volunteers*. Brooklyn: Veteran Association, 1885.

Piston, W. G. and R. W. Hatcher, III. *Wilson's Creek: The Second Battle of the Civil War and the Men Who Fought I.t* Chapel Hill: University of North Carolina Press, 2000.

Purtell, J. *The Tiffany Touch*. New York: Random House, 1971.

Quiner, E. B. *The Military History of Wisconsin*. Chicago: Clarke and Co., 1886.

Randolph, T. J. ed. *Memoir, Correspondence, and Miscellanies, from the Papers of Thomas Jefferson, Volume III*. Charlottesville, VA: F. Carr and Co., 1829.

Report of Committee on Military Surgery to the Surgical Section of the New York Academy of Medicine: Read Before the Academy July 3, 1861. New York: S. S.& W. Wood, 1861.

Revised United States Army Regulations. Washington, D.C.: U. S. Government Printing Office, 1863.

Rice, A. T. *Reminiscences of Abraham Lincoln by Distinguished Men of His Time*. New York: North American Review, 1888.

Richards, J. T. *Abraham Lincoln: The Lawyer Statesman*. New York: Houghton Mifflin, 1916.

Riggs, J. B. *A Guide to Manuscripts in the Eleutherian Mills Historical Library*. Greenville, DE: The Library, 1978.

Roberts, J. *Abraham Lincoln*. Minneapolis, MN: Twenty-first Century Books, 2004.

Sandburg, C. *Abraham Lincoln: The Prairie Years, Volume I*. New York: Harcourt, Brace & World, 1926.

Schisgall, O. *Eyes on Tomorrow: The Evolution of Procter & Gamble*. Chicago: J. G. Ferguson, 1981.

Sears, S. W. *Gettysburg*. Boston: Houghton Mifflin, 2003.

Sherman, W. T. *Memoirs of Gen. W.T. Sherman*, 2 vols. New York: C. L. Webster & Co., 1891.

Smith, G. W. *Medicines for the Union Army: The United States Army Laboratories During the Civil War*. New York: Pharmaceutical Products Press, 2001.

Squibb, E. R. and K. Florey, ed. *The Collected Papers of Edward Robinson Squibb, M.D., 1819-1900*, 2 vols. Princeton, N.J.: Squibb Corp., 1988.

Squibb, E. R. *The Journal of Edward Robinson Squibb, M.D.* 2 vols. Boston: George E. Crosby, Co., 1930.

Stearns, F. P. *Cambridge Sketches.* Philadelphia: J.B. Lippincott Company, 1905.

Stimson, A. L. *History of the Express Business.* New York: Baker & Goldwin, 1881.

Tarbell, I. M. *The Life of Abraham Lincoln.* New York: Lincoln History Society, 1900.

Trudeau, N. A. *Gettysburg: A Testing of Courage.* New York: HarperCollins, 2002.

Tucker, T. W. *Waifs from the Waybills of an Old Expressman.* Boston: Lee and Shephard, 1872.

Tyler, M. W. *Recollections of the Civil War.* New York: G. P. Putnam's, 1912.

Ware, E. F. *The Lyon Campaign in Missouri.* Topeka, KS: Crane & Co., 1907.

Wickware, F. S. *The House of Squibb.* New York: E. R. Squibb & Sons, 1945.

Wiley, B. I. *The Life of Billy Yank: The Common Soldier of the Union.* Baton Rouge: Louisiana State University, 1978.

Wilkie, F. B. and M. E. Banasik, eds. *Missouri in 1861: The Civil War Letters of Franc B. Wilkie, Newspaper Correspondent.* Iowa City, IA: Camp Pope Bookshop, 2001.

Wilkinson, N. B. *Lammot du Pont and the American Explosives Industry, 1850-1884.* Charlottesville: University Press of Virginia, 1984.

Wilson, M. R. *The Business of Civil War: Military Mobilization and the State, 1861-1865.* Baltimore, MD: Johns Hopkins University Press, 2006.

Wittenberg, E. J. ed. *One of Custer's Wolverines: The Civil War Letters of Brevet Brigadier General James H. Kidd, 6th Michigan Cavalry.* Kent, OH: Kent State University Press, 2000.

Wooster, R. *The Civil War 100: A Ranking of the Most Influential People in the War. Between the States* Secaucus, NJ: Carol Publishing Group, 1998.

Wormeley, K. P. *The Other Side of War.* Boston: Ticknor & Co., 1889.

Yates, B. M. *The Perfect Gentleman: The Life and Letters of George Washington Custis Lee,* 2 vols. Fairfax, VA: Xulon Press, 2003.

Zakim, M. *Ready-Made Democracy: A History of Men's Dress in the American Republic, 1760-1860.* Chicago: University of Chicago Press, 2003.

Articles

Albin, M. S. "The Use of Anesthetics During the Civil War, 1861-1865." *Pharmacy in History,* Vol. 42. Nos. 3 and 4, 2000, 99-114.

Alexander, E. P. "Pickett's Charge and Artillery Fighting at Gettysburg." *The Century,* Vol. 33, Issue 3, January 1887, 464-471.

Beckendorf, J. P. "Maj. Wallace's Custer Medal." *North-South Trader's Civil War*, Vol. 31, No. 1, 2005, 22-27.

Churchill, James O. "Wounded at Fort Donelson" in *War Papers and Personal Reminiscences, 1861-1865, Read Before the Commandery of the State of Missouri, Military Order of the Loyal Legion of the United States, Volume I*, (St. Louis: Becktold & Co., 1892), 150-168.

Hancock, H. B. and N. B. Wilkinson. "A Manufacturer in Wartime: Du Pont, 1860-1865." *Business History Review*, Vol. 40, Summer 1966, 213-236.

Hancock, H. B. and N. B. Wilkinson. "'The Devil to Pay! Saltpeter and the Trent Affair." *Civil War History*, Vol. 10, 1964, 20-32.

Hunt, H. J. "The Third Day at Gettysburg." *The Century*, Vol. 33, Issue 3, January 1887, 451-463.

McMurtry, R. G. (ed). "The Clothing Worn by President Abraham Lincoln the Night of His Assassination." *Lincoln Lore*, No. 1569, November 1968, 1-3.

Procter, W. "Editorial Department." *American Journal of Pharmacy*, Vol. 37, January 1865, 74-75.

Rideing, W. H. "An American Enterprise." *Harper's New Monthly Magazine*, August 1875, 314-326.

Shanks, W. F. G. "Recollections of General Sherman." in *Harper's New Monthly Magazine*, Vol. XXX, March 1865, 640-646.

Shoaf, Dana B. "Death of a Regular." *America's Civil War*, July 2002, Vol. 15, No. 3, 50-57.

Smith, G. W. "The Squibb Laboratory in 1863." *Journal of the History of Medicine and Allied Sciences*, July 1958, Vol. 13, 382-94.

Stevens, E. B. and J. A. Murphy. "The Case of Surgeon General Hammond." *The Cincinnati Lancet & Observer*, Vol. VII, 1864. 558-564.

Tobey, J. "A Box From Home." *Rock County Volunteer*, Vol. 18, No. 4, June 2002, 2-5.

Wilkinson, N. B. "Operation Sabotage." *Civil War Times Illustrated*, June 1960, 6-8.

Woodward, C. "Express Operations During the War." *The Express Gazette*, Vol. XXII, No. 5, May 15, 1897, 137-138.

Manuscripts

Borut., M. "The *Scientific American* in Nineteenth Century America." Ph.D. dissertation, New York University, 1977.

"Fact Sheet: Lincoln's Great Coat Tale." Brooks Brothers, n.d.

Lindberg, K. "Uniform and Equipment Descriptions of Units at Wilson's Creek." Wilson's Creek National Battlefield, n.d.

McNinch, M. J. "The du Ponts and the Civil War." July 1996, Hagley Museum and Library (HML).

Parker, N. "Biographical Essay on Lammot du Pont." April 2005, HML.

Terry, C. W. "The Most Commercial of People: Cincinnati, the Civil War, and the Rise of Industrial Capitalism, 1861-1865." Ph.D. dissertation, University of Cincinnati, 2002.

"The Civil War: Its Impact on a Border Community." Cincinnati: Procter & Gamble Educational Services, 1984.

Acknowledgments

THE ROMANTIC NOTION OF WRITING is that of a solitary venture. In fact, it is very much a collaborative effort. To that end, I would like to recognize the archivists and librarians, historians, editors and publishers, fellow writers, friends, and family without whose support and many kindnesses this work would not have been possible. There is significant overlap in the categories and I consider myself most fortunate that over the course of preparing this book I can now count many more people as friends.

I once heard a famous historian state that his favorite people were archivists and librarians. I heartily agree. Assistance from the following corporate archivists was critical to the completion of this book: Drs. Walter Kipp and Ben McDowell, Bristol-Myers Squibb; Mr. Ed Rider, Procter & Gamble; Mr. Ira Galtman, American Express; Ms. Marge McNinch and Jon Williams, Hagley Museum and Library (du Pont); Robert Chandler, Wells Fargo; and Annamarie Sandecki, Tiffany & Co. Librarians all around the country kindly provided material when requested, but a special debt is owed to the reference staff of the Montgomery County (Texas) Memorial Library system.

I would also like to thank Dennis Buttacavoli, John Beckendorf, Terry Reilly, Bob Sullivan (of Sullivan Press), F. Terry Hambrecht, M.D., and Nate Sanders for permission to quote from correspondence or use illustration material from their collections.

I obtained valuable support from a number of historians who reviewed the manuscript in whole or in part and provided advice. Mark Wilson, Assistant Professor, Department of History, University of North Carolina-Charlotte, is an expert in the intersection of American government and business relations. Mark read the bulk of the manuscript and provided excellent advice on the latest scholarship in several areas of interest. Richard R. John, Professor, Department of History, University of Illinois-Chicago, is an expert in the history of business, technology, and communications, and kindly shared his thoughts on the express companies.

Two editorial and publishing teams deserve special mention. Keith Poulter, publisher, and Al Nofi, editor, both at *North & South* magazine, have given me the privilege of publishing several of my pieces over the past several years. Indeed, those short articles are the foundation for this very book. Special thanks are due to Al for kindly agreeing to write the Foreword. Kay and Peter Jorgensen at *The Civil War News* have also been enthusiastic supporters of my writing and research efforts and have been kind enough to give me room in their newspaper for a regular column on Civil War medicine for the past seven years.

Two fellow writers have been especially influential. Darryl Brock was an excellent mentor when I first started doing historical writing more than a decade ago. An experienced writer and researcher in his own right, Darryl shepherded me through my first few writing experiences and provided enthusiastic support and honest appraisals. Guy Hasegawa has been a faithful correspondent and dear friend for nearly a decade. Guy is an expert medical historian and editor and provided unmatched advice from the beginning of this project to its end. Blake Magner, book review editor at the *Civil War News*, shared his insights from his many years of reviewing many hundreds of books, and gave me confidence that I was on the right track. Russell Bonds, Eric Wittenberg, and Thomas Lowry, all authors and historians, also provided kind support and advice.

A number of close friends, co-workers, Civil War Round Table comrades, and other "fellow travelers" have patiently indulged and supported my writing and my interest in history. I especially want to mention my lifelong friend, Curtis Fears. Curtis and I grew up on the same block in Joplin, Missouri as youngsters. Time and travel separated us, but we were happily "re-introduced" about a dozen years ago and have been daily correspondents ever since. Curtis shares my passion for Civil War history, has been a wonderful companion on battlefield trips to Mississippi, Virginia, and Missouri, and his friendship is a true blessing.

I especially want to thank Daniel Hoisington at Edinborough Press for ultimately seeing the promise of this book and kindly, patiently, and expertly shepherding it to publication.

Despite all this help, I take sole responsibility for any errors in fact or interpretation.

Finally, and most important, I must thank my family—parents, brothers, sisters, and in-laws—but especially my wife, Susan, and my darling children, Katherine, Robert, and Michael, to whom this volume is dedicated and whose love and support made it all possible.

Index